JUNIOR CYCLE ENGLISH

William Shakespeare's

The Merchant of Venice

Second Edition

The original New Junior Cycle approach, now with added commentary and exam preparation

Annotations, analysis and activities by
Catherine O'Donovan

EDUCATE.IE
SHAKESPEARE
SERIES

educate.ie

educate.ie

PUBLISHED BY:
Educate.ie
Walsh Educational Books Ltd
Castleisland, Co. Kerry, Ireland
www.educate.ie

DESIGN:
Kieran O'Donoghue

LAYOUT:
Liz White Designs

COVER DESIGN:
Kieran O'Donoghue

PRINTED AND BOUND BY:
Walsh Colour Print, Castleisland, Co. Kerry, Ireland

PHOTOGRAPHS AND ILLUSTRATIONS:
AF Archive/Alamy; AJ Pics/Alamy Stock Photo; Bigstock; Cinematic Collection/Alamy Stock Photo; DEA/G. DAGLI ORTI/ Getty Images; Geraint Lewis/ArenaPAL; Hemis/Alamy; Johan Persson/ArenaPAL; Manuel Harlan/ArenaPAL; Moviestore Collection Ltd/Alamy; Nigel Norrington/ArenaPAL/Topham Partners LLP; PictureLux/The Hollywood Archive/Alamy Stock Photo; Science History Images/Alamy Stock Photo; Shutterstock; The Reading Room/Alamy Stock Photo; Vibrant Pictures/Alamy; Wikimedia Commons

The author and publisher have made every effort to trace all copyright holders. If any have been overlooked we would be happy to make the necessary arrangements at the first opportunity.

ISBN: 978-1-915595-16-4

The Merchant of Venice

Contents

Teacher's Introduction

The *Specification for Junior Cycle English* focuses on the development of language and literacy throughout the three strands: Oral Language, Reading and Writing.

These strands aim to promote **active engagement** with the texts for students. The purpose of this edition of *The Merchant of Venice* is to explore the play in a way that helps to engage learners, while also focusing on the following key objectives:

1. Communicating as a speaker, reader and writer
2. Exploring and using language
3. Understanding the content and structure of language.

This edition of the play is designed to facilitate exploration by including strategies and activities that encourage engagement and interaction with the play. The overarching aim is to encourage students to see the play as a dramatic script to be explored and performed. While there are many activities and exercises included throughout the play text and the portfolio, it is not expected that all will be completed. It is hoped that they will provide suggestions to complement the teacher's own approach to the play, bearing in mind the uniqueness of each class group.

Studying a Shakespearean play can be challenging. This second edition of *The Merchant of Venice* includes the following new features to make the play accessible to students of all levels of ability.

SPOTLIGHT ON ... places emphasis on a particular speech or technique that merits further exploration. It may also link to the portfolio to provide opportunities for more in-depth analysis.

> **SPOTLIGHT ON ...**
>
> **CLASSICAL ALLUSION**
>
> **Classical allusion** is a reference to a character or story from Greek or Roman classical literature. The Prince of Morocco refers to a story about Hercules to illustrate his point about luck.

LOOKING AT LANGUAGE highlights the language devices that students will encounter throughout the play, such as **metaphor**, **oxymoron**, **hyperbole**. It encourages students to explore, examine and appreciate the richness of Shakespeare's text.

> **LOOKING AT LANGUAGE**
> **Hyperbole:** Exaggerated language used for dramatic effect. For example, notice how the Prince of Morocco frequently uses hyperbole in his speech.

PLOT POINT reminds students of what is happening globally in a particular scene and encourages them to consider the wider implications of the action. Taken in conjunction with the annotations, it makes the text accessible for all learners.

> **PLOT POINT**
> Portia warns the Prince of Morocco that he is not obligated to participate in the lottery, but if he does, he must swear that, if unsuccessful, he must never ask another woman to marry him. Do you think that this is fair? Why do you think this condition exists?

CHARACTER NOTE highlights noteworthy aspects of and any development in a character's personality as the play progresses.

> **CHARACTER NOTE**
> After initially declining to dine with Bassanio, Shylock is planning to go. Why is he going and what do you think this reveals about his character?

SHAKESPEARE'S WORLD highlights aspects of Elizabethan England that may provide a context for some of the customs, beliefs and traditions mentioned in the play.

> **SHAKESPEARE'S WORLD**
> Elizabethan masques were a very popular form of entertainment and a very elaborate affair. A masque had music, song, dancing and people in fancy dress and masks. As these mainly took place at night, many people would carry or 'bear' torches, making it quite a spectacular event.

LINKING TO THE EXAM appears at the end of each act and helps students to form links between the text and the kind of questions that may arise in the Junior Cycle English examination. The questions are taken from past examination papers (both ordinary and higher level) or from official sample papers. Students are directed to the portfolio, where they are given advice on how to approach, plan and answer examination questions, as well as opportunities to answer examination questions in full.

> **LINKING TO THE EXAM**
> **Describing Characters and Key Moments** P
> In the exam, you might be asked to give advice to a character in a key moment of the play. Turn to **page 19** of your portfolio to complete a Junior Cycle English question on this topic.

Portfolio

The portfolio is designed to provide a **personal learning log/journal** for students to visit as they read through the play. It allows students to reflect on the characters, plot and key themes of the play, and to take personal ownership of the learning process. The written tasks help them to engage imaginatively with the play and to explore the language of William Shakespeare.

Character File

The Character File section of the portfolio provides a template for students to reflect on their feelings about the main characters as they progress through the play. They are encouraged to record their responses to the characters in each key scene. They may focus on something that stands out to them. They may notice a significant change in the character, or may wish to note something that confuses them about a character in a particular scene.

Student's Introduction

Key Points About *The Merchant of Venice*

Background to the Play

The Merchant of Venice, written between 1596 and 1597, is now a very controversial play because many people feel that it is anti-Jewish (anti-Semitic). It is thought that Shakespeare based the play on a story from an Italian collection of stories called *Il Pecorone* (meaning 'The Simpleton' in English), which was written by Giovanni Fiorentino in 1378.

Venice in the 16th and 17th Centuries

During the late 16th and early 17th centuries, Venice was a wealthy trading city. As most goods were transported by ship, Venice's waterways, as well as its ideal geographical position in Europe, made it a cultural hotspot. Venice was a very **cosmopolitan** (multiracial/international) city because of its trade links with people of all cultures. People of many different religious faiths and nationalities also mixed in Venice at this time, including Christians, Jews, Turks, Africans and Arabs.

Money and Money-Lending (Usury)

In the play, Bassanio wishes to borrow money from his friend, Antonio. However, Antonio does not have the money to lend Bassanio, so Antonio secures a loan from the Jewish moneylender, Shylock. Antonio sees moneylending as a favour, lending money interest-free, whereas Shylock sees it as a business transaction and charges high rates of interest. This causes a lot of tension and conflict between these two characters.

Useful Words

ducat – a gold coin and the currency of Venice at the time the play is set
usury – the practice of lending money at very high rates of interest

Plot Overview

The Bond Plot (Related to the Theme of Conflict and Theme of Money)

In this play, a Christian merchant, Antonio, acquires a loan from a Jew, Shylock. There is a lot of **tension** and **animosity** (hatred) between the two. Instead of charging interest on the loan as would normally be the case, Shylock demands a **pound of Antonio's flesh** if he fails to repay the loan on time.

Shylock is an **outsider** in Venice. He appears to be preoccupied with money and, instead of spending or enjoying his wealth, he hoards it. In a sense, his daughter, Jessica, is also treated like one of his possessions – a treasure to be locked up and guarded closely.

The Casket Plot (Related to the Theme of Love and Marriage)

The secondary (minor) plot concerns a girl from Belmont, Portia, whose father has died. In his will, he has left her instructions about how to find a suitable husband. He has devised a game or lottery in which potential suitors must choose one of three caskets: gold, silver or lead. Whoever chooses the correct casket (the one which contains Portia's portrait) will then win Portia's hand in marriage. Portia is **bound** (limited/confined) by her dead father's wishes and so must follow through with the casket lottery. She has no control over who her future husband will be. The person who will win Portia's hand in marriage will be aware that appearances can be deceiving.

The **elopement** of Jessica and Lorenzo and the **rings** test are also related to the **theme of love and marriage**.

The Merchant of Venice and Anti-Semitism

These days *The Merchant of Venice* is a controversial play. Many people accuse Shakespeare of stereotyping Jewish people in the play through the character of Shylock. In 1594, a Jewish doctor named Roderigo Lopez was accused of trying to poison Queen Elizabeth I. He was tried and executed for this. A playwright called Christopher Marlowe had already written a play called *The Jew of Malta*, so Shakespeare wrote *The Merchant of Venice* at a time when there was demand for plays featuring Jewish people.

Jewish people have experienced a long history of discrimination and persecution in Europe. In England during the Elizabethan period, Jewish people were still demonised and stereotyped because of their religious beliefs.

Throughout the play, Shylock is repeatedly referred to as 'a kind of devil', 'the devil himself', 'the very devil incarnate', 'the devil in the likeness of a Jew' and a 'cruel devil'. In Act 2, Scene 2, Launcelot says of Shylock: 'My master's a very Jew' (line 100). By this he means to call his master a very greedy person. Shylock is rarely referred to by name; mostly, he is simply `the Jew'.

However, some argue that while the character of Shylock is stereotyped and humiliated, Shakespeare also lends him a certain humanity and shows us the extent of Shylock's suffering at the hands of Christians.

The Structure and Language of the Play

- The play is divided into five **acts**. Unlike prose, a play is essentially a script to be performed.
- Each act is divided into **scenes**.
- The language is **archaic** (old-fashioned). Some words will be unfamiliar to you at first, but you will get used to them as the play progresses.
- Have a look at an extract from one of Shylock's speeches (one of the main characters) below. Look at the glossary and see if you can make out what Shylock is saying.

Glossary: hath = has

> *Hath not a Jew eyes? Hath not a Jew hands, organs,*
> *dimensions, senses, affections, passions; fed with*
> *the same food, hurt with the same weapons, subject*
> *to the same diseases, healed by the same means,*
> *warmed and cooled by the same winter and summer as*
> *a Christian is? If you prick us, do we not bleed?*
> *If you tickle us, do we not laugh? If you poison*
> *us, do we not die? And if you wrong us, shall we not*
> *revenge?* (Shylock, Act 3, Scene 1, lines 53–61)

Shakespeare's Theatre

In Elizabethan times (when Shakespeare wrote his plays), the stage in a theatre was usually quite bare. Often the audience had to rely on the characters' lines to figure out whether the scene was set during the day or at night. Shakespeare's Globe Theatre (which has been rebuilt in London close to the site of the original building) was an open-air theatre.

Key Themes in *The Merchant of Venice*

There are many themes in *The Merchant of Venice*, but some of the main ones are:

- Love and Marriage
- Conflict
- Money
- False Appearances.

Your Portfolio

When looking at the play, try to form your own ideas about the **characters** and **themes**, and the **language** used. The activities in the book and portfolio should help you with this.

P = **portfolio activity**

Character File

As you read through the play, record your responses to the main characters in the **Character File** section of your portfolio. Write down anything that you think is important about each character's personality. Use the **list of useful adjectives** in the **Character File** section to help you.

Think about:

- What the character **does** in each key scene
- The **adjectives** you would use to describe the character
- **Something that stands** out to you in a key scene
- How the character **reacts to situations** that arise
- Significant **change** in the character
- Something that **confuses you or surprises you** about the character in a particular scene
- How the character interacts with other characters, i.e. **relationships**.

Important Characters in the Play

- Portia
- Shylock
- Antonio
- Bassanio
- Jessica
- Lorenzo
- Gratiano
- Nerissa

"Prince of Morocco"
Mr Lawson Butt
Shylock (Act I)
"Jessica"
Miss Elfrida Clement
"Shylock"
Mr Bourchier
"Portia"
Miss Violet Vanbrugh
"Antonio"
Mr Jerrold Robertshaw
"Bassanio"
Mr Julian L'Estrange
"Launcelot Gobbo"
Mr Norman Forbes
"Old Gobbo"
Mr O.B. Clarence
"Nerissa"
Miss Muriel Beaumont
Portia. Act II
Ralph Cleaver '05

Overview of the Play

The following grid shows the number of scenes in each act of the play. At the end of each act, write one phrase to summarise each scene of that act on **pages 4–5** of your portfolio. When completed, it will form your own personal overview of the play.

 = **key scene**

ACT 1 	SCENE 1	SCENE 2	SCENE 3 						
ACT 2 	SCENE 1	SCENE 2	SCENE 3	SCENE 4	SCENE 5	SCENE 6 	SCENE 7	SCENE 8	SCENE 9
ACT 3 	SCENE 1	SCENE 2 	SCENE 3	SCENE 4	SCENE 5				
ACT 4 	SCENE 1 	SCENE 2							
ACT 5 	SCENE 1								

Glossary of Important Terms

ASIDE	An aside is a remark that the audience is supposed to hear but that is not supposed to be heard by the other characters on stage.
DENOUEMENT	Denouement refers to the end of the play when the plot is unravelled and key issues are resolved.
DRAMATIC IRONY	Dramatic irony is when the audience or other characters on stage have information or knowledge that the other character(s) do(es) not.
HYBERBOLE	Hyberbole is using exaggerated, over-the-top language for a dramatic effect. For example, in Act 3, Scene 2, Portia says to Bassanio: *I would be trebled twenty times myself,* *A thousand times more fair, ten thousand times more rich,* *That only to stand high in your account* (Act 3, Scene 2, lines 153–155)
IMAGERY	Imagery uses words and phrases to create pictures in your mind. Much of the imagery in the play comes from other language devices such as metaphors, personification, etc. **Imagery can**: • Tell us more about a **character**. • Create a certain **mood or atmosphere**. • Reinforce certain **themes** (of love or conflict, for example). In *The Merchant of Venice*, there is animal imagery, money imagery, ship imagery, etc.
INTERIOR MONOLOGUE	An interior monologue is a piece of dialogue expressing a character's private/inner thoughts.
MALAPROPISM	Malapropism is the incorrect use of a word in place of a word that sounds similar. For example, *I pacifically told her to be there on time* ('pacifically' should be '**specifically**').
METAPHOR	A metaphor is a figure of speech used to make a comparison, usually saying one thing is another, which is not literally true. For example, *Her eyes **are** sparkling diamonds.*
PERSONIFICATION	Personification is when we give non-human things human characteristics. For example, *The wind was **whistling** in the trees. The autumn leaves **danced** in the wind.*
RHETORICAL QUESTION	A rhetorical question is a question that makes a statement and does not require a direct reponse from the listener. For example, *Hath not a Jew eyes?*
SIMILE	A simile is a figure of speech used to compare two things. A simile uses the words 'like', 'as' or 'than'. For example, *Her eyes are **like** sparkling diamonds.* (Compare with metaphor above.)

THE MERCHANT OF VENICE

By William Shakespeare

Setting: Venice and Belmont.

Characters in the Play

Antonio, *a merchant of Venice*
Bassanio, *Antonio's friend and Portia's suitor*

Gratiano
Salerio
Solanio
Lorenzo, *in love with Jessica*
} *friends to Antonio and Bassanio*

Shylock, *a Jew and moneylender*
Jessica, *Shylock's daughter*
Tubal, *a Jew and Shylock's friend*

Launcelot Gobbo, *a clown, first Shylock's servant, later Bassanio's servant*
Gobbo, *Launcelot Gobbo's father*
Leonardo, *Bassanio's servant*

Portia, *an heiress of Belmont*
Nerissa, *Portia's waiting-woman*

Balthasar
Stephano
} *Portia's servants*

The Prince of Morocco
The Prince of Arragon
} *Portia's suitors*

The Duke of Venice

Magnificoes of Venice, a Jailer, Attendants and other Servants

Useful Words

merchant – a person involved in trade and commerce. In Venice, merchants transported their goods to other countries on ships.
suitor – an admirer who would pursue a lady with a view to marrying her
magnificoes – important people

ACT 1

In Act 1, we are introduced to the main characters and the key themes of **money** and **marriage**. **Scene 1** is set in Venice, where we are introduced to Antonio, a merchant from Venice, and Bassanio, his friend. Antonio and Bassanio are two very important characters in the play.

Bassanio intends to seek Portia's hand in marriage, but he needs a loan to allow him to do so. Antonio is not in a position to lend Bassanio the money. He offers to help raise a loan for Bassanio.

The action then moves swiftly to Portia's house in Belmont in **Scene 2**, where we hear about the many suitors lining up to seek Portia's hand in marriage.

In **Scene 3**, the final scene of this act, we move back to Venice where Antonio is discussing terms of a loan from the Jewish moneylender, Shylock.

ACT 1, SCENE 1

Setting: Venice. A street.

In this **scene** you will:

- Meet two main characters: **Antonio** and **Bassanio**.
- Rewrite part of this scene in **modern English** and act it out.
- Explore important **images** in this scene.

Action – What Happens?

In this scene, we meet Antonio, a merchant of Venice, who is talking to two friends, Solanio and Salerio. Antonio is feeling sad, but he doesn't know why. His friends suggest that he is worried about his ships at sea, but Antonio rejects this.

Later on, Bassanio, Lorenzo and Gratiano arrive and Bassanio tells Antonio that he intends to go to Belmont to seek Portia's hand in marriage. He asks Antonio for a loan, but Antonio's money is tied up in his ships. Bassanio has already borrowed money from Antonio in the past to fund his lavish lifestyle. Bassanio believes that if he marries Portia (a wealthy heiress), he will be able to pay Antonio back everything that he has borrowed from him.

Antonio agrees to help Bassanio to get a loan from moneylenders in Venice by acting as a **guarantor** (someone who ensures that the loan will be repaid) for the loan. In this way, Bassanio will be able to get the money he needs to go to Belmont to impress Portia.

Useful Words

argosies – large merchant ships
ado – trouble or difficulty
prodigal – wasteful/extravagant
uttermost – utmost/maximum
venture – enterprise/risk

PLOT POINT

Antonio's sad mood at the start of the scene sets the tone, creating a sense of foreboding (the feeling that something bad might happen).

Enter ANTONIO, SALERIO and SOLANIO.

ANTONIO

In sooth,[1] I know not why I am so sad.
It wearies me, you say it wearies you,
But how I caught it, found it, or came by it,
What stuff[2] 'tis made of, whereof it is born,[3]
I am to learn;[4]
And such a want-wit[5] sadness makes of me
That I have much ado[6] to know myself.

1. *In sooth:* In truth *(another way of saying 'to tell you the truth')*
2. *stuff:* material/substance
3. *whereof it is born:* where it has come from
4. *I am to learn:* I have yet to find out
5. *want-wit:* fool
6. *ado:* trouble or difficulty

SALERIO

Your mind is tossing on the ocean,
There, where your argosies[7] with portly[8] sail,
Like signors[9] and rich burghers[10] on the flood—
Or as it were the pageants[11] of the sea—
Do overpeer[12] the petty traffickers[13]
That curtsy[14] to them, do them reverence,[15]
As they fly by them with their woven wings.[16]

7. *argosies:* large merchant ships
8. *portly:* magnificent
9. *signors:* lords/noblemen who ruled Venice
10. *rich burghers:* wealthy citizen-merchants
11. *pageants:* decorated barges used in parades
12. *overpeer:* tower over
13. *petty traffickers:* small, insignificant trader ships
14. *curtsy:* bow
15. *do them reverence:* show them respect
16. *woven wings:* wing-like sails

SOLANIO

Believe me, sir, had I such venture[17] forth,
The better part of my affections[18] would
Be with my hopes abroad. I should be still[19]
Plucking the grass to know where sits the wind,[20]
Peering in maps for ports and piers and roads,[21]
And every object that might make me fear
Misfortune to my ventures out of doubt
Would make me sad.

17. *venture:* risky investments
18. *affections:* emotions
19. *still:* always
20. *where sits the wind:* what direction the wind is blowing from
21. *roads:* harbours

SALERIO

My wind[22] cooling my broth
Would blow me to an ague[23] when I thought
What harm a wind too great might do at sea.
I should not see the sandy hour-glass run
But I should think of shallows[24] and of flats,[25]
And see my wealthy Andrew,[26] dock'd in sand,
Vailing her high-top[27] lower than her ribs
To kiss her burial.[28] Should I go to church
And see the holy edifice of stone,[29]
And not bethink me straight[30] of dangerous rocks,

22. *wind:* breath
23. *blow me to an ague:* make me shiver *(ague = fever)*
24. *shallows:* shallow waters
25. *flats:* submerged sandbanks
26. *Andrew: name of a ship*
27. *Vailing her high-top:* Lowering her topmast
28. *burial:* burial place *The image here is of the ship capsizing, with its high mast reaching past its hull ribs and falling to its burial place in the sand.*
29. *edifice of stone:* stone structure
30. *bethink me straight:* immediately think about

Which touching but my gentle vessel's side,
Would scatter all her spices on the stream,[31]
Enrobe[32] the roaring waters with my silks,
And, in a word, but even now[33] worth this,
And now worth nothing? Shall I have the thought
To think on this, and shall I lack the thought
That such a thing bechanced[34] would make me sad?
But tell not me.[35] I know Antonio
Is sad to think upon his merchandise.

31. *stream:* water
32. *Enrobe:* Dress/Cover
33. *even now:* only recently
34. *bechanced:* having happened
35. *But tell not me:* Don't tell me.

PLOT POINT

When Antonio tells Salerio and Solanio that he does not know the reason why he is so sad, they try to find reasons: Salerio suggests that he must be concerned about his ships and the potential dangers they face; Solanio tells him that if he were in Antonio's position, he would see signs of potential danger everywhere. Antonio assures them that he is not worried about his ships because all his wealth is not invested in one ship or in one year's trade.

ANTONIO

Believe me, no. I thank my fortune for it,
My ventures are not in one bottom[36] trusted,
Nor to one place; nor is my whole estate
Upon the fortune of this present year.[37]
Therefore my merchandise makes me not sad.

SOLANIO

Why then, you are in love.

36. *bottom:* ship
37. *nor is … present year:* my wealth is not dependent on this year's trade

ANTONIO

Fie, fie![38]

38. *Fie, fie!: An exclamation used to express disgust or outrage. Antonio dismisses Solanio's suggestion that love is the cause of his unhappiness.*

SOLANIO

Not in love neither? Then let us say you are sad
Because you are not merry: and 'twere as easy
For you to laugh and leap, and say you are merry
Because you are not sad. Now, by two-headed Janus,[39]
Nature hath framed[40] strange fellows in her time:
Some that will evermore peep through their eyes[41]
And laugh like parrots at a bagpiper,[42]
And other of such vinegar[43] aspect
That they'll not show their teeth in way of smile
Though Nestor[44] swear the jest be laughable.[45]

39. *Janus: Roman God who had two faces – one looking to the past and one to the future. Janus is often referred to as the god of new beginnings.*
40. *framed:* created
41. *peep through their eyes:* will laugh so much that he can barely see through his eyes
42. *laugh like parrots at a bagpiper: A bagpiper's music was considered terrible.*
43. *vinegar:* sour/moody
44. *Nestor: Nestor was a Greek man who was always serious and never smiled.*
45. *swear the jest be laughable:* Even Nestor *(who never smiled)* found the joke *(jest)* funny.

'two-headed Janus'

Enter BASSANIO, LORENZO and GRATIANO.

Here comes Bassanio, your most noble kinsman,
Gratiano, and Lorenzo. Fare ye well.
We leave you now with better company.

SALERIO

I would have stay'd till I had made you merry,
If worthier friends had not prevented me.

ANTONIO

Your worth is very dear in my regard.
I take it your own business calls on you
And you embrace th'occasion to depart.[46]

SALERIO

Good morrow,[47] my good lords.

BASSANIO

Good signors both, when shall we laugh?[48] Say, when?
You grow exceeding strange.[49] Must it be so?[50]

SALERIO

We'll make our leisures to attend on yours.[51]

Exeunt SALERIO and SOLANIO.

LORENZO

My lord Bassanio, since you have found Antonio,
We two will leave you; but at dinner-time,
I pray you have in mind where we must meet.

BASSANIO

I will not fail you.

GRATIANO

You look not well, Signor Antonio.
You have too much respect upon the world.[52]
They lose it that do buy it with much care.[53]
Believe me, you are marvellously changed.

ANTONIO

I hold[54] the world but as the world, Gratiano—
A stage where every man must play a part,
And mine a sad one.

GRATIANO

Let me play the fool.
With mirth and laughter let old wrinkles come,
And let my liver[55] rather heat with wine
Than my heart cool with mortifying[56] groans.

46. *And … depart:* You are taking the opportunity to leave now.
47. *Good morrow:* Good day
48. *when shall we laugh?:* When will we have fun together?
49. *You grow exceeding strange:* You have become more like a stranger.
50. *Must it be so?:* Does this have to be the case?
51. *We'll … yours:* We are free to meet whenever you are.
52. *You … world:* You are too anxious about your business affairs.
53. Those who worry too much about their wealth, lose it. *Gratiano then comments on how he has noticed a big change in Antonio, which suggests that Antonio is not normally so sad.*
54. *hold:* regard/view
55. *liver: In Elizabethan times, the liver was considered the centre of emotion/passion.*
56. *mortifying:* deadly

Why should a man whose blood is warm within,[57]
Sit like his grandsire cut in alabaster?[58]
Sleep when he wakes, and creep into the jaundice
By being peevish?[59] I tell thee what, Antonio—
I love thee, and 'tis my love that speaks—[60]
There are a sort of men whose visages[61]
Do cream and mantle like a standing pond,
And do a wilful stillness entertain,[62]
With purpose to be dress'd in an opinion[63]
Of wisdom, gravity, profound conceit,[64]
As who should say[65] 'I am Sir Oracle,
And when I ope[66] my lips let no dog bark.'
O my Antonio, I do know of these
That therefore only are reputed wise
For saying nothing, when I am very sure,
If they should speak, would almost damn those ears
Which, hearing them, would call their brothers fools.
I'll tell thee more of this another time.
But fish not with this melancholy bait[67]
For this fool gudgeon,[68] this opinion.—
Come, good Lorenzo.— Fare ye well a while.
I'll end my exhortation[69] after dinner.

LORENZO [*to ANTONIO and BASSANIO*]
Well, we will leave you then till dinner-time.
I must be one of these same dumb[70] wise men,
For Gratiano never lets me speak.

GRATIANO
Well, keep me company but two years moe,[71]
Thou shalt not know the sound of thine own tongue.

ANTONIO
Fare you well. I'll grow a talker for this gear.[72]

GRATIANO
Thanks, i'faith,[73] for silence is only commendable
In a neat's[74] tongue dried and a maid not vendible.[75]

Exeunt GRATIANO and LORENZO.

57. *within:* inside
58. *Sit ... alabaster?:* Sit like a statue?
59. *creep ... peevish?:* bring jaundice *(liver disease)* upon himself by being irritable/bad-humoured
60. *I love thee ... speaks:* I am only telling you this because I love you.
61. *visages:* faces
62. *do ... entertain:* deliberately appear silent or serious
63. *dress'd in an opinion:* gain a reputation for
64. *There are a sort ... conceit:* There are some men whose faces become frothy like a stagnant pool and they take on a deliberate fixed expression designed to make them appear really important, full of great wisdom and seriousness
65. *As who should say:* As if to say
66. *ope:* open

SHAKESPEARE'S WORLD

At the time when Shakespeare was writing his plays, the Elizabethans believed that people's personalities or temperaments could be affected by certain bodily fluids, called the 'four humours': blood, yellow bile, black bile and phlegm. An imbalance in the levels of these fluids could determine a person's mood. Here, Gratiano is saying that he would rather be happy than melancholy.

67. *But fish not ... bait:* Don't try to gain a reputation for being wise by appearing sad
68. *gudgeon:* a small fish which is easy to catch
69. *exhortation:* sermon/speech
70. *dumb:* silent
71. *moe:* more
72. *for this gear:* as a result of this talk
73. *i'faith:* indeed
74. *a neat's:* an ox's
75. *vendible:* sellable *(i.e. marriageable) Gratiano is talking nonsense here.*

ANTONIO

Is that anything now?[76]

BASSANIO

Gratiano speaks an infinite deal of nothing, more than any man in all Venice. His reasons[77] are as two grains of wheat hid in two bushels[78] of chaff:[79] you shall seek all day ere[80] you find them, and when you have[81] them they are not worth the search.

ANTONIO

Well, tell me now what lady is the same
To whom you swore a secret pilgrimage,[82]
That you today promised to tell me of?

BASSANIO

'Tis not unknown to you, Antonio,
How much I have disabled mine estate,[83]
By something showing a more swelling port[84]
Than my faint[85] means would grant continuance,[86]
Nor do I now make moan to be abridged
From such a noble rate;[87] but my chief care[88]
Is to come fairly off from[89] the great debts
Wherein my time, something too prodigal,[90]
Hath left me gaged.[91] To you, Antonio,
I owe the most in money and in love,
And from your love I have a warranty[92]
To unburden[93] all my plots and purposes[94]
How to get clear of all the debts I owe.

ANTONIO

I pray you,[95] good Bassanio, let me know it,
And if it stand as you yourself still[96] do,
Within the eye of honour, be assured
My purse,[97] my person,[98] my extremest means[99]
Lie all unlock'd to your occasions.[100]

BASSANIO

In my school-days, when I had lost one shaft,[101]
I shot his fellow[102] of the selfsame flight

76. *Is that anything now?:* Is there any sense at all in what he is saying?
77. *reasons:* sensible remarks
78. *bushels:* barrels
79. *chaff:* husks/shells *(i.e. you have to look really hard to find any sense in his words)*
80. *ere:* before
81. *have:* find
82. *pilgrimage:* sacred or holy journey
83. *disabled mine estate:* destroyed my fortune
84. *swelling port:* extravagant lifestyle
85. *faint:* humble
86. *grant continuance:* allow to continue
87. *Nor … rate:* Nor am I complaining about having to cut back on my excessive lifestyle.
88. *my chief care:* my main concern
89. *come fairly off from:* release myself from
90. *prodigal:* extravagant/wasteful
91. *gaged:* bound/pledged/indebted
92. *warranty:* permission/sanction
93. *unburden:* reveal
94. *plots and purposes:* plans

CHARACTER NOTE

It is clear that Bassanio is a spendthrift who lives beyond his means. He has borrowed from Antonio before and already owes him money. He tells Antonio that he has a plan to clear all his debts.

95. *I pray you:* Please
96. *still:* always
97. *purse:* money
98. *my person:* I myself
99. *my extremest means:* everything that I own
100. *Lie … occasions:* Are all at your disposal.
101. *shaft:* arrow
102. *his fellow:* another one

The selfsame way, with more advised[103] watch,
To find the other forth;[104] and by adventuring[105] both
I oft found both. I urge this childhood proof[106]
Because what follows is pure innocence.
I owe you much, and, like a wilful youth,
That which I owe is lost; but if you please

To shoot another arrow that self[107] way
Which you did shoot the first, I do not doubt,
As I will watch the aim, or[108] to find both
Or bring your latter hazard[109] back again
And thankfully rest debtor for the first.

ANTONIO
You know me well, and herein spend but time
To wind about my love with circumstance;[110]
And out of doubt you do me now more wrong
In making question of my uttermost[111]
Than if you had made waste of all I have.
Then do but say to me what I should do
That in your knowledge may by me be done,
And I am pressed unto it.[112] Therefore speak.

103. *advised:* careful

104. *To ... forth:* To get the other one back
105. *adventuring:* risking
106. *I urge ... proof:* I am telling you about this childhood story/example

107. *self:* same

108. *or:* either

109. *your latter hazard:* your most recent loan

110. *To wind ... circumstance:* You are trying to win me over with your long-winded story

111. *And out ... uttermost:* you are doing me a greater wrong now by assuming that I wouldn't do all I can to help you

112. *I am ... it:* And I am more than willing to do it.

LOOKING AT LANGUAGE

Analogy: A comparison of two seemingly different things in order to explain a point or clarify an idea. However, there will be important similarities between both things. For example, Bassanio is describing his method of finding lost arrows in childhood in order to clarify his plan to repay Bassanio the money he has lent him. Can you explain this analogy? (Look back over lines 140–152.)

BASSANIO

In Belmont is a lady richly left,[113]
And she is fair, and, fairer than that word,
Of wondrous virtues. Sometimes[114] from her eyes
I did receive fair speechless messages.
Her name is Portia, nothing undervalued
To[115] Cato's daughter,[116] Brutus' Portia;
Nor is the wide world ignorant of her worth,
For the four winds blow in from every coast
Renownèd suitors,[117] and her sunny locks
Hang on her temples like a golden fleece,
Which makes her seat of Belmont Colchos' strand,[118]
And many Jasons come in quest of her.
O my Antonio, had I but the means
To hold a rival place with one of them,
I have a mind presages me such thrift[119]
That I should questionless be fortunate.[120]

ANTONIO

Thou know'st that all my fortunes are at sea,
Neither have I money nor commodity[121]
To raise a present[122] sum; therefore go forth—
Try[123] what my credit can in Venice do;
That shall be racked[124] even to the uttermost
To furnish thee to[125] Belmont, to fair Portia.
Go presently enquire, and so will I,
Where money is; and I no question make
To have it of my trust or for my sake.[126]

Exeunt.

113. *richly left:* who has received a great inheritance

114. *Sometimes:* At times

PLOT POINT

Bassanio tells Antonio of his desire to travel to Belmont to woo the beautiful heiress, Portia. Having received loving looks from her, he is confident that he will succeed in wooing her. However, he just needs the necessary 'means' or funds to get there.

115. *nothing undervalued to:* no less worthy than
116. *Cato's daughter, Portia, was renowned for her fidelity to her husband, Brutus, and was considered a model of female virtue.*
117. *Renownèd suitors:* Distinguished, highly-esteemed admirers
118. *Colchos: The coast of Colchos is where Jason won the golden fleece.*

LOOKING AT LANGUAGE

Classical allusion: When a text makes reference to a person or story in classical literature. For example, Portia is compared to Cato's daughter (line 166); Bassanio refers the Greek myth of Jason who went in quest of the golden fleece (line 172).

119. *I … thrift:* I see such riches for myself
120. *That … fortunate:* I have no doubt that I will succeed.

121. *commodity:* goods

122. *present:* immediate

123. *Try:* Test/Find out

124. *racked:* stretched

125. *To furnish thee to:* To help get you to

126. *I no question … sake:* I have no doubt that I will get it either because of my good credit, or as a personal favour.

OVERVIEW OF ACT 1, SCENE 1

- At the start of this opening scene, Antonio is **sad** and **melancholy** (depressed) but he cannot explain why:

  In sooth, I know not why I am so sad. (line 1)
- Salerio suggests that it is the thought of his ships at sea that is making Antonio depressed, saying that if he were in Antonio's position, everything would remind him of this fact:

  My wind cooling my broth
  Would blow me to an ague when I thought
  What harm a wind too great might do at sea. (lines 22–24)
- Antonio disputes this, assuring Salerio and Solanio that his 'ventures are not in one bottom trusted' (line 42) and that his fortune does not depend solely on the present year's trading.
- Antonio also rejects Solanio's claim that he must therefore be in love.
- Next, Bassanio, Lorenzo and Gratiano enter the scene. Salerio and Solanio decide to leave and agree to meet Bassanio again at a time that suits him.
- Lorenzo also decides to depart, saying that he will meet Antonio and Bassanio at dinner-time. Gratiano, however, is in no hurry to leave and instead comments on Antonio's sad appearance, saying that he 'look[s] not well' (line 73). Antonio replies:

  I hold the world but as the world, Gratiano—
  A stage where every man must play a part,
  And mine a sad one. (lines 77–79)

  These lines seem to sum up Antonio's character – he is realistic (or pessimistic) and resigned to his fate.
- In Gratiano's long-winded speech that **ensues** (follows), he suggests that people who appear sad and silent do so in order to gain a reputation for being very profound and wise. He advises Antonio to cast aside this appearance:

  But fish not with this melancholy bait
  For this fool gudgeon, this opinion. (lines 101–102)
- When Gratiano and Lorenzo finally leave, Bassanio seems to sum up Gratiano's personality perfectly:

  Gratiano speaks an infinite deal of nothing, more
  than any man in all Venice. (lines 114–115)
- Finally, Bassanio can speak to Antonio alone about his proposed plan to win the hand of 'fair' (line 162) Portia, a rich heiress who lives in Belmont. When Antonio asks Bassanio to tell him about his 'secret pilgrimage' (line 120), Bassanio **digresses** (strays from the subject) at first. Bassanio tells an elaborate story about his childhood when, if he lost one arrow, he would send another arrow in exactly the same direction. He often found both arrows when he did this. (*Often,* but not *always!*)
- Bassanio is, in an indirect way, preparing Antonio for his request for money. Antonio has already given Bassanio money in the past. Bassanio used this money to fund his very extravagant lifestyle, which he describes as a 'swelling port' (line 124). This money is like the first arrow. Now, if Antonio will agree to lend him more money (a second arrow), he feels that he will be in a position to **recoup** (get back) all the money that Antonio has lent him – or at least the second loan.
- Antonio is almost insulted that Bassanio would resort to long and drawn-out stories to ask him for money and tells him to come to the point directly:

  Then do but say to me what I should do
  That in your knowledge may by me be done (lines 158–159)

- Bassanio has devised an **ingenious** (clever) plan to help him to 'get clear of all the debts [he] owe[s]' (line 134). He has decided to seek Portia's hand in marriage, a 'lady richly left' (line 161), who is 'fair' (line 162) and 'of wondrous virtues' (line 163). He is confident that he will succeed. When he met Portia in the past, he felt that she found him attractive:

  from her eyes
  I did receive fair speechless messages. (lines 163–164)

- Unfortunately, Bassanio lacks the funds necessary to get himself to Belmont. He therefore asks Antonio to lend him the money he needs.
- However, Antonio is not in a position to give him the money as 'all [his] fortunes are at sea' (line 177), and he has neither 'money nor commodity' (line 178) to raise the amount.
- Antonio offers to help Bassanio raise the money by acting as a **guarantor** (someone who ensures that the loan will be repaid) for a loan:

  Try what my credit can in Venice do;
  That shall be racked even to the uttermost
  To furnish thee to Belmont, to fair Portia. (lines 180–182)

Themes

- The key themes of **money** and **love** are introduced in this scene. Bassanio is depicted as an extravagant spendthrift who borrows money to fuel his lavish lifestyle. Antonio, it seems, has already lent him a considerable amount of money:

  To you, Antonio,
  I owe the most in money and in love (lines 130–131)

- Bassanio is certainly enticed by the fact that Portia is a wealthy heiress. This could be the answer to all his financial problems. If Antonio could lend him *'the means'* (line 173) to get to Belmont, he is confident of success:

  I have a mind presages me such thrift
  That I should questionless be fortunate. (lines 175–176)

  In this way, the theme of money is **inextricably** (meaning it is not possible to separate) linked to the theme of love.

REVIEWING

1. Why, according to Salerio and Solanio, is Antonio sad?
2. What would remind Salerio of his ships if he were in Antonio's situation?
3. How does Antonio respond to Salerio's suggestions?
4. What favour does Bassanio ask of Antonio?
5. What is Antonio's response to his request?

ORAL LANGUAGE

Conversation Between Antonio and Bassanio

Pair Activity

With your partner, look back over the conversation between Antonio and Bassanio in lines 119–185 and:

(a) Summarise the main points of the conversation.

(b) Write the conversation in modern English and perform it together.

EXPLORING

Language and Imagery P

This scene is rich in imagery that helps to tell us more about characters and the key themes.

(a) Bassanio uses **classical imagery** when discussing his voyage to Belmont, drawing parallels between himself and Jason from the **myth of Jason and the Golden Fleece**.

(b) There are also many **images of ships** in this scene. They remind us how important ships are for business and enterprise in Venice. These images also alert us to the risks and dangers involved.

Turn to **page 6** of your portfolio to complete the tasks on imagery in this scene.

REFLECTING

1. Character File P

Turn to the Character File section of your portfolio to record your first impressions of **(a) Antonio** (**page 111**) and **(b) Bassanio** (**page 117**).

2. My Reflection on Act 1, Scene 1 P

Turn to **page 8** of your portfolio to complete your reflection on this scene.

3. Key Quotes P

Turn to **page 9** of your portfolio to complete the task on key quotes from this scene.

VENETIA

ACT 1, SCENE 2

Setting: Belmont, a room in Portia's house.

In this **scene** you will:

- Meet the character of **Portia**.
- Write a **diary entry**.
- Draw a **caricature** based on Portia's suitors.

Action – What Happens?

In this scene, we are introduced to Portia and Nerissa. Portia is a wealthy heiress and Nerissa is Portia's waiting-woman and **confidante** (close friend). Portia is sad, weary and disillusioned. Before Portia's father died, he devised a lottery for suitors who wish to marry her. He placed her portrait in one of three chests (or caskets) of gold, silver and lead. The person who chooses the correct casket, the one which contains Portia's portrait, gets her hand in marriage.

Nerissa lists all the suitors who have come to seek Portia's hand. Portia outlines the flaws she sees with each. None of the suitors interests Portia in the least. Later on in the scene, Portia is relieved to learn that all five suitors are departing.

Nerissa reminds Portia of a young Venetian named Bassanio who came to Belmont in the past. It is clear that Portia remembers him well and considers him worthy of praise.

The scene ends with a messenger coming to announce the expected arrival of another suitor – the Prince of Morocco.

Useful Words

death's-head – a skull

suitor – admirer/wooer

determinations – plans

dumb-show – mimed play

ACT 1, SCENE 2

Enter PORTIA and NERISSA.

PORTIA

By my troth,[1] Nerissa, my little body is aweary of this great world.

NERISSA

You would be, sweet madam, if your miseries were in the same abundance as your good fortunes are;[2] and yet, for aught I see, they are as sick that surfeit[3] with too much as they that starve with nothing.[4] It is no mean[5] happiness therefore, to be seated[6] in the mean.[7] Superfluity[8] comes sooner by white hairs, but competency[9] lives longer.[10]

PORTIA

Good sentences,[11] and well pronounced.

NERISSA

They would be better if well followed.

'By my troth, Nerissa, my little body is aweary of this great world.'

(Portia, lines 1–2)

1. *By my troth:* Truly

CHARACTER NOTE

When we are first introduced to Portia, she seems tired and unhappy. This reminds us of Antonio's sadness in the previous scene. Look back over Antonio's first lines in Act 1, Scene 1 (p. 3). What similarities do you notice?

2. *if your miseries … are:* if your problems were as great as your good fortune
3. *as sick that surfeit:* have too much to eat
4. *for aught … nothing:* it seems to me that those that have too much are as badly off as those that have too little
5. *mean:* small
6. *seated:* located
7. *mean:* middle
8. *Superfluity:* Having too much of something
9. *competency:* just enough
10. *Superfluity … longer:* Having too much makes you age more quickly than having a moderate amount.
11. *Good sentences:* Great wisdom/advice

PORTIA

If to do were as easy as to know what were good to do,[12] chapels had been[13] churches, and poor men's cottages princes' palaces. It is a good divine[14] that follows his own instructions.[15] I can easier teach twenty what were good to be done than to be one of the twenty to follow mine own teaching. The brain may devise laws for the blood,[16] but a hot temper leaps o'er a cold decree.[17][18] Such a hare is madness, the youth, to skip o'er the meshes[19] of good counsel,[20] the cripple.[21] But this reasoning is not in the fashion to choose me a husband. O me, the word 'choose'! I may neither choose who I would[22] nor refuse who I dislike; so is the will[23] of a living daughter curbed[24] by the will[25] of a dead father. Is it not hard, Nerissa, that I cannot choose one nor refuse none?

NERISSA

Your father was ever[26] virtuous,[27] and holy men at their death have good inspirations; therefore the lottery, that he hath devised in these three chests of gold, silver and lead, whereof[28] who chooses his meaning chooses you, will, no doubt, never be chosen by any rightly but one who shall rightly love.[29] But what warmth is there in your affection towards any of these princely suitors that are already come?[30]

PORTIA

I pray thee, over-name them, and as thou namest them I will describe them; and, according to my description, level[31] at my affection.

NERISSA

First, there is the Neapolitan[32] prince.

PORTIA

Ay, that's a colt[33] indeed, for he doth[34] nothing but talk of his horse, and he makes it a great appropriation[35] to his own good parts that he can shoe him himself. I am much afeard my lady his mother played false with a smith.[36]

12. *If … do:* It is easier to know what should be done than to actually do it *Portia comments on how hard it is to actually follow advice. She goes on to claim that it is easier to give advice to twenty people than to follow it herself.*
13. *had been:* would be
14. *divine:* clergyman
15. *instructions:* teaching
16. *blood:* emotions/passions
17. *decree:* law/judgement
18. *The brain … decree:* While our mind tries to control our emotions, there are times when these emotions overtake our reason.
19. *meshes:* snares/traps
20. *good counsel:* good advice
21. *Such a hare … cripple: According to Portia, young people are like hares avoiding the traps ('meshes') of good advice given by their elders.*
22. *who I would:* who I would like
23. *will:* wish
24. *curbed:* controlled/restricted
25. *will:* testament *Portia laments the fact that her choice of husband has been restricted by conditions laid down by her dead father.*
26. *ever:* always
27. *virtuous:* good/moral
28. *whereof:* whereby
29. *whereof … love:* the correct chest or casket will only be chosen by one that truly loves you *Nerissa is assuring Portia that her father has arranged this in her best interest, confident that the man who succeeds will be the most suitable match for his daughter.*
30. *But what warmth … come?:* Tell me what you think about those noble suitors who have come already.
31. *level:* guess
32. *Neapolitan:* from Naples
33. *colt:* a foolish young man
34. *doth:* does
35. *appropriation:* addition
36. *I am … smith:* I suspect his mother had an affair with a blacksmith *(who made horse shoes).*

NERISSA

Then there is the County Palatine.[37]

37. *County Palatine:* a count/lord who had royal powers

PORTIA

He doth nothing but frown, as who should say[38] 'An[39] you will not have me, choose'.[40] He hears merry tales and smiles not. I fear he will prove the weeping philosopher[41] when he grows old, being so full of unmannerly[42] sadness in his youth. I had rather be married to a death's-head with a bone[43] in his mouth than to either of these. God defend me from these two!

38. *as who should say:* as if to say
39. *'An:* If
40. *choose:* do as you wish
41. *The weeping philosopher: This refers to Heraclitus – a melancholy (sad) Greek philosopher.*
42. *unmannerly:* excessive
43. *death's-head … bone:* skull and bones

NERISSA

How say you by[44] the French lord, Monsieur le Bon?

44. *How say you by:* What do you think about

PORTIA

God made him, and therefore let him pass for a man. In truth, I know it is a sin to be a mocker, but he — why, he hath a horse better than the Neapolitan's, a better bad habit of frowning than the Count Palatine. He is every man in no man. If a throstle[45] sing, he falls straight a-cap'ring.[46][47] He will fence[48] with his own shadow. If I should marry him, I should marry twenty husbands. If he would despise me, I would forgive him, for if he love me to madness, I shall never requite him.[49]

45. *throstle:* thrush *(a bird)*
46. *a-cap'ring:* leaping
47. *he falls straight a-cap'ring:* he will dance at the drop of a hat
48. *fence:* fight
49. *If he would … him:* I wouldn't mind if he hated me, because I certainly would never return his love.

NERISSA

What say you then to Falconbridge, the young baron of England?

PORTIA

You know I say nothing to him, for he understands not me, nor I him. He hath[50] neither Latin, French, nor Italian, and you will come into the court and swear that I have a poor pennyworth[51] in the English. He is a proper man's picture,[52] but alas, who can converse with a dumb-show?[53] How oddly he is suited![54] I think he bought his doublet[55] in Italy, his round hose[56] in France, his bonnet[57] in Germany, and his behaviour everywhere.

50. *hath:* has
51. *poor pennyworth:* bad command of
52. *a proper man's picture:* handsome
53. *dumb-show:* play without speech *(mime)*
54. *suited:* dressed
55. *doublet:* upper garment *(jacket)*
56. *round hose:* puffed pants
57. *bonnet:* hat

NERISSA

What think you of the Scottish lord, his neighbour?

PORTIA

That he hath a neighbourly charity[58] in him, for he borrowed a box of the ear[59] of the Englishman and swore he would pay him again[60] when he was able. I think the Frenchman became his surety[61] and sealed under for another.[62]

58. *That … charity:* He has a kind, considerate nature *(Portia is being sarcastic)*
59. *a box of the ear:* got a slap
60. *pay him again:* pay him back *(i.e. retaliate)*
61. *surety:* substitute/representative
62. *I think … another:* The Frenchman guaranteed the Scot's promise of a slap and promised to give the Englishman another slap from himself.

SHAKESPEARE'S WORLD

Even though Scotland and England are now part of the United Kingdom, historically there was a lot of animosity between the two countries. In Elizabethan times France was an ally of Scotland against England. In his play *Henry V*, Shakespeare refers to the famous Battle of Agincourt (1415), which was one of England's most historic victories against France.

NERISSA

How like you the young German, the Duke of Saxony's nephew?

PORTIA

Very vilely in the morning when he is sober, and most vilely in the afternoon when he is drunk.[63] When he is best, he is a little worse than a man, and when he is worst, he is little better than a beast. An the worst fall that ever fell,[64] I hope I shall make shift[65] to go without him.

63. *Very vilely … drunk:* This man behaves very badly when he is sober, and worse when he is drunk.
64. *An … fell:* If the worst came to worst
65. *make shift:* manage

NERISSA

If he should offer to choose, and choose the right casket,[66] you should refuse to[67] perform your father's will if you should refuse to accept him.

66. *casket:* chest
67. *you should refuse to:* you would be refusing to

PORTIA

Therefore, for fear of the worst, I pray thee[68] set a deep glass of Rhenish wine[69] on the contrary[70] casket; for if the devil be within and that temptation without, I know he will choose it.[71] I will do any thing, Nerissa, ere I will be married to a sponge.[72]

68. *I pray thee:* please
69. *Rhenish wine:* strong white wine from Germany
70. *contrary:* wrong
71. *for if … choose it:* if he has the desire within himself to drink and sees the tempting glass of wine, I know he'll want to choose that one
72. *sponge:* drunkard

NERISSA

You need not fear, lady, the having any of these lords. They have acquainted me with their determinations,[73] which is indeed to return to their home and to trouble you with no more suit, unless you may be won by some other sort than your father's imposition depending on the caskets.[74]

73. *They have … determinations:* They have let me know their intentions/plans
74. *unless … caskets:* unless you may be won by some other way than the conditions set for you by your father in his will

75. *Sibylla: Sibylla was a woman in classical mythology who asked Apollo to allow her to live for as many years as the grains of sand in her hands. Her wish was granted, and she lived a very long life, but she did not ask for eternal youth.*
76. *chaste:* pure/virginal
77. *Diana: Roman goddess of chastity (virginity)*
78. *wooers:* suitors

PORTIA

If I live to be as old as Sibylla,[75] I will die as chaste[76] as Diana,[77] unless I be obtained by the manner of my father's will. I am glad this parcel of wooers[78] are so reasonable, for there is not one among them but I dote on his very absence; and I pray God grant them a fair departure.

NERISSA

Do you not remember, lady, in your father's time, a Venetian, a scholar and a soldier, that came hither[79] in company of the Marquis of Montferrat?

79. *hither:* here

PORTIA

Yes, yes, it was Bassanio—as I think, so was he called.

NERISSA

True, madam. He of all the men that ever my foolish eyes looked upon was the best deserving a fair lady.

PLOT POINT

It now emerges that Bassanio has previously visited Belmont and is remembered fondly by Portia. This suggests that his trip is not in vain as he is already a favourite of Portia's.

SPOTLIGHT ON ... STAGECRAFT

This modern production used Las Vegas as the setting for the play. Why do you think the director might have chosen this setting? Do you think this was a good idea?

PORTIA

I remember him well, and I remember him worthy of thy praise.

Enter a SERVANT.

How now, what news?

SERVANT

The four strangers[80] seek for you, madam, to take their leave, and there is a forerunner[81] come from a fifth, the Prince of Morocco, who brings word the Prince his master will be here tonight.

80. *four strangers: There were six suitors mentioned.*

81. *forerunner:* messenger

PORTIA

If I could bid the fifth welcome with so good heart as I can bid the other four farewell, I should be glad of his approach. If he have the condition of a saint and the complexion of a devil, I had rather he should shrive me than wive me.[82] Come, Nerissa. Sirrah, go before. Whiles we shut the gates upon one wooer, another knocks at the door.

82. *If he have ... me:* Even if he is as pure as a saint and as black as a devil, I would rather he hear my confession than marry me. *This comment from Portia is inherently racist.*

Exeunt.

OVERVIEW OF ACT 1, SCENE 2

- Portia's first words echo those of Antonio from the previous scene and set a sombre (sad) tone. She tells Nerissa, her waiting-woman and confidante, 'my little body is aweary of this great world' (lines 1–2). However, unlike Antonio, Portia proves herself light-hearted and spirited in this scene too.
- Portia's father has restricted her choice of potential husband and this has contributed to her **malaise** (unhappiness):

  > *I may neither choose who I would nor refuse who*
  > *I dislike; so is the will of a living daughter curbed*
  > *by the will of a dead father.* (lines 23–25)

- Nerissa lists the suitors who have all come to seek Portia's hand in marriage. This gives Portia the opportunity to mock each one. It is important to remember that this kind of cultural stereotyping was not unusual in Shakespeare's time. By criticising (or mocking) each suitor, Portia is emphasising their cultural or racial differences.

- Portia finds fault with each admirer. For example:
    - **The Neapolitan Prince**, *'doth nothing but talk of his horse'* (lines 39–40)
    - **The County Palatine**, *'hears merry tales and smiles not'* (lines 46–47)
    - **The French lord, Monsieur le Bon**, *'is every man in no man'* (line 57) (he has no distinctive personality of his own)
    - **Falconbridge, the young baron of England**, *'hath neither Latin, French, nor Italian'* (lines 66–67) (he does not understand her language) and even though he is handsome, she would rather not be married to a 'dumb-show' (i.e. a silent man) (line 70)
    - **The Scottish lord** is too cowardly
    - **The young German, the Duke of Saxony's nephew**, is described as a drunkard, a *'sponge'* (line 95).
- Portia shows her good humour and high spirits when she remarks that, in order to ensure that the young German would not choose the correct casket, she would place a glass of wine on the wrong 'contrary' (line 92) casket, knowing this would **deflect** (draw) his attention from the right one.
- Portia is extremely **dutiful** because, even though she dislikes the prospect of not being able to choose her own husband, she will obey her father's wishes no matter what:

  If I live to be as old as Sibylla, I will die as chaste
  as Diana, unless I be obtained by the manner of
  my father's will. (lines 102–104)

  This means that, even if Portia lives for a thousand years, she will marry only if the conditions of her father's will are respected.
- Towards the end of the scene, Nerissa reminds Portia of a young Venetian 'scholar and a soldier' (line 109) she once met called Bassanio:

  He of all the men that ever my foolish
  eyes looked upon was best deserving a fair lady. (lines 112–113)
- The scene ends with news that the Prince of Morocco will arrive later. Portia's response is racist:

  If he have the
  condition of a saint and the complexion of a devil,
  I had rather he should shrive me than wive me. (lines 123–125)

REVIEWING

1. Explain the lottery that Portia's father outlined in his will.
2. How does Portia feel about this arrangement?
3. It is clear that Portia will **abide by** (follow) her father's wishes. Where do we see evidence of this in the scene?
4. What plan does Portia have in mind to avoid marrying the young German?
5. How does Portia react to the news that the suitors are going to depart?
6. What is Nerissa's opinion of Bassanio?

EXPLORING

Portia's Suitors – 'parcel of wooers' P

Pair Activity

Turn to **page 10** of your portfolio to complete the exercise on the suitors.

CREATING

Complete either **task A or task B below:**

Task A – Portia's Diary P

Imagine you are Portia. Write a diary entry in which you record your private thoughts and feelings about the lottery your late father has devised to help you find a suitable husband. Refer to the suitors in this scene. Turn to **page 11** of your portfolio to help you.

OR

Task B – Cartoon Caricature of a Suitor P

A caricature is a cartoon picture in which the prominent features of a person are exaggerated for comic effect. Turn to **page 12** of your portfolio to draw a caricature of **one or more** of the suitors from this scene. Label your picture with quotes and arrows.

Example of a caricature – an unflattering 1819 caricature of the Prince Regent by George Cruikshank

REFLECTING

1. Character File P

Turn to the Character File section of your portfolio (**page 123**) to record your first impressions of **Portia**. (**Hint:** You might write down **something you admire** and **something you do not admire** about her in this scene.)

2. My Reflection on Act 1, Scene 2 P

Turn to **page 13** of your portfolio to record your responses to aspects of this scene.

ACT 1, SCENE 3

Setting: Venice. A street

In this **scene** you will:

- Meet the character of **Shylock**.
- Explore and perform one of Shylock's important **speeches**.
- Examine **imagery**, **language** and **conflict** in the scene.

Action – What Happens?

We meet Shylock (a Jewish moneylender) in this scene. Bassanio wants Shylock to give him a loan. Shylock is hesitant at first, but he agrees to lend Bassanio 3,000 **ducats** (gold coins) if Antonio guarantees the loan.

When Shylock meets Antonio, he accuses Antonio of treating him badly in the past. Shylock says that Antonio has used **offensive language** against him and spat on him. According to Shylock, Antonio has been abusive towards him because he charges interest on loans (something that Antonio does not do) and because he is Jewish. However, to prove that he does not hold a grudge against Antonio, Shylock offers to lend Bassanio the money interest-free.

Shylock says that if Antonio does not repay the loan on time, he will take a **pound of flesh** from any part of Antonio's body he wishes. Antonio agrees, thinking this is just good sport, but Bassanio is sceptical and does not trust these terms.

Useful Words

ducats – gold coins

bond – financial contract/loan agreement

usance – interest

forfeit – penalty

Rialto – the Venetian stock exchange

eanlings – lambs

Enter BASSANIO and SHYLOCK.

SHYLOCK

Three thousand ducats,[1] well.

BASSANIO

Ay, sir, for three months.

SHYLOCK

For three months, well.

BASSANIO

For the which, as I told you, Antonio shall be bound.[2]

SHYLOCK

Antonio shall become bound, well.

BASSANIO

May you stead[3] me? Will you pleasure[4] me? Shall I know your answer?

PLOT POINT

When we join the action, Bassanio is already negotiating a loan from Shylock, a Jewish moneylender. Shylock will become a very important character as the play progresses.

1. *ducats:* gold coins
2. *shall be bound:* act as guarantor *(be held responsible for repaying the loan)*
3. *stead:* facilitate
4. *pleasure:* please

SHYLOCK

Three thousand ducats for three months, and Antonio bound.

BASSANIO

Your answer to that.

SHYLOCK

Antonio is a good man.

BASSANIO

Have you heard any imputation[5] to the contrary?

SHYLOCK

Ho, no, no, no, no! My meaning in saying he is a good man is to have you understand me that he is sufficient.[6] Yet his means are in supposition.[7] He hath an argosy[8] bound to Tripolis, another to the Indies. I understand moreover upon the Rialto,[9] he hath a third at Mexico, a fourth for England, and other ventures he hath squandered abroad.[10] But ships are but boards, sailors but men.[11] There be land-rats and water-rats, water-thieves and land-thieves—I mean pirates—and then there is the peril of waters, winds, and rocks.[12] The man is, notwithstanding,[13] sufficient. Three thousand ducats. I think I may take his bond.

BASSANIO

Be assured you may.

SHYLOCK

I will be assured[14] I may, and that I may be assured, I will bethink me.[15] May I speak with Antonio?

BASSANIO

If it please you to dine with us.

SHYLOCK

Yes, to smell pork, to eat of the habitation[16] which your prophet the Nazarite conjured the devil into.[17] I will buy with you, sell with you, talk with you,

5. *imputation:* implication or suggestion
6. *sufficient:* financially solvent
7. *in supposition:* in doubt/at risk
8. *argosy:* large merchant ship
9. *Rialto: the Venetian stock exchange where merchants congregated*
10. *and other … abroad:* other investments scattered abroad
11. *But ships … men:* Ships are only made of wood and men are fallible. *In other words, there is a lot of danger out there.*
12. *There be … rocks: Shylock is listing all the potential dangers that ships and sailors can encounter, including rats, pirates, stormy weather and rocks.*
13. *notwithstanding:* in spite of all this
14. *assured: given financial guarantees*
15. *I will bethink me:* I will think carefully about it.
16. *habitation:* pigsty
17. *your prophet … into:* Christ, from Nazareth, who turned devils into a herd of swine. *Shylock, being Jewish, does not eat pork. He will not share a meal with Christians for fear pork would be consumed.*

walk with you, and so following, but I will not
eat with you, drink with you, nor pray with you.
What news on the Rialto? Who is he comes here?

Enter ANTONIO.

BASSANIO
This is Signor Antonio.

SHYLOCK
[*aside*] How like a fawning publican[18] he looks!
I hate him for he is a Christian;
But more, for that in low simplicity[19]
He lends out money gratis,[20] and brings down
The rate of usance[21] here with us in Venice.
If I can catch him once upon the hip,[22]
I will feed fat the ancient grudge I bear him.[23]
He hates our sacred nation,[24] and he rails
Even there where merchants most do congregate
On me,[25] my bargains, and my well-won thrift[26]
Which he calls interest. Cursèd be my tribe
If I forgive him!

BASSANIO
Shylock, do you hear?

SHYLOCK
I am debating of my present store,[27]
And by the near guess of my memory,
I cannot instantly raise up the gross[28]
Of full three thousand ducats. What of that?[29]
Tubal, a wealthy Hebrew of my tribe,
Will furnish me.[30] But soft[31]—how many months
Do you desire? [*to ANTONIO*] Rest you fair, good signor.
Your worship was the last man in our mouths.[32]

ANTONIO
Shylock, albeit[33] I neither lend nor borrow
By taking nor by giving of excess,
Yet to supply the ripe wants[34] of my friend,
I'll break a custom. [*to BASSANIO*] Is he yet possessed
How much ye would?[35]

SPOTLIGHT ON … ASIDE

Aside: A short remark, made by a character on stage, which is supposed to be heard by the audience but not the other character(s) on stage. When reading Shylock's aside (lines 36–47), consider what it reveals about his intentions. What two reasons does he give for 'hating' Antonio? What else does he reveal about Antonio?

18. *fawning publican:* grovelling tax-collector
19. *low simplicity:* simple honesty *Antonio doesn't charge interest. Shylock sees this as being naïve or foolish.*
20. *gratis:* interest-free
21. *usance:* interest
22. *If I … hip:* If I could get him at a disadvantage
23. *I will … him:* I could feed my hatred for him.
24. *sacred nation: the Jewish people*
25. *He hates … me:* he publicly humiliates me
26. *well-won thrift:* well-earned profit *Shylock sees the money he earns from lending money as profit for doing good business and not as interest.*
27. *I am … store:* I am thinking about the money/funds I have available to me at the moment
28. *gross:* full amount
29. *What of that?:* What does that matter?
30. *furnish me:* give me the money
31. *soft:* wait
32. *Your worship … mouths:* We were just talking about you.
33. *albeit:* although
34. *ripe wants:* immediate/urgent needs
35. *Is he … would?:* Does he know yet how much you want?

SHYLOCK

Ay, ay, three thousand ducats.

ANTONIO

And for three months.

SHYLOCK

I had forgot—three months. [to *BASSANIO*] You told me so.—
Well then, your bond; and let me see—but hear you,[36]
Methoughts you said you neither lend nor borrow
Upon advantage.[37]

ANTONIO

I do never use it.[38]

SHYLOCK

When Jacob grazed his uncle Laban's sheep[39]—
This Jacob from our holy Abram was,
As his wise mother wrought in his behalf,
The third possessor;[40] ay, he was the third—

ANTONIO

And what of him? Did he take interest?

SHYLOCK

No, not take interest, not, as you would say,
Directly int'rest. Mark[41] what Jacob did:
When Laban and himself were compromised[42]
That all the eanlings[43] which were streaked and pied[44]
Should fall as Jacob's hire,[45] the ewes, being rank,[46]
In end of autumn turnèd to the rams,
And when the work of generation[47] was
Between these woolly breeders in the act,
The skilful shepherd peeled me certain wands,[48]
And in the doing of the deed of kind[49]
He stuck them up before the fulsome ewes,[50]
Who then conceiving, did in eaning time
Fall[51] parti-coloured lambs, and those were Jacob's.
This was a way to thrive; and he was blest;
And thrift is blessing, if men steal it not.[52]

36. *hear me:* listen to me

37. *advantage:* interest

38. *I do … it:* I don't ever charge interest.

39. *When … sheep: Shylock is referring to the story of Jacob and his uncle Laban in the Bible.*

40. *third possessor:* third in line to inherit the property

PLOT POINT

In the Bible story from the Book of Genesis, Jacob and his uncle Laban came to an agreement that Jacob would keep all the striped or spotted sheep. When mating time came, Jacob cleverly arranged some sticks close to the ewes to give them the appearance of being striped, thereby increasing his flock. Shylock sees profit as a blessing if it is not obtained illegally. Antonio, meanwhile, wonders if Shylock has mentioned this story to defend his own practice of charging interest.

41. *Mark:* Note
42. *compromised:* agreed
43. *eanlings:* lambs
44. *streaked and pied:* striped and spotted
45. *hire:* income
46. *rank:* in heat *(ready to mate)*
47. *generation:* mating
48. *wands:* thin branches/rods
49. *the deed of kind:* the deed of nature *(i.e. procreation)*
50. *fulsome ewes:* plump ewes/ewes that were in heat
51. *Fall:* Deliver/Give birth to
52. *And thrift … stealing:* Profit is a blessing if it is not obtained by stealing.

ANTONIO

This was a venture, sir, that Jacob served for[53]—
A thing not in his power to bring to pass,
But swayed and fashioned[54] by the hand of heaven.
Was this inserted to make interest good?[55]
Or is your gold and silver ewes and rams?

SHYLOCK

I cannot tell. I make it breed as fast.
But note me, signor—

ANTONIO

Mark you this, Bassanio,
The devil can cite Scripture for his purpose.[56]

53. *served for:* gave his service for

54. *fashioned:* created

55. *Was ... good?:* Did you deliberately tell us this to defend your charging interest?

56. *The devil ... purpose:* Even the devil can use the Bible to suit his purposes.

An evil soul producing holy witness[57]
Is like a villain with a smiling cheek,
A goodly[58] apple rotten at the heart.
O, what a goodly outside falsehood hath!

SHYLOCK

Three thousand ducats. 'Tis a good round sum.
Three months from twelve—then let me see the rate.

ANTONIO

Well, Shylock, shall we be beholding[59] to you?

SHYLOCK

Signor Antonio, many a time and oft
In the Rialto you have rated me[60]
About my moneys and my usances.[61]
Still[62] have I borne[63] it with a patient shrug,
For suff'rance[64] is the badge[65] of all our tribe.

57. *holy witness:* biblical evidence

58. *goodly:* attractive-looking

CHARACTER NOTE

Notice how antagonistic Antonio is from the outset. He suggests to Bassanio that Shylock harbours bad intentions, comparing him to an apple that looks good on the outside but is rotten to the core.

59. *beholding:* indebted

60. *rated me:* berated me *(you have scolded me; Shylock takes the opportunity in this important speech to remind Antonio of his ill-treatment of him in the past.)*
61. *usances:* rates of interest
62. *Still:* Always
63. *borne:* tolerated
64. *suff'rance:* patience/endurance
65. *badge:* feature/characteristic

You call me misbeliever, cut-throat dog,
And spit upon my Jewish gaberdine,[66]
And all for use of that which is mine own.
Well then, it now appears you need my help.
Go to, then, you come to me, and you say
'Shylock, we would have moneys'—you say so,
You, that did void your rheum[67] upon my beard,
And foot[68] me as you spurn a stranger cur[69]
Over your threshold.[70] Moneys is your suit.[71]
What should I say to you? Should I not say
'Hath a dog money? Is it possible
A cur can lend three thousand ducats?' Or
Shall I bend low and in a bondman's[72] key,
With bated breath and whisp'ring humbleness,[73]
Say this:
'Fair sir, you spat on me on Wednesday last;
You spurned me such a day; another time
You called me dog; and for these courtesies
I'll lend you thus much moneys'?

ANTONIO

I am as like[74] to call thee so again,
To spit on thee again, to spurn thee too.
If thou wilt lend this money, lend it not
As to thy friends; for when did friendship take
A breed for barren metal of his friend?[75]
But lend it rather to thine[76] enemy,
Who if he break, thou mayst with better face
Exact the penalty.[77]

SHYLOCK

Why, look you, how you storm![78]
I would be friends with you, and have your love,
Forget the shames that you have stained me with,
Supply your present wants, and take no doit
Of usance[79] for my moneys, and you'll not hear me.[80]
This is kind I offer.[81]

BASSANIO

This were[82] kindness.

66. *gaberdine:* long coat

67. *void your rheum:* spit

68. *foot:* kick
69. *cur:* dog
70. *threshold:* doorstep
71. *suit:* request

72. *bondman's:* slave's

73. *whisp'ring humbleness:* in a submissive voice

SPOTLIGHT ON ... LANGUAGE

Shylock's monologue:
A monologue is a speech that is spoken aloud on stage to one or more characters. It often reveals something about the character's emotional state. What is revealed, in your opinion, about Shylock's emotional state of mind in this monologue? Before you read on, do you think Shylock will lend Antonio the money?

74. *as like:* likely

75. *for when ... friend?:* when did friends ever try to make money from each other?
76. *thine:* your
77. *But lend ... penalty:* Lend instead to your enemy as, if he fails to repay, it is easier to demand a penalty.

PLOT POINT

Antonio is in no way apologetic about how he has treated Shylock in the past. In fact, he says he would spit on and insult him again. He asks Shylock to lend the money as if lending to an enemy as, if Antonio defaults (is unable to repay the loan), it will be easier to demand a penalty.

78. *Why, ... storm!:* Look how angry you are!

79. *and take ... moneys:* and take not even an iota (small amount) of interest
80. *you'll not hear me:* you won't listen to me
81. *This is ... offer:* This is a generous offer.

82. *were:* would be

SHYLOCK

This kindness will I show.
Go with me to a notary,[83] seal me there
Your single bond,[84] and, in a merry sport,[85]
If you repay me not on such a day,
In such a place, such sum or sums as are
Expressed in the condition, let the forfeit[86]
Be nominated for an equal pound
Of your fair flesh to be cut off and taken
In what part of your body pleaseth me.

ANTONIO

Content,[87] in faith,[88] I'll seal to such a bond,
And say there is much kindness in the Jew.

BASSANIO

You shall not seal to such a bond for me.
I'll rather dwell in my necessity.[89]

83. *notary: a person who prepares legal documents*

84. *single bond: a bond signed by a single debtor*
85. *in a merry sport:* just for fun

86. *forfeit:* penalty

PLOT POINT

Shylock claims that he will not charge Antonio interest but, just for fun, if he fails to repay on time, the penalty will be a pound of Antonio's flesh.

87. *Content:* Agreed
88. *in faith:* indeed

89. *I'll rather … necessity:* I would rather do without.

SPOTLIGHT ON … STAGECRAFT

There are three different images of actors playing Shylock on pages 29, 30 (character on right) and here. Which one most closely resembles the image of the character you have in your mind?

ANTONIO

Why, fear not, man; I will not forfeit it:
Within these two months—that's a month before
This bond expires—I do expect return
Of thrice[90] three times the value of this bond.

90. *thrice:* three

SHYLOCK

O father Abram,[91] what these Christians are,
Whose own hard dealings teaches them suspect
The thoughts of others![92] Pray you[93] tell me this:
If he should break his day, what should I gain
By the exaction of the forfeiture?[94]
A pound of man's flesh taken from a man
Is not so estimable,[95] profitable neither,
As flesh of muttons, beefs, or goats. I say,
To buy his favour I extend this friendship.
If he will take it, so. If not, adieu,[96]
And, for my love, I pray you wrong me not.

91. *Abram: Abraham, father of the Jewish people*
92. *what these … others!:* Christians are so hard on each other that they suspect the worst in everybody!
93. *Pray you:* Please
94. *what should … forfeiture?:* what do I have to gain from taking this penalty?
95. *estimable:* valuable
96. *adieu:* goodbye

ANTONIO

Yes Shylock, I will seal unto this bond.

SHYLOCK

Then meet me forthwith[97] at the notary's.
Give[98] him direction[99] for this merry bond,
And[100] I will go and purse[101] the ducats straight,
See to my house—left in the fearful[102] guard
Of an unthrifty knave[103]—and presently[104]
I will be with you.

97. *forthwith:* immediately
98. *Give:* To give
99. *direction:* instructions
100. *And:* And then
101. *purse:* collect
102. *fearful:* awful
103. *unthrifty knave:* careless rascal
104. *presently:* immediately

ANTONIO

Hie[105] thee, gentle Jew.

Exit SHYLOCK.

The Hebrew will turn Christian, he grows kind.

105. *Hie:* Hurry

BASSANIO

I like not fair terms and a villain's mind.[106]

ANTONIO

Come on. In this there can be no dismay.[107]
My ships come home a month before the day.[108]

Exeunt.

106. *I like not … mind:* I don't trust this arrangement./It is too good to be true.
107. *dismay:* worry/cause for concern
108. *a month before the day:* a month before the day the bond is due to be repaid

PLOT POINT

Despite Antonio's confidence that his ships will return a month before the bond is due, the audience shares Bassanio's sense of apprehension (anxiety or fearful doubt) (line 175).

OVERVIEW OF ACT 1, SCENE 3

KEY SCENE – TERMS OF THE LOAN

Part 1 (lines 1–99) – Shylock contemplates lending Bassanio the money.

- At the start of this scene, Bassanio is negotiating a loan of 3,000 ducats from Shylock, a Jewish moneylender. It appears as if Shylock is teasing Bassanio, repeating what he says in order to keep Bassanio in suspense.
- Bassanio declares that Antonio 'shall become bound' (line 5). This means that Antonio is guaranteeing the loan. In the event that the loan is not paid back, Antonio would be **liable** (responsible) and given a penalty.
- Shylock is very aware of Antonio's financial position, and claims that 'his means are in supposition' (line 15). Shylock also says that 'ships are but boards, sailors but men' (lines 19–20), meaning that ships and men are vulnerable to external forces. Shylock elaborates on this, **citing** (mentioning) the 'peril (danger) of waters, winds, and rocks' (lines 22–23). This sets an **ominous** (gloomy/sinister) tone in the play as we realise that Antonio's ships are at the mercy of **the elements** (bad weather).

Part 2 (lines 100–138) – The past conflict between Shylock and Antonio is revealed.

- It is not long before Antonio appears on the scene to help Bassanio secure a loan. The tension between Shylock and Antonio is immediately **palpable** (noticeable), symbolising the resentment Jewish people and Christians had towards each other at this time.
- In an **aside** (something said by a character which is not meant to be heard by other characters on stage) Shylock says that he hates Antonio:

  I hate him for he is a Christian;
  But more, for that in low simplicity
  He lends out money gratis, and brings down
  The rate of usance here with us in Venice. (lines 37–40)

  Shylock hates Antonio mainly because he does not charge interest when he lends money and this has a negative effect on Shylock's business. He does this, Shylock claims, out of 'low simplicity' (line 38).
- Shylock's intention to deliberately get revenge on Antonio is made clear in the following lines:

  If I can catch him once upon the hip,
  I will feed fat the ancient grudge I bear him. (lines 41–42)
- If only Shylock could catch Antonio at a disadvantage – this would certainly help to 'feed fat' the bitter resentment Shylock feels towards Antonio. While we may be surprised initially by Shylock's strong language, we later learn why his **antipathy** (hatred) for Antonio runs so deep.
- Shylock asks Antonio why he now comes to him for help. He takes this opportunity to justify his practice of charging interest on the money he lends. Shylock refers to the Bible story of Jacob and his uncle Laban. Shylock uses this story to suggest that those who are **ingenious** (clever/inventive) or **enterprising** (resourceful/imaginative) are rewarded. Just as Jacob increased his wealth using his resourcefulness, Shylock makes his wealth 'breed' (line 91) too. Shylock firmly believes that 'thrift is blessing, if men steal it not' (line 85), meaning that wealth is good so long as it is not obtained by illegal means.

- Antonio interprets the Bible story differently, claiming that the success was 'swayed and fashioned (created) by the hand of heaven' (line 88). He is suggesting that Shylock is twisting the meaning of the Bible to suit his own intentions. Antonio also accuses Shylock of being a devil, saying that he is like an apple that is appealing on the outside but rotten to the core:

  An evil soul producing holy witness
  Is like a villain with a smiling cheek,
  A goodly apple rotten at the heart. (lines 94–96)

- Shylock now launches a vicious attack on Antonio, confronting him about his abusive treatment in the past. Antonio, it appears, has publicly abused and humiliated Shylock 'many a time and oft in the Rialto' (lines 101–102), the Venetian stock exchange. He accuses Antonio of calling him a 'misbeliever, cut-throat dog' (line 106) and of spitting on him and kicking him. Shylock is **incredulous** (in disbelief) that this same person is coming to him looking for help:

  you come to me, and you say
  'Shylock, we would have moneys'—you say so,
  You, that did void your rheum upon my beard,
  And foot me as you spurn a stranger cur (lines 110–113)

- It is important to note that Antonio does not deny these accusations. In fact, he says that he would do it again: 'To spit on thee again, to spurn thee too' (line 126).

Part 3 (lines 139–176) – Antonio accepts the terms of Shylock's bond.

- Antonio asks Shylock to lend the money, not as a friend, but as an enemy as he thinks it would be easier for Shylock to demand the penalty from someone he dislikes:

  But lend it rather to thine enemy,
  Who if he break, thou mayst with better face
  Exact the penalty. (lines 130–132)

- In response to this, Shylock claims that he wishes to be friends with Antonio and forgive him for all past **grievances** (wrongs/insults): 'I would be friends with you, and have your love' (line 134). To prove it, he says that he will lend the loan interest-free and 'take no doit of usance for my moneys' (lines 136–137). He suggests going to a notary (a person who prepares legal documents) to seal the deal.

  Shylock then suggests that just for fun, what he calls a 'merry sport' (line 141), there should be a penalty for not repaying the loan:

  let the forfeit
  Be nominated for an equal pound
  Of your fair flesh to be cut off and taken
  In what part of your body pleaseth me. (lines 144–147)

  Antonio agrees and seems to be taken in by Shylock's apparent kindness:

  I'll seal to such a bond,
  And say there is much kindness in the Jew. (lines 148–149)

- Bassanio, however, is not convinced that this arrangement is a wise one and asks Antonio not to accept this condition. Antonio tries to **allay** (ease/reduce) Bassanio's fears by telling him that he should not worry; his ships are expected home a month before the term of the loan expires:

  Come on. In this there can be no dismay.
  My ships come home a month before the day. (lines 176–177)

REVIEWING

1. What are the terms of the loan? (How **much** is it for and **how long** before it must be repaid?)
2. Explain what Shylock means when he says Antonio's 'means are in supposition' (line 15).
3. What are the **two main reasons** Shylock gives for hating Antonio? (Look at lines 36–47.)
4. What is the penalty (or **forfeit**) for not repaying the loan on time?
5. Do you think Shylock is doing this just for a 'merry sport' as he says? Explain your answer.

ORAL LANGUAGE

Shylock's Speech P

Group Activity

In groups of **four**, read back over Shylock's speech (lines 101–124) and **summarise** the main points of what he is saying by writing a sentence (or two) to sum up each colour-coded section. Turn to **page 14** of your portfolio to complete the grid.

Next, prepare the piece to be **read aloud** in your group. Each person should read one section. Decide on what Shylock's **tone of voice** should be in each section. Will it change or stay the same? Discuss this with the group.

EXPLORING

1. Language and Imagery P

(a) The scene has many examples of **insulting language** which reflects the racial and religious tensions of the time. Find **two** examples and state the **effect** of each one. Turn to **page 15** of your portfolio to help you.

(b) The scene is also rich in **imagery** – imagery of false appearances, biblical imagery, animal imagery and ship/weather imagery. Imagery can tell us more about a **character** or **theme**, or it can help to create a certain **mood** or **atmosphere**. Turn to **page 15** of your portfolio to complete the exercise on the imagery in this scene.

2. Director's Notebook – Staging a Scene P

Imagine you are directing Act 1, Scene 3. How would you stage the scene to show the **conflict** between Shylock and Antonio? Write your response on **page 16** of your portfolio.

REFLECTING

1. Character File P

Do you feel sympathy for **Shylock** in this scene or do you see him as a scheming villain? Turn to **page 131** of your portfolio to record your responses to Shylock.

You can also record your impressions of **Antonio** (**page 112**) and **Bassanio** (**page 118**) based on this scene.

2. My Reflection on Act 1, Scene 3 P

Turn to **page 17** of your portfolio to complete the reflection on this scene.

3. Key Quotes P

Turn to **page 18** of your portfolio to complete the task on key quotes from this scene.

LOOKING BACK AT ACT 1

1. Overview P

Pair Activity

With your partner, turn to **page 4** of your portfolio to write **one sentence or phrase** in the box for each scene in Act 1. This sentence or phrase should **sum up the main action** in that scene.

2. Individual Assignment

Choose one of the following activities:

(a) Discuss the **theme of conflict** in Act 1.

(b) Research the **treatment of Jewish people** in Italy and/or England during the Elizabethan period. Present your findings to the class. What facts did you find most surprising?

LINKING TO THE EXAM

Describing Characters and Key Moments P

In the exam, you might be asked to give advice to a character in a key moment of the play. Turn to **page 19** of your portfolio to complete a Junior Cycle English question on this topic.

ACT 2

The action in Act 2 moves between Belmont, where the Prince of Morocco and the Prince of Arragon are due to try their luck with the caskets, and Venice, where Bassanio is preparing to embark on his journey. Bassanio plans a farewell feast for all of his friends and Shylock.

Launcelot Gobbo, Shylock's servant, is also introduced in this act. Launcelot wants to leave Shylock's service to become Bassanio's servant. Launcelot acts as a go-between, inviting Shylock to supper with Bassanio and sending messages between Jessica and Lorenzo. Later in Act 2, we witness the **elopement** (running away to get married in secret) of Jessica and Lorenzo.

Towards the end of this act, suspense is high with the Prince of Morocco and the Prince of Arragon each choosing a casket, and the news that a Venetian merchant ship has been shipwrecked. We also learn that Bassanio has cancelled his farewell celebrations and is to set sail immediately for Belmont.

ACT 2, SCENE 1

Setting: Belmont, a room in Portia's house.

In this **scene** you will:

- Consider the character of the **Prince of Morocco**.
- Learn about **hyperbole** and find examples.

Action – What Happens?

In this scene, the Prince of Morocco arrives at Belmont to try to win Portia's hand in marriage. He asks her not to judge him by the colour of his skin and states that he would do anything in order to marry her. Portia reminds him that she is bound by her dead father's wishes and that he must take his chance like the other suitors. She warns him that if he decides to take part in the lottery, he must never propose marriage to anyone else in the future. The Prince of Morocco is willing to take the risk.

Useful Words

complexion – the natural colour or appearance of a person's skin

incision – a cut made in skin or flesh **scimitar** – a curved sword **hue** – colour

Flourish of cornets.[1] *Enter the PRINCE OF MOROCCO, a tawny Moor all in white, and three or four followers accordingly,*[2] *with PORTIA, NERISSA, and their train.*[3]

MOROCCO

Mislike me not for my complexion,[4]
The shadowed livery[5] of the burnished[6] sun,
To whom I am a neighbour and near bred.[7]
Bring me the fairest creature northward born,[8]
Where Phoebus' fire[9] scarce thaws the icicles,
And let us make incision for your love
To prove whose blood is reddest, his or mine.[10]
I tell thee, lady, this aspect[11] of mine
Hath feared the valiant.[12] By my love I swear,
The best-regarded virgins of our clime[13]
Have loved it too. I would not change this hue[14]
Except to steal your thoughts,[15] my gentle queen.

PORTIA

In terms of choice I am not solely led
By nice direction of a maiden's eyes.[16]
Besides, the lottery of my destiny
Bars me the right of voluntary choosing.[17]
But if my father had not scanted[18] me,
And hedged[19] me by his wit,[20] to yield myself
His wife who wins me by that means I told you,[21]
Yourself, renownèd prince, then stood as fair
As any comer I have looked on yet
For my affection.[22]

MOROCCO

Even for that[23] I thank you.
Therefore I pray you lead me to the caskets
To try my fortune. By this scimitar,[24]
That slew the Sophy[25] and a Persian prince
That won three fields[26] of Sultan Solyman,[27]
I would o'erstare the sternest eyes that look,
Outbrave the heart most daring on the earth,
Pluck the young sucking cubs from the she-bear,
Yea, mock the lion when a[28] roars for prey,
To win thee, lady.[29] But alas the while,

1. *Flourish of cornets: A fanfare of instruments (resembling trumpets) used to signify the arrival of someone important.*
2. *accordingly: of similar dress and appearance*
3. *train:* attendants
4. *my complexion:* the colour of my skin
5. *livery:* dark clothing/uniform
6. *burnished:* shining
7. *near bred:* a close relative

PLOT POINT

Morocco is asking Portia to reserve her judgement of him and not judge him on the colour of his skin. He argues that he wouldn't change his skin colour except to gain her affection.

8. *the fairest ... born:* the lightest-skinned person from the North
9. *Phoebus' fire:* the sun's heat *Phoebus was also known as Apollo, god of the sun.*
10. *Bring me ... mine:* Bring me the lightest-skinned person and let me make a cut in order to draw blood and you will see that my blood is redder than his. *Red blood was seen as a sign of bravery.*
11. *aspect:* appearance
12. *Hath feared the valiant:* Has made brave men afraid.
13. *The ... clime:* The most admired ladies of our region
14. *hue:* colour
15. *steal your thoughts:* gain your affection

CHARACTER NOTE

Portia reminds Morocco that she has no control over whom she marries as she is bound by her father's lottery. She reassures him that if this were not the case, he would have as good a chance of marrying her as any. What is your impression of Portia here? Is she being dutiful? Sincere? Insincere?

16. *I am not ... eyes:* I am not relying only on what I see before me.
17. *Bars me ... choosing:* Prevents me from choosing who I like.
18. *scanted:* limited
19. *hedged:* restricted
20. *wit:* wisdom
21. *to yield ... you:* to become the wife of the person who wins me by the method I told you about
22. *Yourself ... affection:* then you would stand as good a chance as any admirer of winning my love
23. *Even for that:* Even for that compliment
24. *scimitar:* curved sword
25. *Sophy:* Shah *(monarch)* of Persia
26. *fields:* battles
27. *Sultan Solyman: a Turkish ruler*

LOOKING AT LANGUAGE

Hyperbole: Exaggerated language used for dramatic effect. For example, notice how the Prince of Morocco frequently uses hyperbole in his speech.

28. *a:* he
29. *I would ... lady: The Prince of Morocco is listing all the brave things he would do to win Portia.*

If Hercules[30] and Lichas[31] play at dice
Which is the better man, the greater throw
May turn by fortune from the weaker hand.[32]
So is Alcides[33] beaten by his page,[34]
And so may I, blind Fortune leading me,
Miss that which one unworthier may attain,
And die with grieving.[35]

PORTIA

You must take your chance,
And either not attempt to choose at all,
Or swear before you choose, if you choose wrong
Never to speak to lady afterward
In way of marriage.[36] Therefore be advised.[37]

MOROCCO

Nor will not.[38] Come, bring me unto my chance.

PORTIA

First, forward to the temple.[39] After dinner
Your hazard[40] shall be made.

MOROCCO

Good fortune then,
To make me blest or cursèd'st among men.

Flourish of cornets. Exeunt.

30. *Hercules: a mythological hero famous for his strength*
31. *Lichas: Hercules' servant*
32. *If Hercules … hand: The Prince of Morocco is saying that fortune or luck is unpredictable and the most worthy person may not necessarily have good luck or fortune.*
33. *Alcides: another name for Hercules*
34. *page:* servant
35. *And so … grieving:* In a similar way, I might chance my luck, but I might miss out to someone inferior to me and die of a broken heart.

PLOT POINT

Portia warns the Prince of Morocco that he is not obligated to participate in the lottery, but if he does, he must swear that, if unsuccessful, he must never ask another woman to marry him. Do you think that this is fair? Why do you think this condition exists?

36. *Or swear … marriage:* You must swear an oath before you choose that you must never ask any other woman to be your wife if you are unsuccessful.
37. *advised:* warned
38. *Nor will not:* No, I will never ask another woman to be my wife if I fail.
39. *First … temple:* Go to the temple first to swear the oath.
40. *hazard:* choice *(of casket)*

SPOTLIGHT ON …

CLASSICAL ALLUSION

Classical allusion is a reference to a character or story from Greek or Roman classical literature. The Prince of Morocco refers to a story about Hercules to illustrate his point about luck.

OVERVIEW OF ACT 2, SCENE 1

- In this scene, the Prince of Morocco makes a grand entrance with a fanfare announcing his arrival. Immediately he asks Portia not to judge him by his dark-skinned appearance, emphasising instead how brave he is:

  Mislike me not for my complexion (line 1)

- He challenges Portia to find the fairest-skinned (lightest-skinned) person 'northward born' (line 4) to see whose blood is redder. Red blood was a sign of **valour** (great courage). He says that he would be willing to change the colour of his skin to secure Portia's love:

  I would not change this hue
  Except to steal your thoughts, my gentle queen. (lines 11–12)

- Portia reminds the Prince of Morocco that 'the lottery of [her] destiny' (line 15) forbids her 'right of voluntary choosing' (line 16), but assures him that if this were not the case, he would stand as good a chance as any other of winning her affection.
- The Prince of Morocco is heartened by this response and goes on to stress all the daring things he would undertake in order to win Portia's love. For example:

  I would o'erstare the sternest eyes that look,
  Outbrave the heart most daring on the earth (lines 27–28)

- Portia warns the Prince that if he decides to participate in the lottery, he must take an oath swearing to never marry in the future. However, this does not **faze him** (put him off) and he goes to the temple to take the oath. The scene ends on a note of suspense as we are told that the Prince of Morocco will try his luck after dinner.

REVIEWING

1. Why does the Prince of Morocco mention the colour of his skin to Portia?
2. For what reason would the Prince of Morocco be willing to change his skin colour?
3. What warning does Portia give him about taking his chance with the caskets?
4. How does the Prince of Morocco respond to Portia's warning?

EXPLORING

1. Hyperbole P

Pair Activity

What is hyperbole?

Hyberbole is using exaggerated, over-the-top language for a dramatic effect, e.g. 'I wouldn't do that in a million years!'

Can you find any examples of **hyperbole** (exaggeration) in Morocco's language? Turn to **page 23** of your portfolio to complete the grid.

2. Classical Allusion P

Why do you think that the Prince of Morocco refers to Hercules? What effect does this classical allusion have? Turn to **page 23** of your portfolio to complete the task.

REFLECTING

1. Is the Prince of Morocco a Suitable Match for Portia? P

Turn to **page 24** of your portfolio to write a short paragraph outlining the reasons why you think that the Prince of Morocco may or may not be a suitable match for Portia.

2. Character File P

Turn to the Character File section of your portfolio and record your impressions of **Portia** (**page 124**) based on this scene.

PREDICTING

Which Casket Contains Portia's Portrait? P

The next time we meet the Prince of Morocco, he will be getting ready to choose his casket. Turn to **page 24** of your portfolio to see if you can guess which casket contains Portia's portrait.

ACT 2, SCENE 2

Setting: Venice. A street.

In this **scene** you will:

- Read **Launcelot's soliloquy** aloud.
- Learn about **malapropisms** and find examples.

Action – What Happens?

In this scene we meet Shylock's servant, Launcelot Gobbo, who is debating whether to leave Shylock's service. By chance he meets his father, Old Gobbo, who is nearly blind. Old Gobbo does not recognise his son. Launcelot plays a cruel trick on him and tells him his son is dead. After a while, he reveals his true identity to his father and tells him that he is unhappy working for Shylock. Later, they meet Bassanio and his men, who are getting ready to go to Belmont. With the help of his father, Old Gobbo, Launcelot succeeds in securing a position as Bassanio's servant.

Useful Words

fiend – an evil spirit or devil

gear – matter

sand-blind – half-blind

high-gravel-blind – almost totally blind

ergo (Latin) – therefore

anon – at once

suit – a favour/request

fairer table – luckier palm (of a hand)

Enter LAUNCELOT GOBBO, the clown, alone.

LAUNCELOT

Certainly my conscience will serve[1] me to run from this Jew my master. The fiend[2] is at mine[3] elbow and tempts me, saying to me 'Gobbo, Launcelot Gobbo, good Launcelot,' or 'good Gobbo,' or 'good Launcelot Gobbo—use your legs, take the start,[4] run away.' My conscience says 'No, take heed, honest Launcelot, take heed, honest Gobbo,' or, as aforesaid, 'honest Launcelot Gobbo—do not run, scorn running with thy heels.'[5] Well, the most courageous fiend bids me pack.[6] '*Via!*'[7] says the fiend; 'Away!' says the fiend. 'For the heavens,[8] rouse up a brave mind,' says the fiend, 'and run.' Well, my conscience, hanging about the neck of my heart, says very wisely to me, 'My honest friend Launcelot'—being an honest man's son, or rather an honest woman's son, for indeed my father did something smack,[9] something grow to; he had a kind of taste[10]—well, my conscience says, 'Launcelot, budge not'; 'Budge!' says the fiend. 'Budge not', says my conscience. 'Conscience,' say I, 'you counsel[11] well;' 'Fiend,' say I, 'you counsel well.' To be ruled by my conscience, I should stay with the Jew my master who, God bless the mark,[12] is a kind of devil; and to run away from the Jew, I should be ruled by the fiend who, saving your reverence,[13] is the devil himself. Certainly the Jew is the very devil incarnation;[14] and in my conscience, my conscience is but a kind of hard conscience, to offer to counsel me to stay with the Jew. The fiend gives the more friendly counsel. I will run, fiend. My heels are at your commandment. I will run.

Enter Old GOBBO, with a basket.

GOBBO

Master young man, you, I pray you,[15] which is the way to Master Jew's?

1. *serve:* allow
2. *fiend:* devil/evil spirit
3. *mine:* my
4. *take the start:* go
5. *scorn running with thy heels:* reject running completely *(pun)*
6. *pack:* leave
7. *Via!:* Away!
8. *For the heavens:* For heaven's sake
9. *smack:* dishonest
10. *had a kind of taste:* was promiscuous *(Old Gobbo cheated on Launcelot's mother.)*
11. *counsel:* advise
12. *God bless the mark: This was a phrase used as an apology before saying something rude or offensive.*
13. *saving your reverence: Similar to 'God bless the mark,' 'save your reverence' was also used as an apology before saying something rude or offensive.*
14. *the very devil incarnation: Launcelot means to say 'incarnate' instead of 'incarnation,' meaning Shylock is the devil in human form.*

LOOKING AT LANGUAGE

Soliloquy: A speech spoken by a character to him- or herself. It gives the audience an insight into the character's thoughts and feelings at that particular time. In his soliloquy, Launcelot is conflicted about whether or not to leave his master Shylock, whom he claims has mistreated him. His conscience would like him to stay, but the 'fiend' tells him to leave. How is Shylock depicted in this soliloquy?

15. *I pray you:* please

LAUNCELOT

[*aside*] O heavens, this is my true-begotten[16] father who, being more than sand-blind,[17] high-gravel-blind,[18] knows me not. I will try confusions with him.[19]

GOBBO

Master young gentleman, I pray you, which is the way to Master Jew's?

LAUNCELOT

Turn up on your right hand at the next turning, but at the next turning of all on your left, marry at the very next turning, turn of no hand[20] but turn down indirectly to the Jew's house.

GOBBO

By God's sonties,[21] 'twill be a hard way to hit.[22] Can you tell me whether one Launcelot that dwells[23] with him, dwell with him or no?

LAUNCELOT

Talk you of young Master Launcelot? [*aside*] Mark me now, now will I raise the waters.[24] [*to GOBBO*] Talk you of young Master Launcelot?

GOBBO

No master, sir, but a poor man's son. His father, though I say't, is an honest exceeding poor man and, God be thanked, well to live.[25]

LAUNCELOT

Well, let his father be what a[26] will, we talk of young Master Launcelot.

GOBBO

Your worship's friend, and Launcelot, sir.

LAUNCELOT

But I pray you, *ergo*[27] old man, *ergo* I beseech you,[28] talk you of young Master Launcelot?

16. *my true-begotten: Launcelot is a little confused here. Launcelot was 'begotten', or brought into the world, by his father Old Gobbo.*
17. *sand-blind:* partly blind
18. *high-gravel-blind:* almost totally blind
19. *I will … him:* I will try to confuse him.
20. *turn of no hand:* don't turn at all *Launcelot is trying to confuse Old Gobbo by giving him ridiculous directions.*
21. *sonties:* saints
22. *hit:* reach
23. *dwells:* lives
24. *will I raise waters:* I will make him cry
25. *well to live:* well-to-do *This seems to contradict his previous comment that he is a 'poor man'.*
26. *a:* he
27. *ergo:* therefore *Launcelot is trying to appear like a gentleman and so is speaking in this way.*
28. *I beseech you:* I beg you

29. *an't:* if it

30. *father: 'Father' was a common way to address an old man.*
31. *the Sisters Three: These were three sisters in Greek mythology and it was thought that they determined the life and destiny of everybody.*

32. *Marry:* By Mary! *(a common exclamation)*
33. *staff: a long stick used as support when walking*
34. *prop:* a support beam
35. *The boy ... prop:* I was depending on that boy to support me in my old age.

36. *cudgel:* short stick
37. *hovel-post:* shed post

38. *Alack: An exclamation used to express regret or dismay.*

LOOKING AT LANGUAGE

Dramatic irony: Occurs when the audience or certain characters on stage have information that the other characters on stage do not have. It can be used for a variety of purposes: for dramatic or comedic effect. Why do you think Launcelot pretends not to know his father in this scene?

39. *It is ... child: Launcelot is reversing the commonly known phrase 'A wise child knows his own father.'*

40. *a man's son may: Meaning 'a man's son may be hidden'.*

GOBBO

Of Launcelot, an't[29] please your mastership.

LAUNCELOT

Ergo Master Launcelot. Talk not of Master Launcelot, father,[30] for the young gentleman, according to fates and destinies and such odd sayings—the Sisters Three[31] and such branches of learning—is indeed deceased; or, as you would say in plain terms, gone to heaven.

GOBBO

Marry,[32] God forbid! The boy was the very staff[33] of my age, my very prop.[34 35]

LAUNCELOT

[*aside*] Do I look like a cudgel[36] or a hovel-post,[37] a staff or a prop? [*to GOBBO*] Do you know me, father?

GOBBO

Alack[38] the day, I know you not, young gentleman. But I pray you tell me, is my boy—God rest his soul—alive or dead?

LAUNCELOT

Do you not know me, father?

GOBBO

Alack, sir, I am sand-blind. I know you not.

LAUNCELOT

Nay, indeed, if you had your eyes, you might fail of the knowing me. It is a wise father that knows his own child.[39] Well, old man, I will tell you news of your son. [*kneeling*] Give me your blessing. Truth will come to light; murder cannot be hid long—a man's son may,[40] but in the end truth will out.

GOBBO

Pray you, sir, stand up. I am sure you are not Launcelot, my boy.

LAUNCELOT

Pray you, let's have no more fooling about it, but give me your blessing. I am Launcelot, your boy that was, your son that is, your child that shall be.

GOBBO

I cannot think you are my son.

LAUNCELOT

I know not what I shall think of that, but I am Launcelot, the Jew's man, and I am sure Margery your wife is my mother.

GOBBO

Her name is Margery indeed. I'll be sworn, if thou be Launcelot, thou art mine own flesh and blood. Lord worshipped might he be, what a beard hast thou got! Thou hast got more hair on thy chin than Dobbin my fill-horse[41] has on his tail.

41. *fill-horse:* cart-horse

LAUNCELOT

It should seem then that Dobbin's tail grows backward. I am sure he had more hair of[42] his tail than I have of my face when I last saw him.

GOBBO

Lord, how art thou changed! How dost thou and thy master agree?[43] I have brought him a present. How 'gree[44] you now?

LAUNCELOT

Well, well: but for mine own part, as I have set up my rest[45] to run away, so I will not rest till I have run some ground. My master's a very Jew.[46] Give him a present?—give him a halter![47] I am famished in his service. You may tell[48] every finger I have with my ribs. Father, I am glad you are[49] come. Give me your present to one Master Bassanio, who indeed gives rare new liveries.[50] If I serve not him, I will run as far as God has any ground.[51] O rare fortune![52] Here comes the man. To[53] him, father, for I am a Jew if I serve the Jew any longer.[54]

Enter BASSANIO with LEONARDO and other followers.

BASSANIO

[*to one of his men*] You may do so, but let it be so hasted[55] that supper be ready at the farthest[56] by five of the clock. See these letters delivered, put the liveries to making,[57] and desire[58] Gratiano to come anon[59] to my lodging.

Exit one of his men.

LAUNCELOT

To him, father.

GOBBO

God bless your worship.

BASSANIO

Gramercy.[60] Wouldst thou aught[61] with me?[62]

42. *of:* on
43. *How dost … agree?:* How do you and your master get along?
44. *'gree:* agree
45. *set up my rest:* decided
46. *a very Jew:* an absolutely greedy person
47. *halter:* a noose *(a rope for around his neck to hang himself with)*
48. *tell:* count
49. *are:* have
50. *liveries:* servants' uniforms
51. *If I … ground:* If I can't serve him, I'll run to the ends of the earth.
52. *O rare fortune!:* What a lucky coincidence! *(Launcelot sees Bassanio approaching.)*
53. *To:* Let's go to
54. *for I … longer:* I will become a Jew if I stay in Shylock's service any longer.

PLOT POINT

Bassanio arrives on the scene and Launcelot takes the opportunity to ask him if he can join his service. Having heard Launcelot recommended by Shylock, Bassanio agrees.

55. *hasted:* hurried
56. *farthest:* latest
57. *put the … making:* make the new servants' uniforms
58. *desire:* tell
59. *anon:* immediately
60. *Gramercy:* Thank you.
61. *aught:* anything
62. *Wouldst thou … me?:* What can I do for you?

GOBBO

Here's my son, sir, a poor boy—

LAUNCELOT

Not a poor boy, sir, but the rich Jew's man that would, sir, as my father shall specify—

GOBBO

He hath a great infection,[63] sir, as one would say, to serve—

LAUNCELOT

Indeed, the short and the long is, I serve the Jew, and have a desire, as my father shall specify—

GOBBO

His master and he, saving your worship's reverence,[64] are scarce cater-cousins[65]—

LAUNCELOT

To be brief, the very truth is that the Jew, having done me wrong, doth cause me, as my father—being, I hope, an old man—shall frutify[66] unto you.

GOBBO

I have here a dish of doves that I would bestow upon your worship, and my suit[67] is—

LAUNCELOT

In very brief, the suit is impertinent[68] to myself, as your worship shall know by this honest old man; and though I say it, though old man, yet, poor man, my father.

BASSANIO

One speak for both. What would you?[69]

LAUNCELOT

Serve you, sir.

63. *infection: Launcelot means to say 'affection' (desire or wish) instead of 'infection'.*

64. *saving … reverence:* begging your pardon

65. *scarce cater-cousins:* are hardly good friends

66. *frutify: Launcelot means to say 'certify' (prove) instead of 'frutify'.*

67. *suit:* request/favour

68. *impertinent: Launcelot means to say 'pertinent' (important) instead of 'impertinent' (rude).*

69. *What would you?:* What do you desire?

GOBBO

That is the very defect[70] of the matter, sir.

BASSANIO

I know thee well. Thou hast obtained thy suit.
Shylock thy master spoke with me this day,
And hath preferred[71] thee, if it be preferment[72]
To leave a rich Jew's service to become
The follower of so poor a gentleman.

LAUNCELOT

The old proverb[73] is very well parted between my master Shylock and you, sir: you have the grace of God, sir, and he hath enough.

BASSANIO

Thou speak'st it well. Go, father, with thy son.
Take leave of thy old master and inquire
My lodging out. Give him a livery
More guarded[74] than his fellows':[75] see it done.

LAUNCELOT

Father, in. I cannot get a service, no, I have ne'er a tongue in my head—well! If any man in Italy have a fairer table[76] which doth offer to swear upon a book,[77] I shall have good fortune. Go to, here's a simple line of life, here's a small trifle of wives—alas, fifteen wives is nothing! Eleven widows and nine maids is a simple coming-in[78] for one man, and then to 'scape[79] drowning thrice, and to be in peril of my life with the edge of a feather-bed[80]—here are simple 'scapes. Well, if Fortune be a woman, she's a good wench for this gear[81] Father, come. I'll take my leave of the Jew in the twinkling.[82]

Exeunt LAUNCELOT and OLD GOBBO.

BASSANIO

I pray thee, good Leonardo, think on this.
These things being bought and orderly bestowed,[83]

70. *defect: Old Gobbo is also mixing up his words. He means to say 'effect' (that's the point of the matter) instead of 'defect'.*
71. *preferred:* recommended
72. *preferment:* a promotion
73. *The old proverb: This proverb is 'The grace of God is gear (property) enough.'*
74. *guarded:* decorated
75. *fellows':* than his fellow servants' uniforms
76. *fairer table:* luckier palm
77. *If any man … book: Launcelot uses his palm to swear upon the holy Bible. Here he is mocking his father, who presumably told him in the past that he would never secure a 'service' or a good position. He is examining the lines on his palm which he says predict good fortune for him in the future.*
78. *coming-in:* income
79. *'scape:* escape
80. *and to be … feather-bed: Launcelot seems to be suggesting that the only dangers he will face in life will be insignificant ones relating to marriage.*
81. *gear:* matter
82. *twinkling:* in the twinkling of an eye/very quickly
83. *orderly bestowed:* properly stowed/placed on the ship *Bassanio is getting ready to set sail to Belmont.*

Return in haste, for I do feast tonight
My best-esteemed acquaintance.[84] Hie[85] thee, go.

LEONARDO

My best endeavours shall be done herein.

Enter GRATIANO.

GRATIANO

Where's your master?

LEONARDO

Yonder, sir, he walks.

Exit.

GRATIANO

Signor Bassanio!

BASSANIO

Gratiano!

GRATIANO

I have a suit to you.[86]

BASSANIO

You have obtained it.

GRATIANO

You must not deny me. I must go with you to Belmont.

BASSANIO

Why then, you must. But hear thee, Gratiano,
Thou art too wild, too rude and bold of voice[87]—
Parts[88] that become thee happily enough,
And in such eyes as ours appear not faults;
But where thou art not known, why, there they show
Something too liberal.[89] Pray thee, take pain
To allay with some cold drops of modesty
Thy skipping spirit, lest through thy wild behavior
I be misconstered[90] in the place I go to,
And lose my hopes.[91]

84. *My best-esteemed acquaintance:* My most respected friends.
85. *Hie:* Hurry
86. *I have … you:* I have a favour to ask.
87. *bold of voice:* loud
88. *Parts:* Attributes
89. *Why then … liberal: Bassanio is saying that Gratiano is fun and loud-mouthed and people who know him are used to this, but this behaviour might not be seen as acceptable to those who don't know him (i.e. people in Belmont might find him offensive and undisciplined).*
90. *misconstered:* misconstrued/misunderstood
91. *Pray thee, … hopes: Bassanio is asking Gratiano to tone down his behaviour in case he ruins his chances with Portia in Belmont.*

SPOTLIGHT ON ... STAGECRAFT

What do you think this image reveals about Gratiano's character? Look at the actor's facial expressions and pose.

GRATIANO

Signor Bassanio, hear me.
If I do not put on a sober habit,[92]
Talk with respect, and swear but now and then,
Wear prayer-books in my pocket, look demurely,[93]
Nay more, while grace is saying hood mine eyes
Thus with my hat,[94] and sigh and say 'Amen',
Use all the observance of civility,[95]
Like one well studied in a sad ostent[96]
To please his grandam,[97] never trust me more.[98]

92. *sober habit:* respectable clothes or good behaviour
93. *demurely:* reserved
94. *hood mine ... hat:* cover my eyes with my hat *Hats were taken off for grace before meals.*
95. *Use all ... civility:* have such good manners
96. *in a sad ostent:* in solemn appearance
97. *grandam:* grandmother
98. *more:* again

BASSANIO

Well, we shall see your bearing.[99]

99. *bearing:* behaviour

GRATIANO

Nay, but I bar tonight.[100] You shall not gauge[101] me
By what we do tonight.

100. *I bar tonight:* I am excluding tonight.
101. *gauge:* judge

BASSANIO

No, that were pity.
I would entreat[102] you rather to put on
Your boldest suit of mirth,[103] for we have friends
That purpose merriment. But fare you well.
I have some business.

102. *entreat:* ask
103. *mirth:* fun/enjoyment

GRATIANO

And I must to Lorenzo and the rest.
But we will visit you at supper-time.

Exeunt.

OVERVIEW OF ACT 2, SCENE 2

- This is a scene of **comedy** which forms a contrast to the more serious scenes that have gone before it. In this scene, we meet Launcelot Gobbo who is Shylock's servant. At the start of the scene he is conflicted about whether or not he should leave Shylock's service. His conscience is telling him to stay, but the 'fiend' (devil) is urging him to go:

  To be ruled by my conscience, I should stay
  with the Jew my master who, God bless the mark,
  is a kind of devil; and to run away from the Jew,
  I should be ruled by the fiend who, saving your
  reverence, is the devil himself. Certainly the Jew is
  the very devil incarnation (lines 21–26)

- It is clear that Launcelot has a very negative opinion of Shylock, saying that he is 'a kind of devil' and 'the very devil incarnation'. It is not surprising then that, by the end of his speech, he has made up his mind to leave.
- Next, Launcelot Gobbo meets an almost-blind old man whom he recognises as his own father, Old Gobbo. Old Gobbo doesn't recognise his son and asks him for directions to Shylock's house. Launcelot, being a comedic character, takes the opportunity to play a cruel trick on his father, saying that he 'will try confusions with him' (line 35). He proceeds to give the old man nonsensical directions and then tells him that Launcelot Gobbo has died:

> *is indeed*
> *deceased; or, as you would say in plain*
> *terms, gone to heaven.* (lines 60–62)

- However, Launcelot soon reveals his true identity to his father:

> *I am Launcelot, your boy that*
> *was, your son that is, your child that shall be.* (lines 81–82)

- Old Gobbo comments on how Launcelot has changed and is anxious to know how he and Shylock get along. When Old Gobbo says that he has brought Shylock a gift, Launcelot is outraged. He claims that Shylock has mistreated him by not giving him enough food to eat and suggests that he deserves a noose rather than a present:

> *Give him*
> *a present?—give him a halter! I am famished in*
> *his service. You may tell every finger I have with my*
> *ribs.* (lines 100–103)

- Launcelot suggests that his father should offer the gift to Bassanio and just at that moment, Bassanio appears on the scene. Launcelot recognises his good luck:

> *O rare fortune! Here comes*
> *the man. To him, father, for I am a Jew if I serve*
> *the Jew any longer.* (lines 106–108)

- Here Launcelot wants his father to **intercede** (negotiate) on his behalf to obtain a new position as one of Bassanio's servants, saying that if he stays with Shylock any longer, he will become like him. It seems as if Launcelot is indeed very fortunate as Bassanio has received his loan and is busy making preparations for his voyage to Belmont. Bassanio's preparations include hiring servants and getting their uniforms or 'liveries' ready.
- Bassanio proves himself patient and courteous when approached by Launcelot and his father, Old Gobbo. He readily **accedes** (agrees) to Launcelot's request, telling him that he heard Shylock speak highly of him earlier. He even promises Launcelot a livery that is 'More guarded' (line 148) or distinguished than his other servants' liveries.
- Launcelot is elated to have achieved his '**suit**' (request) and gloats to his father about how lucky he is and what a great future he foresees for himself. He is excited as he goes to take his 'leave of the Jew' (line 159).
- Bassanio tells Leonardo to place the items he has bought for his journey to Belmont safely on the ship and to return quickly, as he has planned a feast for his friends that night before he sets sail for Belmont.
- Another person now enters the scene requesting a 'suit' of Bassanio. This time it is Gratiano who pleads with Bassanio to take him to Belmont. Bassanio agrees to his request, but advises him to be on his best behaviour for fear that Gratiano's behaviour may compromise his own suit with Portia.

Bassanio claims that Gratiano is 'too wild, too rude and bold of voice' (line 171). His positive attributes are welcome among his friends, but where he is not known they may 'show something too liberal' (lines 174–175), meaning that his behaviour could be interpreted as rude and undisciplined. Gratiano assures Bassanio that he will be on his best behaviour and 'Use all the observance of civility' (line 185) there.

- However, Gratiano says that his good behaviour will not come into effect until after the feast that night and urges Bassanio not to judge him on this behaviour. Bassanio reassures him that he won't, telling him 'to put on your boldest suit of mirth, for we have friends that purpose merriment' (lines 191–193).
- The scene ends with the friends parting, but agreeing to meet again at supper-time.

REVIEWING

1. What is Launcelot so conflicted about at the start of the scene?
2. Who does Launcelot meet?
3. Why does Launcelot not reveal his true identity immediately?
4. Is Shylock a good master according to Launcelot? Give reasons for your answer.
5. Why does Bassanio agree to take Launcelot on as a servant?
6. What has Bassanio planned for that evening?
7. Why is Bassanio worried about bringing Gratiano with him to Belmont?
8. How does Gratiano convince Bassanio to bring him along?

ORAL LANGUAGE

Launcelot's Soliloquy

Group Activity

What is a soliloquy?

A soliloquy is a speech spoken by a character who is alone on stage. It gives us an **insight into the character's thoughts and feelings** at that particular time.

In groups of **three**, read back over Launcelot's speech at the start of the scene (lines 1 to 30). Divide the speech into three parts – (i) Launcelot, (ii) Launcelot's 'conscience' and (iii) the 'fiend'.

Next, prepare the piece to be read aloud in your group. Decide as a group who will perform each part and focus on **tone** and **gestures**. Consider the following when you are preparing the reading:

- **Launcelot** – Try to communicate Launcelot's sense of inner conflict and confusion.
- **Launcelot's 'conscience'** – Try to appeal to Launcelot's better nature to convince him to stay.
- **The 'fiend'** – Try to convince Launcelot to leave.

EXPLORING

Launcelot and Old Gobbo's Language

Much of the humour from this scene comes from Launcelot and Old Gobbo's **malapropisms**.

What is malapropism?

Malapropism is the incorrect use of a word in place of a word that sounds similar. Many people use malapropisms in everyday language, for example:

- 'I ***pacifically*** told her to be there on time.' ('pacifically' should be '**specifically**')
- 'We had no fire ***distinguisher*** in the apartment.' ('distinguisher' should be '**extinguisher**')

1. Looking at Malapropisms P

Turn to **page 25** of your portfolio to complete a short exercise on malapropisms in this scene.

2. Research: Malapropisms P

Pair Activity

What are the **most common malapropisms** people use? There are numerous examples of comedies where characters mix up their words. Are there words that you commonly mix up? Discuss this with your partner and write examples on **page 26** of your portfolio.

REFLECTING

Character File P

Turn to the Character File section of your portfolio and record your impressions of **(a) Bassanio** (**page 119**) and **(b) Gratiano** (**page 138**) based on this scene.

ACT 2, SCENE 3

Setting: Venice. A room in Shylock's house.

In this **scene** you will:

- Consider the character of **Jessica**.

Action – What Happens?

In this **scene**, Launcelot is saying goodbye to Jessica, Shylock's daughter. Jessica is very sad to see him go as she found that he helped to make her life bearable. She gives him a **ducat** (gold coin) and asks him to deliver a letter to her love, Lorenzo, who is a Christian.

It is obvious that Jessica has no real love for her father; she clearly disapproves of his behaviour. By the end of the scene, Jessica is planning to escape from her father, convert to Christianity and marry Lorenzo.

Useful Words

heinous – wicked

strife – conflict

Enter JESSICA and LAUNCELOT.

JESSICA

I am sorry thou wilt leave my father so.
Our house is hell, and thou, a merry devil,
Didst rob it of some taste[1] of tediousness.[2]
But fare thee well. There is a ducat for thee.
And, Launcelot, soon at supper shalt thou see
Lorenzo, who is thy new master's guest.
Give him this letter, do it secretly;
And so farewell. I would not have my father
See me in talk with thee.

1. ***taste:*** sense
2. ***tediousness:*** weariness/boredom

PLOT POINT

Jessica asks Launcelot to deliver a letter to Lorenzo, a Christian. It is clear that Jessica is unhappy living with her father, Shylock, whom she seems to despise. She is planning to marry Lorenzo and become a Christian.

LAUNCELOT

Adieu![3] Tears exhibit[4] my tongue. Most beautiful
pagan; most sweet Jew; if a Christian do not
play the knave and get thee,[5] I am much deceived.
But adieu. These foolish drops do something drown
my manly spirit. Adieu.

3. ***Adieu!:*** Goodbye!
4. ***exhibit:*** *Launcelot means to say 'inhibit' (stop) instead of 'exhibit'. Launcelot is saying that he cannot say goodbye because he is so upset.*
5. ***play the knave and get thee:*** use trickery to make you fall in love with him

Exit LAUNCELOT.

JESSICA

Farewell, good Launcelot.
Alack,[6] what heinous[7] sin is it in me
To be ashamed to be my father's child!
But though I am a daughter to his blood,
I am not to his manners.[8] O Lorenzo,
If thou keep promise, I shall end this strife,[9]
Become a Christian and thy loving wife.

6. ***Alack:*** Alas *(an expression of regret or sorrow)*
7. ***heinous:*** wicked/evil
8. ***manners:*** behaviour
9. ***strife:*** struggle or inner conflict *Jessica is torn between her duty to her father and her love for Lorenzo.*

Exit.

OVERVIEW OF ACT 2, SCENE 3

- In this scene we are introduced to Shylock's daughter, Jessica. Launcelot is saying goodbye to Jessica as he is leaving to work as Bassanio's servant.
- Jessica reveals a lot about her home life through her interaction with Launcelot. She informs us that her house 'is hell' (line 2) and tells Launcelot that he made it tolerable – 'Didst rob it of some taste of tediousness' (line 3). She also asks Launcelot to deliver a letter to her love, Lorenzo and gives him a ducat.

- Launcelot, in his typical over-the-top fashion, tells Jessica that he is too overwhelmed with emotion to speak.
- After Launcelot leaves, we get an insight into Jessica's inner turmoil. Jessica has a duty to her father but she is ashamed of him:

  Alack, what heinous sin is it in me
  To be ashamed to be my father's child! (lines 16–17)

- It is clear that she strongly disapproves of her father's behaviour and that she and Lorenzo have previously discussed eloping together. By the end of the scene, Jessica is hoping that Lorenzo will keep his promise to marry her. She will then be liberated from the 'hell' she is living in. Jessica is also willing to convert to Christianity. All of this reflects badly on Shylock.
- Shylock is unaware of the betrayal his daughter is planning:

  O Lorenzo,
  If thou keep promise, I shall end this strife,
  Become a Christian and thy loving wife. (lines 19–21)

REVIEWING

1. Why is Jessica so sad to see Launcelot leave her house?
2. What favour does Jessica ask of Launcelot?
3. What do you think Lorenzo has promised Jessica?
4. What would Jessica be willing to do for Lorenzo if he keeps his promise?

ORAL LANGUAGE

Discussing Jessica's Decision P

Pair Activity

Do you think that Jessica is right to leave her father's house, convert to Christianity and marry Lorenzo? Record your responses on **page 27** of your portfolio.

REFLECTING

Character File P

Turn to **page 132** of your portfolio to continue recording your impressions of **Shylock**. What does Jessica say about Shylock in this scene? Record one quote and write what you think the quote reveals about Shylock's personality.

ACT 2, SCENE 4

Setting: Venice. A street.

In this **scene** you will:

- Write **Jessica's letter** to Lorenzo.

Action – What Happens?

In this short scene, we learn that Lorenzo, Solanio and Salerio are arranging a masque for Bassanio's feast that night. Launcelot gives Lorenzo the letter from Jessica which reveals her plan to disguise herself as a boy and elope with him. Jessica also informs Launcelot in her letter that she has stolen gold and jewels to take with her.

Useful Words

torch-bearer – a person who carries a lighted torch

Marry – By Mary (a mild oath meaning 'indeed')

Enter GRATIANO, LORENZO, SALERIO and SOLANIO.

LORENZO
Nay, we will slink away in[1] supper-time,
Disguise us at my lodging, and return
All in an hour.

GRATIANO
We have not made good preparation.

SALERIO
We have not spoke us yet of[2] torchbearers.

SOLANIO
'Tis vile, unless it may be quaintly ordered,[3]
And better in my mind not undertook.

LORENZO
'Tis now but four o'clock. We have two hours
To furnish us.[4]

Enter LAUNCELOT with a letter.

Friend Launcelot, what's the news?

LAUNCELOT
An[5] it shall please you to break up[6]
this, it shall seem to signify.[7]

LORENZO
I know the hand.[8] In faith, 'tis a fair hand,
And whiter than the paper it writ on
Is the fair hand that writ.

GRATIANO
Love-news, in faith.

LAUNCELOT
By your leave, sir.[9]

LORENZO
Whither[10] goest thou?

1. *in:* during

SHAKESPEARE'S WORLD

Elizabethan masques were a very popular form of entertainment and a very elaborate affair. A masque had music, song, dancing and people in fancy dress and masks. As these mainly took place at night, many people would carry or 'bear' torches, making it quite a spectacular event.

2. *We have … of:* We have not yet arranged for
3. *quaintly ordered:* cleverly managed
4. *To furnish us:* To get everything we need.
5. *An:* If
6. *break up:* open (the seal of the letter)
7. *it shall … signify:* it will tell you all you want to know
8. *hand:* handwriting
9. *By your leave, sir:* Please excuse me.
10. *Whither:* Where

LAUNCELOT

Marry, sir, to bid my old master the Jew to sup[11]
tonight with my new master the Christian.

11. *to sup:* to have supper

LORENZO

Hold[12] here, take this. Tell gentle Jessica
I will not fail her. Speak it privately.

12. *Hold:* Wait

Exit LAUNCELOT.

Go gentlemen,
Will you prepare you for this masque tonight?
I am provided of a torch-bearer.[13]

13. *I am ... torch-bearer:* I have got a torch-bearer. *(Lorenzo has Jessica in mind.)*

SALERIO

Ay, marry, I'll be gone about it straight.[14]

14. *straight:* immediately

SOLANIO

And so will I.

LORENZO

Meet me and Gratiano
At Gratiano's lodging some hour hence.[15]

15. *hence:* from now

SALERIO

'Tis good we do so.

Exeunt SALERIO and SOLANIO.

GRATIANO

Was not that letter from fair Jessica?

LORENZO

I must needs tell thee all. She hath directed[16]
How I shall take her from her father's house,
What gold and jewels she is furnished with,[17]
What page's suit[18] she hath in readiness.
If e'er the Jew her father come to heaven,
It will be for his gentle daughter's sake;
And never dare misfortune cross her foot

16. *directed:* written

17. *furnished with:* supplied with

18. *page's suit:* a young boy's outfit

Unless she do it under this excuse:
That she is issue to a faithless Jew.[19]
Come, go with me. Peruse this[20] as thou goest.
Fair Jessica shall be my torch-bearer.

Exeunt.

19. *Unless she ... Jew:* The only reason Jessica might experience bad luck is through being the daughter of an unbelieving Jew.
20. *Peruse this:* Read this (letter)

PLOT POINT

Jessica has arranged to disguise herself as a torch-bearer in order to elope with Lorenzo.

OVERVIEW OF ACT 2, SCENE 4

- In this scene, Lorenzo, Gratiano, Solanio and Salerio are making preparations for a masque that night at Bassanio's feast. Gratiano is worried that they are not adequately prepared, but Lorenzo assures them that they can do it.
- Launcelot enters and gives Lorenzo Jessica's letter. Lorenzo gives Launcelot money, asking him to give a message to Jessica that he will not 'fail her' (line 20). Launcelot then leaves to go to invite Shylock to supper with Bassanio.
- Jessica's letter reveals the plan to **elope** with Lorenzo. She will disguise herself as a **page** (boy). She also informs Lorenzo that she has stolen 'gold and jewels' (line 31) from her father. Lorenzo plans to disguise Jessica as his torch-bearer that night.

REVIEWING

1. How does Lorenzo react to the letter that Launcelot gives him?
2. Where does Launcelot say he has to go next?
3. When and where have Lorenzo, Solanio and Salerio agreed to meet again?
4. Who is going to be the torch-bearer? How will this be arranged, in your opinion?

CREATING

Jessica's Letter to Lorenzo P

Turn to **page 28** of your portfolio to write Jessica's letter to Lorenzo. Read lines 29–32 of this scene again before you write the letter.

ACT 2, SCENE 5

Setting: Venice. Shylock's house.

In this **scene** you will:

- Learn about **dramatic irony** and discuss examples.
- Reflect on the character of **Shylock**.

Action – What Happens?

In this scene, Launcelot has come to take his leave of Shylock and to invite him to supper with Bassanio that evening. Although Shylock is reluctant at first, he decides to go anyway, just to eat at Bassanio's expense. He warns Jessica to lock up the windows and doors of the house and not to look out the windows. Contrary to what Shylock says, Launcelot tells Jessica to look out the window later on as Lorenzo will be coming by. The scene ends with Jessica longing to be free from her father's house.

Useful Words

gormandize – over-eat

wherefore – why

apparel – clothing

fife – flute

ACT 2, SCENE 5

PLOT POINT

At the start of the scene, Launcelot has told Shylock that he has become Bassanio's servant.

Enter SHYLOCK and LAUNCELOT.

SHYLOCK

Well, thou shalt see, thy eyes shall be thy judge,
The difference of[1] old Shylock and Bassanio.—
What, Jessica!—Thou shalt not gormandize,
As thou hast done with me—What, Jessica!—
And sleep and snore, and rend apparel out.[2]—
Why, Jessica, I say!

LAUNCELOT

Why, Jessica!

SHYLOCK

Who bids thee call? I do not bid thee call.

LAUNCELOT

Your worship was wont[3] to tell me that
I could do nothing without bidding.[4]

Enter JESSICA.

JESSICA

Call you? What is your will?

SHYLOCK

I am bid forth to supper, Jessica.
There are my keys. But wherefore[5] should I go?
I am not bid for love. They flatter me,
But yet I'll go in hate, to feed upon[6]
The prodigal[7] Christian. Jessica, my girl,
Look to my house. I am right loath[8] to go.
There is some ill a-brewing towards my rest,[9]
For I did dream of money-bags tonight.[10]

LAUNCELOT

I beseech[11] you, sir, go. My young master doth expect
your reproach.[12]

SHYLOCK

So do I his.

1. *of:* between
2. *rend apparel out:* wear out your clothes
3. *wont:* accustomed
4. *Your worship … bidding:* You used to tell me that I could do nothing on my own initiative.

LOOKING AT LANGUAGE

Foreshadowing: An advance warning or hint about something that will happen later in the story. Can you find the example of foreshadowing in Shylock's lines 11–18? What effect does foreshadowing have here, in your opinion?

CHARACTER NOTE

After initially declining to dine with Bassanio, Shylock is planning to go. Why is he going and what do you think this reveals about his character?

5. *wherefore:* why
6. *to feed upon:* to eat at the expense of
7. *prodigal:* wasteful
8. *right loath:* very reluctant
9. *There is … rest:* I feel there is some danger lurking that makes me uneasy
10. *tonight:* last night *Shylock had a dream/premonition that something bad would happen.*
11. *beseech:* beg
12. *reproach: Launcelot means to say 'approach' instead of 'reproach'.*

LAUNCELOT

And they have conspired[13] together. I will not say you shall see a masque, but if you do, then it was not for nothing that my nose fell a-bleeding on Black Monday[14] last at six o'clock i' the morning, falling out[15] that year on Ash Wednesday was four year in th'afternoon.[16]

13. *conspired:* planned

14. *Black Monday:* Easter Monday
15. *falling out:* coming on
16. *And they … th'afternoon: Launcelot is mocking Shylock's tendency to be superstitious. Most of what Launcelot is saying is nonsensical.*

SPOTLIGHT ON … LANGUAGE

What words or phrases does Shylock use to describe the masque? What do these tell you about his attitude towards the masque?

SHYLOCK

What, are there masques? Hear you me, Jessica,
Lock up my doors; and when you hear the drum
And the vile squealing of the wry-neck'd fife,[17]
Clamber[18] not you up to the casements[19] then,
Nor thrust your head into the public street
To gaze on Christian fools with varnished[20] faces,
But stop my house's ears—I mean my casements.
Let not the sound of shallow fopp'ry[21] enter
My sober[22] house. By Jacob's staff I swear,
I have no mind of feasting forth[23] tonight:
But I will go. Go you before me, sirrah.
Say I will come.

17. *wry-neck'd fife:* twisted neck flute *The image here is of the person playing the flute bending their head or neck to the side as they play.*
18. *Clamber:* Climb
19. *casements:* windows
20. *varnished:* painted/masked
21. *fopp'ry:* fun/light-heartedness
22. *sober:* serious/solemn

23. *forth:* away from home

SPOTLIGHT ON … LANGUAGE

Jonathan Pryce and real-life daughter Phoebe (seen here) won acclaim for their roles as Shylock and Jessica in The Globe Theatre's 2015 production. Choose a line from the scene that you think would be suitable to accompany this image.

LAUNCELOT

I will go before, sir.
[*aside to JESSICA*] Mistress, look out at window for all this,[24]
There will come a Christian by
Will be worth a Jewess' eye.

Exit.

SHYLOCK

What says that fool of Hagar's offspring,[25] ha?

JESSICA

His words were 'Farewell mistress'; nothing else.

SHYLOCK

The patch[26] is kind enough, but a huge feeder,
Snail-slow in profit, and he sleeps by day
More than the wild-cat. Drones hive not with me;[27]
Therefore I part with him, and part with him
To one that would have him help to waste
His borrowed purse. Well, Jessica, go in.
Perhaps I will return immediately.
Do as I bid you. Shut doors after you.
Fast bind, fast find[28]—
A proverb never stale in thrifty mind.

Exit.

JESSICA

Farewell; and if my fortune be not crossed,[29]
I have a father, you a daughter, lost.

Exit.

24. *for all this:* despite all this *(despite what Shylock has told her)*

25. *What says … offspring: Shylock is implying that he is disowning Launcelot in the same way that Abraham disowned Ishmael, the child he had with Hagar. The reference comes from the Bible.*

26. *patch:* fool/clown

27. *Drones hive … me:* Bees who do no work *Shylock is saying that he will not support people who do not work hard in his house.*

28. *Fast bind, fast find: A proverb meaning if you secure something well it will remain safe.*

29. *Farewell; … crossed:* Goodbye and if all goes well

SPOTLIGHT ON … CHARACTERS

At the end of the scene, Jessica expresses her desire to flee her father's house to elope with the man she loves, a Christian called Lorenzo. How does Jessica compare to Portia? Think about the father/daughter relationship and the theme of marriage.

OVERVIEW OF ACT 2, SCENE 5

- This is a **domestic scene** where we observe the interaction between Shylock and his daughter, Jessica. Launcelot has come to take his leave of his old master, Shylock, and invite him to supper with his new master, Bassanio. Shylock warns Launcelot that Bassanio might not be as accommodating a master as he is:

  Thou shalt not gormandize,
  As thou hast done with me (lines 3–4)

- Shylock has reservations about accepting the invitation to go to supper with Bassanio, but his desire to feast at Bassanio's expense outweighs his fears about going:

  But wherefore should I go?
  I am not bid for love. They flatter me,
  But yet I'll go in hate, to feed upon
  The prodigal Christian. (lines 12–15)

- Shylock expresses his insecurities and worries about leaving his house. He reveals that he had a dream about money-bags, which seems to indicate that his chief concern is for the safety of his wealth. The dream is oddly **portentous** (sinister/predictive) as it also reminds us that Jessica is planning to desert her father and steal his money and jewels.
- When Launcelot reveals that there will also be a masque, Shylock becomes quite protective of his daughter. He warns her not to put her head out of the window 'To gaze on Christian fools with varnished faces' (line 33). He does not want his daughter to be contaminated by the 'shallow fopp'ry' (line 35) or **revelries** (celebrations) of the Christians who will be involved in the celebrations. This idea is reinforced by Shylock's use of **personification** when describing his house:

  But stop my house's ears (line 34)

- Shylock instructs Jessica to close the 'ears', or windows, of the house so that they do not **admit** (let in) any sounds. This warning to Jessica is sadly ironic as we are aware that she is planning to elope with Lorenzo, a Christian, that very night. Shylock's absence from the house will make her escape easier. This is an example of **dramatic irony** as the audience is aware of something that Shylock is not. In this case, dramatic irony can increase the **tension** or **suspense** of the play, or even cause us to sympathise with Shylock, knowing the fate that is about to **befall** (happen to) him (i.e. he is about to lose his riches and his daughter).

REVIEWING

1. What warning does Shylock give to Launcelot about becoming Bassanio's servant?
2. Shylock decides to go to supper despite his doubts. Why does he decide to go?
3. Why does Shylock tell Jessica to shut up his windows and doors?
4. What is Shylock's opinion of Launcelot?
5. What message does Launcelot give Jessica?
6. What is Jessica's response to Launcelot's message?

ORAL LANGUAGE

Discussing Dramatic Irony

Pair Activity

What is dramatic irony?

Dramatic irony occurs when the audience or a character on stage has information that other characters do not have. For example, in this scene, the audience is aware that Jessica is planning to leave her father's house and marry a Christian, but Shylock is completely unaware of this fact.

1. Discuss one other example of **dramatic irony** from this scene.
2. Do you think that this is an effective dramatic device to use at this point in the play?
3. Can you think of any film, television programme or other play that has made use of dramatic irony? Briefly describe the scenario and say whether you as a viewer/audience member thought that it was an effective device.

REFLECTING

Character File P

Turn to the Character File section of your portfolio to write your response to **Shylock** (**page 133**) in this scene. Use quotations to help you.

ACT 2, SCENE 6

Setting: Venice. Shylock's house.

In this **scene** you will:

- Focus on **imagery**.
- Reflect on the character of **Jessica**.

Action – What Happens?

Gratiano and Salerio are waiting for Lorenzo to arrive so they can help Jessica to escape. Lorenzo finally arrives and apologises for being late. He then calls up to Jessica who is dressed as a page boy. When Lorenzo tells her that she is to be a torch-bearer, she is embarrassed to have the torch highlight her new disguise. Jessica throws down a casket (or box) of gold and jewels, saying that she will steal more gold coins before descending. Later, Antonio arrives, informing Gratiano that the masque has been cancelled and that Bassanio is going to set sail immediately. Gratiano welcomes this news.

Useful Words

bark – ship

obscured – hidden

office – task/duty

garnish – dress/outfit

dwells – lives

ACT 2, SCENE 6

Enter GRATIANO and SALERIO, masqued.

GRATIANO

This is the penthouse[1] under which Lorenzo
Desired us to make stand.

SALERIO

His hour is almost past.

GRATIANO

And it is marvel he out-dwells his hour,
For lovers ever run before the clock.[2]

SALERIO

O, ten times faster Venus' pigeons[3] fly
To seal love's bonds new-made, than they are wont
To keep obligèd[4] faith unforfeited![5]

GRATIANO

That ever holds.[6] Who riseth from a feast
With that keen appetite that he sits down?
Where is the horse that doth untread[7] again
His tedious measures[8] with the unbated fire[9]
That he did pace them first?[10] All things that are
Are with more spirit chasèd than enjoyed.[11]
How like a younker[12] or a prodigal
The scarfèd bark[13] puts from her native bay,[14]
Hugged and embracèd by the strumpet wind!
How like the prodigal[15] doth she return,
With over-weathered ribs[16] and raggèd sails,
Lean, rent[17] and beggared by the strumpet wind!

SALERIO

Here comes Lorenzo. More of this hereafter.[18]

Enter LORENZO.

LORENZO

Sweet friends, your patience for my long abode.[19]
Not I but my affairs have made you wait.
When you shall please to play the thieves for wives

1. *penthouse:* projecting roof/porch of Shylock's house
2. *And it ... clock:* It is amazing that he is late considering that lovers are usually early.
3. *Venus' pigeons:* the doves who draw Venus' chariot *Venus was the goddess of love.*
4. *obligèd:* pledged *(married)*
5. *O, ten ... unforfeited!: Salerio claims that the doves drawing Venus' chariot fly faster to lovers at the start of their relationship than to lovers who have been married for a while. In other words, time flies at the start of a relationship when the passion and excitement of new love is strongest.*
6. *ever holds:* remains true
7. *untread:* retrace
8. *measures:* paces
9. *unbated fire:* intensity/enthusiasm
10. *Where is ... first?:* What horse can retrace his paces again with the same energy he did at the start?
11. *All things ... enjoyed:* The reality of something may not be as exciting as chasing after it.
12. *younker:* fashionable youth
13. *The scarfèd bark:* the ship adorned with flags and sails
14. *puts from her native bay:* sails out from the harbour
15. *prodigal:* the prodigal son *(Bible story in which the prodigal son left his wealthy father's house and wasted all his money. He returned home with nothing.)*
16. *over-weathered ribs:* weather-beaten timbers
17. *rent:* torn
18. *hereafter:* later
19. *long abode:* delay

I'll watch[20] as long for you then.[21] Approach.
Here dwells[22] my father[23] Jew. [*calling*] Ho, who's within?

20. *watch:* wait
21. *When you … then:* When you have to steal wives for yourselves, I'll wait as long for you.
22. *dwells:* lives
23. *father:* father-in-law

Enter JESSICA, above, in boy's clothes.

JESSICA

Who are you? Tell me, for more certainty,
Albeit[24] I'll swear that I do know your tongue.[25]

24. *Albeit:* Although
25. *tongue:* voice

LORENZO

Lorenzo, and thy love.

JESSICA

Lorenzo, certain, and my love indeed,
For who love I so much? And now who knows
But you, Lorenzo, whether I am yours?

SHAKESPEARE'S WORLD

In Shakespeare's time, the female roles in the theatre would have been played by young males between the ages of about 12–20. So, during this scene, the young boy playing Jessica would have had to dress as a boy!

LORENZO

Heaven and thy thoughts are witness that thou art.

JESSICA

Here, catch this casket. It is worth the pains.[26]
I am glad 'tis night, you do not look on me,
For I am much ashamed of my exchange;[27]
But love is blind, and lovers cannot see
The pretty follies that themselves commit;[28]
For if they could, Cupid[29] himself would blush
To see me thus transformèd to a boy.

26. *pains:* effort
27. *exchange:* change of dress
28. *But love … commit:* Lovers cannot see the silly things that they do for each other.
29. *Cupid:* God of love *(often depicted as blind)*

LORENZO

Descend, for you must be my torch-bearer.

SPOTLIGHT ON … STAGECRAFT

Jessica is very self-conscious about having to dress as a boy. Think about how Jessica's rapid transformation could be effectively achieved on stage in this scene. What costumes or props (stage objects) do you think would facilitate her transformation?

JESSICA

What, must I hold a candle to my shames?
They in themselves, good sooth,[30] are too too light.[31]
Why, 'tis an office[32] of discovery, love,
And I should be obscured.[33]

30. *good sooth:* in truth
31. *light: There are two possible meanings of 'light' here – bright or frivolous/irresponsible.*
32. *office:* task
33. *What, … obscured: Jessica is worried that the task of holding the torch will draw attention to her when she feels that she should be 'obscured' or hidden.*

LORENZO

So are you, sweet,
Even in the lovely garnish[34] of a boy.

34. *garnish:* dress/outfit

35. *For the … runaway:* it is getting late

36. *stayed:* waited

37. *make fast:* lock
38. *gild:* cover
39. *straight:* right away

But come at once,
For the close night doth play the runaway,[35]
And we are stayed[36] for at Bassanio's feast.

JESSICA

I will make fast[37] the doors, and gild[38] myself
With some more ducats, and be with you straight.[39]

Exit above.

GRATIANO

Now, by my hood, a gentile and no Jew.[40]

LORENZO

Beshrew me[41] but I love her heartily,
For she is wise, if I can judge of her;
And fair she is, if that mine eyes be true;
And true she is, as she hath proved herself;
And therefore like herself, wise, fair, and true,
Shall she be placèd in my constant soul.

Enter JESSICA, below.

What, art thou come? On, gentlemen, away!
Our masquing mates by this time for us stay.

Exit with JESSICA and SALERIO.

Enter ANTONIO.

ANTONIO

Who's there?

GRATIANO

Signor Antonio!

ANTONIO

Fie, fie, Gratiano! Where are all the rest?
'Tis nine o'clock. Our friends all stay for you.[42]
No masque tonight. The wind is come about.[43]
Bassanio presently[44] will go aboard.
I have sent twenty[45] out to seek for you.

GRATIANO

I am glad on't.[46] I desire no more delight[47]
Than to be under sail and gone tonight.

Exeunt.

40. *no Jew: Jessica does not behave like a Jewish person who was stereotyped as being miserly and frugal.*

41. *Beshrew me:* Curse me

CHARACTER NOTE

In Lorenzo's speech here (lines 52–57), he is speaking aloud about Jessica. What qualities does he admire in her?

42. *all stay for you:* are all waiting for you

43. *The wind ... about:* The wind has changed.

44. *presently:* immediately

45. *twenty:* twenty men

46. *on't:* of it

47. *I desire ... delight:* Nothing would make me happier.

PLOT POINT

There is a sense of urgency at the end of the scene as Antonio informs Gratiano that the wind has changed, so the masque has been cancelled and Bassanio is to set sail for Belmont immediately.

OVERVIEW OF ACT 2, SCENE 6

KEY SCENE – THE ELOPEMENT

Part 1 (lines 1–20) – Gratiano and Salerio wait for Lorenzo under the porch of Shylock's house.

- The main action of this scene concerns Jessica's betrayal. Not only is she deserting her father, but she is stealing his valuables and **eloping** (running away to get married secretly) with a Christian.
- The scene opens with Gratiano and Salerio waiting for Lorenzo outside Shylock's house. Lorenzo is late. Gratiano argues that it is unusual for someone in love to be late:

  All things that are
  Are with more spirit chasèd than enjoyed. (lines 12–13)

- Gratiano suggests that people are more interested in the 'chase' or pursuing love rather than the reality of love when they succeed in wooing someone. Is Gratiano subtly hinting that Lorenzo is not as committed to Jessica as Jessica is to him?

Part 2 (lines 21–59) – Lorenzo arrives and Jessica escapes with a casket filled with her father's riches.

- When Lorenzo eventually arrives on the scene, he does not offer any explanation for his lateness, apart from **cryptically** (mysteriously) saying, 'Not I but my affairs have made you wait' (line 22). One wonders what 'affairs' could possibly have made him late considering the importance of the task he is undertaking – ensuring the escape of his wife-to-be. Nonetheless, Lorenzo does seem genuinely **enamoured of** (filled with love for) Jessica when she enters the scene.
- Before she descends, Jessica throws down a casket laden with gold and jewels she has stolen from her father. She is quite embarrassed by her transformation into a boy, but doesn't seem to be ashamed about the impact her theft will have on her father:

  For I am much ashamed of my exchange (line 35)

- Jessica thinks she should be 'obscured' (line 44) or hidden, rather than hold a torch at the feast her father will be attending that evening. Lorenzo playfully reassures her that she is sufficiently disguised 'in the lovely garnish of a boy' (line 45). Before she actually descends, Jessica decides to steal even more money from her father.
- Jessica's actions cause Gratiano to remark:

  Now, by my hood, a gentile and no Jew. (line 51)

  This suggests that Jessica is the opposite of the stereotypical Jew, who was thought miserly, as she is displaying great generosity **dispensing** (giving out/distributing) her father's wealth.

- Lorenzo responds by saying how much he loves Jessica:

  Beshrew me but I love her heartily,
  For she is wise, if I can judge of her;
  And fair she is, if that mine eyes be true;
  And true she is, as she hath proved herself (lines 52–55)

  Indeed, this episode does prove that Jessica is devoted to Lorenzo.

Part 3 (lines 60–67) – Antonio informs Gratiano that they will set sail for Belmont immediately.

- As Lorenzo, Jessica and Salerio exit the scene, Antonio enters and tells Gratiano that the masque has been cancelled. A change in the direction of the wind means that Bassanio must set sail for Belmont immediately. This is welcome news for Gratiano as he is more than ready to depart:

  I am glad on't. I desire no more delight
  Than to be under sail and gone tonight. (lines 66–67)

THEMES

- The themes of **betrayal**, **marriage** and **false appearances** all feature in this scene through the elopement of Jessica and Lorenzo. Jessica has betrayed her father and her religion by eloping with Lorenzo. Not only that, but she has stolen his precious gold and jewels. Jessica's disguise relates to the theme of false appearances – things not being what they seem.
- The theme of marriage is seen through Jessica's elopement with Lorenzo. This is a union that will not be supported by her father. Jessica, by 'gilding' herself with coins and jewels and being the daughter of a rich Jew, is certainly an attractive **prospective** (potential/possible) wife, much like the wealthy Portia in Belmont. In this way, the themes of **marriage** and **money** are also **interlinked** (connected) in this scene.

REVIEWING

1. What reason does Lorenzo give for being late?
2. What joke does he make to his friends by way of an apology?
3. What does Jessica throw down to Lorenzo?
4. Why is Jessica embarrassed and ashamed in this scene?
5. What news does Antonio bring Gratiano at the end of the scene?
6. What do you think Gratiano might mean by his response to Antonio (lines 66–67)?

ORAL LANGUAGE

Discussing

Pair Activity

All things that are
Are with more spirit chasèd than enjoyed.
Gratiano (lines 12–13)

1. Discuss with your partner whether or not you think the quote above is true. Is the 'chase' more exciting than the reality of getting something (or someone) you want?
2. Can you think of any examples, either from your own life or from people in general, to prove or disprove this notion? (Think about Christmas presents, celebrities, etc.)

EXPLORING

Ship Imagery P

Images of ships pervade this play. In lines 14 –19, Gratiano creates a vivid image of a ship leaving the harbour in all its splendour and returning ragged and weather-beaten. The ship is **personified** (given human qualities), which helps bring the image to life.

Turn to **page 29** of your portfolio to complete an exercise on the image of the ship from this scene.

REFLECTING

Character File P

What is your impression of Jessica in this scene? Do you agree with Lorenzo's description of her as 'wise, fair and true'? (Look back at lines 52–57 to help you.) Turn to the Character File section of your portfolio to write your response to **Jessica** (**page 139**) in this scene.

Do you think Lorenzo is genuinely in love with Jessica? Turn to **page 141** of your portfolio to record your impression of **Lorenzo** in this scene.

ACT 2, SCENE 7

Setting: Belmont. A room in Portia's house.

In this **scene** you will:

- Read, examine and perform the Prince of Morocco's **speech**.
- Consider **Portia's final lines**.
- **Reflect** on the Prince of Morocco's choice of casket.

Action – What Happens?

The action moves swiftly in this scene from Venice to Belmont, where the Prince of Morocco is about to choose a casket in the hope of winning Portia's hand in marriage. The Prince of Morocco reads the inscriptions carefully before making his choice.

Useful Words

hazard – risk

throughway – main road

dross – worthless junk/rubbish

complexion – skin-colour

ACT 2, SCENE 7

PLOT POINT

The scene is full of suspense as the Prince of Morocco makes his choice. His choice of casket, his reasoning and his use of language give us an insight into his character. Notice that the Prince of Morocco delivers a monologue as he chooses a casket.

1. *discover:* reveal
2. *several:* different
3. *who:* which
4. *bears:* carries/contains
5. *Who chooseth:* Whoever chooses
6. *blunt:* plainly spoken
7. *hazard:* risk
8. *withal:* with it
9. *survey:* examine
10. *back again:* over again (in reverse order)
11. *threatens:* is menacing
12. *advantages:* rewards
13. *A golden … dross:* A noble mind like mine doesn't even consider worthless junk like lead.
14. *nor:* neither
15. *aught:* anything
16. *hue:* colour
17. *And weigh … hand:* And consider your worth in an impartial manner.
18. *If thou … estimation:* If you are to judge yourself
19. *Thou dost … lady:* You are deserving enough, but maybe not good enough for Portia.
20. *And yet … myself:* To be worried about whether I am good enough for her is doing myself a disservice.

Flourish of cornets. Enter PORTIA, with the PRINCE OF MOROCCO, and their trains.

PORTIA

Go, draw aside the curtains, and discover[1]
The several[2] caskets to this noble prince.
Now make your choice.

MOROCCO

This first of gold who[3] this inscription bears:[4]
'Who chooseth[5] me shall gain what many men desire.'
The second, silver, which this promise carries:
'Who chooseth me shall get as much as he deserves.'
This third, dull lead, with warning all as blunt:[6]
'Who chooseth me must give and hazard[7] all he hath.'
How shall I know if I do choose the right?

PORTIA

The one of them contains my picture, Prince.
If you choose that, then I am yours withal.[8]

MOROCCO

Some god direct my judgement! Let me see.
I will survey[9] th'inscriptions back again.[10]
What says this leaden casket?
'Who chooseth me must give and hazard all he hath.'
Must give, for what? For lead? Hazard for lead?
This casket threatens.[11] Men that hazard all
Do it in hope of fair advantages.[12]
A golden mind stoops not to shows of dross.[13]
I'll then nor[14] give nor hazard aught[15] for lead.
What says the silver with her virgin hue?[16]
'Who chooseth me shall get as much as he deserves.'
'As much as he deserves': pause there, Morocco,
And weigh thy value with an even hand.[17]
If thou be'st rated by thy estimation[18]
Thou dost deserve enough, and yet 'enough'
May not extend so far as to the lady.[19]
And yet to be afeard of my deserving
Were but a weak disabling of myself.[20]
As much as I deserve—why, that's the lady!

I do in birth deserve her, and, in fortunes,
In graces, and in qualities of breeding;
But more than these, in love I do deserve.
What if I strayed no further, but chose here?[21]
Let's see once more this saying graved in gold:
'Who chooseth me shall gain what many men desire.'
Why, that's the lady! All the world desires her.
From the four corners of the earth they come
To kiss this shrine, this mortal-breathing[22] saint.
The Hyrcanian deserts[23] and the vasty[24] wilds
Of wide Arabia are as throughfares[25] now
For princes to come view fair Portia.
The watery kingdom,[26] whose ambitious head[27]
Spits in the face of heaven, is no bar
To stop the foreign spirits,[28] but they come
As o'er a brook[29] to see fair Portia.
One of these three contains her heavenly picture.
Is't like[30] that lead contains her? 'Twere damnation
To think so base[31] a thought. It were too gross
To rib her cerecloth in the obscure grave.[32]
Or shall I think in silver she's immured,[33]
Being ten times undervalued to tried[34] gold?
O sinful thought! Never so rich a gem
Was set in worse than gold. They have in England
A coin that bears the figure of an angel
Stamped in gold, but that's insculped[35] upon;
But here an angel in a golden bed
Lies all within.[36] Deliver me the key.
Here do I choose, and thrive I as I may![37]

PORTIA

There, take it, Prince; and if my form[38] lie there,
Then I am yours.

MOROCCO unlocks the golden casket.

21. *What if … here?:* What if I didn't consider the other caskets and just chose this one?

LOOKING AT LANGUAGE

Hyperbole: Exaggerated language used for dramatic effect. Notice how the Prince of Morocco continues to use hyperbole (exaggeration) here to show how eager the suitors coming in pursuit of Portia are.

22. *mortal-breathing:* living
23. *Hyrcanian deserts: area of land south of the Caspian Sea*
24. *vasty:* vast/huge
25. *throughfares:* main roads/pathways
26. *The watery kingdom:* The sea
27. *ambitious head:* swelling waves of a storm
28. *foreign spirits:* suitors
29. *As o'er a brook:* As if they were crossing a brook or stream
30. *like:* likely/probable
31. *base:* low
32. *It were … grave:* Lead is not good enough to cover her funeral shroud in a dark grave. *(Shrouds often contained a layer of lead.)*
33. *immured:* enclosed
34. *tried:* purified

SPOTLIGHT ON … IMAGERY

Religious imagery: The Prince of Morocco uses religious imagery here to show how precious Portia is. Can you find examples (lines 48–60)?

35. *insculped:* engraved
36. *within:* inside
37. *and thrive … may!:* let's see how I get on
38. *form:* image

MOROCCO

O hell! What have we here?
A carrion Death,[39] within whose empty eye
There is a written scroll. I'll read the writing.
'All that glisters[40] is not gold;
Often have you heard that told.
Many a man his life hath sold
But my outside to behold.[41 42]
Gilded[43] tombs do worms infold.[44]
Had you been[45] as wise as bold,
Young in limbs, in judgement old,[46]
Your answer had not been inscrolled.[47]
Fare you well; your suit is cold.'[48]
Cold indeed, and labour lost.[49]
Then farewell heat, and welcome frost.
Portia, adieu.[50] I have too grieved a heart
To take a tedious leave.[51] Thus losers part.

Exit with his train. Flourish of cornets.

PORTIA

A gentle riddance. Draw the curtains, go.
Let all of his complexion[52] choose me so.

Exeunt.

39. *A carrion Death:* A skull
40. *glisters:* glitters
41. *behold:* see
42. *Many a man … behold:* Many men have lost their lives for the sight of gold.
43. *Gilded:* Golden
44. *Gilded tombs … infold:* Golden tombs contain worms inside.
45. *Had you been:* If you had been
46. *old:* wise
47. *Your answer … inscrolled:* You would not be reading this answer.
48. *your suit is cold:* you've missed your chance
49. *labour lost:* all that effort wasted
50. *adieu:* goodbye
51. *I have … leave:* I am too upset for a long goodbye.
52. *complexion:* skin-colour

OVERVIEW OF ACT 2, SCENE 7

- This is the first casket scene. The Prince of Morocco is the first suitor to make his choice. A sense of ceremony and suspense **pervades** (runs through) the scene as he surveys the three caskets.
- The Prince of Morocco rejects the lead casket, saying that a noble person such as he would never stoop so low as to pick lead:

  A golden mind stoops not to shows of dross. (line 20)
- Next, he considers the silver casket, but also rejects it. He responds to the inscription on the silver casket by saying that he deserves Portia and is careful not to allow himself to feel unworthy of her:

  I do in birth deserve her, and, in fortunes,
  In graces, and in qualities of breeding;
  But more than these, in love I do deserve. (lines 32–34)

- The Prince of Morocco is almost happy to choose then and there, but decides to inspect the gold casket once more. His response to the inscription 'Who chooseth me shall gain what many men desire' (line 37) is that many men desire the lady. He takes this to mean that Portia's picture is enclosed in the gold casket. He uses **religious imagery** and **hyperbole** (exaggeration) to suggest how desirable she really is. The Prince of Morocco refers to Portia as a 'shrine, this mortal-breathing saint' (line 40) to whom suitors come from far and wide over land and sea to woo.
- Eventually, having reviewed all three options once again, the Prince of Morocco is confident that Portia's image is in the gold casket. However, he is bitterly disappointed to discover that he has made the wrong choice, that his 'suit is cold' (line 73).
- Inside the casket is a skull with a scroll in its eye-socket. He reads the message, which is like a **taunt** (tease) to him at this point. The first line – 'All that glisters is not gold' (line 65) – is a reminder not to judge too much on appearances. This is ironic, as previously the Prince of Morocco pleaded with Portia not to judge him on the colour of his skin.
- The Prince of Morocco leaves very quickly saying that he is too upset for a long, drawn-out goodbye:

  I have too grieved a heart
  To take a tedious leave. (lines 76–77)

  When he leaves, Portia is relieved, expressing a racist remark about the colour of the Prince of Morocco's skin – 'Let all of his complexion choose me so' (line 79). This means that she hopes that no one of the Prince of Morocco's dark skin colour will succeed in choosing her.

THEMES

The key themes in this scene are **marriage** and **false appearances**. The scroll enclosed in the gold casket warns against judging on appearances, that 'All that glisters is not gold' (line 65). The theme of **marriage** is very much apparent in the lottery that Portia's father has ingeniously devised for her to find a suitable husband.

REVIEWING

1. How will the Prince of Morocco know if he has chosen the correct casket?
2. Which casket does he eventually choose and why?
3. What is the Prince of Morocco's reaction to what he finds inside the casket?
4. How does Portia feel about the outcome for the Prince of Morocco? Use a quote to support your answer.

EXPLORING

1. Performing Morocco's Speech P

Group Activity

In groups of **four**, prepare a reading of the Prince of Morocco's speech, which captures his reaction to the caskets:

- **Part 1 (lines 15–21)** contemplating the **lead** casket
- **Part 2 (lines 22–35)** contemplating the **silver** casket
- **Part 3 (lines 36–47)** contemplating the **gold** casket
- **Part 4 (lines 48–60)** reviewing the caskets and coming to his final decision.

1. Everyone in the group should choose a different part of the speech to **read aloud**. Pay close attention to the language and imagery used in each part.
2. **Summarise** the main points of your part in your portfolio on **pages 31 and 32**.
3. Share your summary with the rest of your group.
4. What impression do you have of the Prince of Morocco after reading his speech? Record your thoughts on **page 33** of your portfolio.

2. Director's Notebook – Portia's Final Lines P

Portia's final lines in this scene are often cut from modern productions of the play. If you were the director, would you keep or cut these lines? Write your response on **page 33** of your portfolio.

REFLECTING

1. Reflecting on the Caskets P

Turn to **page 34** of your portfolio to record your response to the Prince of Morocco choosing the gold casket.

2. Character File P

Turn to **page 125** of the Character File section of your portfolio to write a brief note about how **Portia** comes across in this scene. Use a quote if possible.

ACT 2, SCENE 8

Setting: Venice. A street.

In this **scene** you will:

- Write and perform a **short script**.

Action – What Happens?

In this scene, Salerio and Solanio discuss the recent happenings in Venice. First, they discuss Shylock's reaction to his daughter's escape. They talk about how Shylock called on the Duke of Venice to help him find his daughter. Next, Salerio mentions that he heard a rumour that a merchant ship was lost at sea in the English Channel. He fears that this ship could belong to Antonio, but does not wish to upset him by telling him about it now. Salerio also talks about Bassanio and Antonio's sincere and emotional farewell to each other.

Useful Words

gondola – a boat used on the canals in Venice

passion – outburst

Enter SALERIO and SOLANIO.

SALERIO

Why, man, I saw Bassanio under sail.
With him is Gratiano gone along,
And in their ship I am sure Lorenzo is not.

SOLANIO

The villain Jew with outcries raised[1] the Duke,
Who went with him to search Bassanio's ship.

SALERIO

He came too late. The ship was under sail.
But there the Duke was given to understand
That in a gondola[2] were seen together
Lorenzo and his amorous[3] Jessica.
Besides, Antonio certified[4] the Duke
They were not with Bassanio in his ship.

SOLANIO

I never heard a passion[5] so confused,
So strange, outrageous, and so variable[6]

1. *raised:* roused/awakened

PLOT POINT

Salerio and Solanio reveal significant plot developments. Here, they report Shylock's reaction to Jessica's elopement and to theft of his jewels and money.

2. *gondola: a boat used on the canals in Venice*
3. *amorous:* loving
4. *certified:* assured
5. *passion:* outburst
6. *variable:* changing

'in a gondola were seen together Lorenzo and his amorous Jessica' (lines 8–9)

As the dog Jew did utter in the streets.
'My daughter! O my ducats! O my daughter!
Fled with a Christian! O my Christian ducats!
Justice! The law! My ducats, and my daughter!
A sealèd bag, two sealèd bags of ducats,
Of double ducats, stolen from me by my daughter!
And jewels, two stones, two rich and precious stones,
Stolen by my daughter! Justice! Find the girl!
She hath the stones upon her, and the ducats!'

SALERIO

Why, all the boys in Venice follow him,
Crying, 'His stones, his daughter, and his ducats!'

SOLANIO

Let good Antonio look he keep his day,[7]
Or he shall pay for this.

SALERIO

Marry, well remembered.
I reasoned[8] with a Frenchman yesterday,
Who told me, in the narrow seas that part
The French and English[9] there miscarrièd[10]
A vessel[11] of our country richly fraught.[12]
I thought upon Antonio when he told me,
And wished in silence that it were not his.

SOLANIO

You were best to tell Antonio what you hear—
Yet do not suddenly, for it may grieve him.

SALERIO

A kinder gentleman treads[13] not the earth.
I saw Bassanio and Antonio part.
Bassanio told him he would make some speed
Of his return.[14] He answered, 'Do not so.
Slubber not business[15] for my sake, Bassanio,
But stay the very riping of the time;[16]
And for the Jew's bond which he hath of me,
Let it not enter in your mind[17] of love

7. *keep his day:* repay his debt on time
8. *reasoned:* spoke
9. *the narrow … English:* the English Channel
10. *miscarrièd:* became shipwrecked/destroyed
11. *vessel:* ship
12. *richly fraught:* laden with valuable goods

PLOT POINT

Salerio has heard news that a merchant ship has been destroyed in the English Channel. He fears that the ship could belong to Antonio, but does not want to worry him about it yet. This creates a sense of foreboding.

13. *treads:* walks
14. *make some … return:* hurry back
15. *Do not … business:* Do not rush your business.
16. *But stay … time:* Take the time you need to successfully complete your business.
17. *enter in your mind:* interrupt your thoughts

18. *chiefest:* main
19. *ostents:* displays
20. *Be merry, …there:* Be happy and let your main focus be on love and displays of affection which are appropriate there.
21. *him: Bassanio*
22. *affection wondrous sensible:* incredibly heartfelt emotion
23. *wrung:* shook

Be merry, and employ your chiefest[18] thoughts
To courtship and such fair ostents[19] of love
As shall conveniently become you there.'[20]
And even there, his eye being big with tears,
Turning his face, he put his hand behind him[21]
And, with affection wondrous sensible,[22]
He wrung[23] Bassanio's hand; and so they parted.

SOLANIO

I think he only loves the world for him.[24]
I pray thee let us go and find him out,
And quicken his embracèd heaviness[25]
With some delight or other.

SALERIO

Do we so.

Exeunt.

24. *I think … him:* I think Antonio's friendship with Bassanio is the only thing in the world that makes him happy.
25. *quicken his embracèd heaviness:* lighten his sad mood

SPOTLIGHT ON … CHARACTERS

In this scene, Salerio and Solanio discuss Shylock and Antonio. Do you notice a difference in the way they describe Shylock and Antonio, or in their attitude towards the characters?

OVERVIEW OF ACT 2, SCENE 8

- In this short scene, we find out quite a lot of news from Salerio and Solanio. The action is so well **recounted** (told) that these recent events are brought vividly to life for the audience.
- First, we get an account of Shylock's reaction to his daughter's escape. Shylock, in a fit of rage and panic, 'raised the Duke' (line 4) and went straight to Bassanio's ship to search for his daughter. However, by the time they got there, Bassanio's ship had already set sail. Antonio reassured Shylock and the Duke that Shylock's daughter was not on board the ship. We hear that Jessica and Lorenzo were recently seen in a **gondola** (a particular boat used on the canals in Venice).
- Next, a note of **foreboding** (worry or fear) sounds as Salerio **recounts** (tells about) a conversation he had with a Frenchman who told him that a Venetian merchant ship had been shipwrecked in the English Channel:

  there miscarrièd
  A vessel of our country richly fraught. (lines 29–30)

  Salerio fears that this ship belongs to Antonio, but does not wish to 'grieve' him with this news just yet, especially considering how upset he is about Bassanio's departure.
- Salerio depicts a very moving farewell where Antonio told Bassanio to put the bond out of his mind and focus all his thoughts on winning the fair Portia. Salerio describes how Antonio was overwrought with emotion – 'his eye being big with tears' (line 46) – and shook Bassanio's hand before he left for Belmont.
- Solanio says that Antonio 'only loves the world for [Bassanio]' (line 50), which shows how much Antonio values their friendship. Both Solanio and Salerio decide to cheer him up 'With some delight or other' (line 53). However, it is interesting that neither Solanio nor Salerio have any compassion for Shylock who has lost his daughter and his valuables in this scene.

REVIEWING

1. How did Shylock react when he found his daughter and his money gone?
2. What happened when the Duke and Shylock went to search Bassanio's ship?
3. What rumour did they hear about the whereabouts of Jessica?
4. What does Solanio mean when he says:

   Let good Antonio look he keep his day,
   Or he shall pay for this. (lines 25–26)

5. What news did Salerio hear from a Frenchman about a ship? What is his fear regarding this news?
6. What did Antonio say to Bassanio as he was about to set sail?

ORAL LANGUAGE

Drama Script

Pair Activity

Prepare a **short script** to dramatise the scene described by Solanio when Shylock finds out that his daughter and money are missing.

Write out your script and perform it aloud in pairs. Use the detail from this scene to help you, but you can add in your own ideas too.

REFLECTING

Character File P

Turn to the Character File section of your portfolio to record your impressions of **(a) Antonio** (**page 113**) and **(b) Shylock** (**page 134**) based on this scene. Use quotes where possible.

ACT 2, SCENE 9

Setting: Belmont. A room in Portia's house.

In this **scene** you will:

- Write an **interior monologue**.
- **Reflect** on the Prince of Arragon's choice of casket.

Action – What Happens?

In this scene, the Prince of Arragon has come to try his luck with the caskets. Immediately, he appears pompous and full of self-importance, convinced that he deserves Portia. Like the Prince of Morocco before him, he considers each inscription carefully and is confident that he has made the correct choice.

Useful Words

nuptial rites – wedding ceremony

unfold – reveal

a martlet – a swallow (bird)

schedule – written scroll

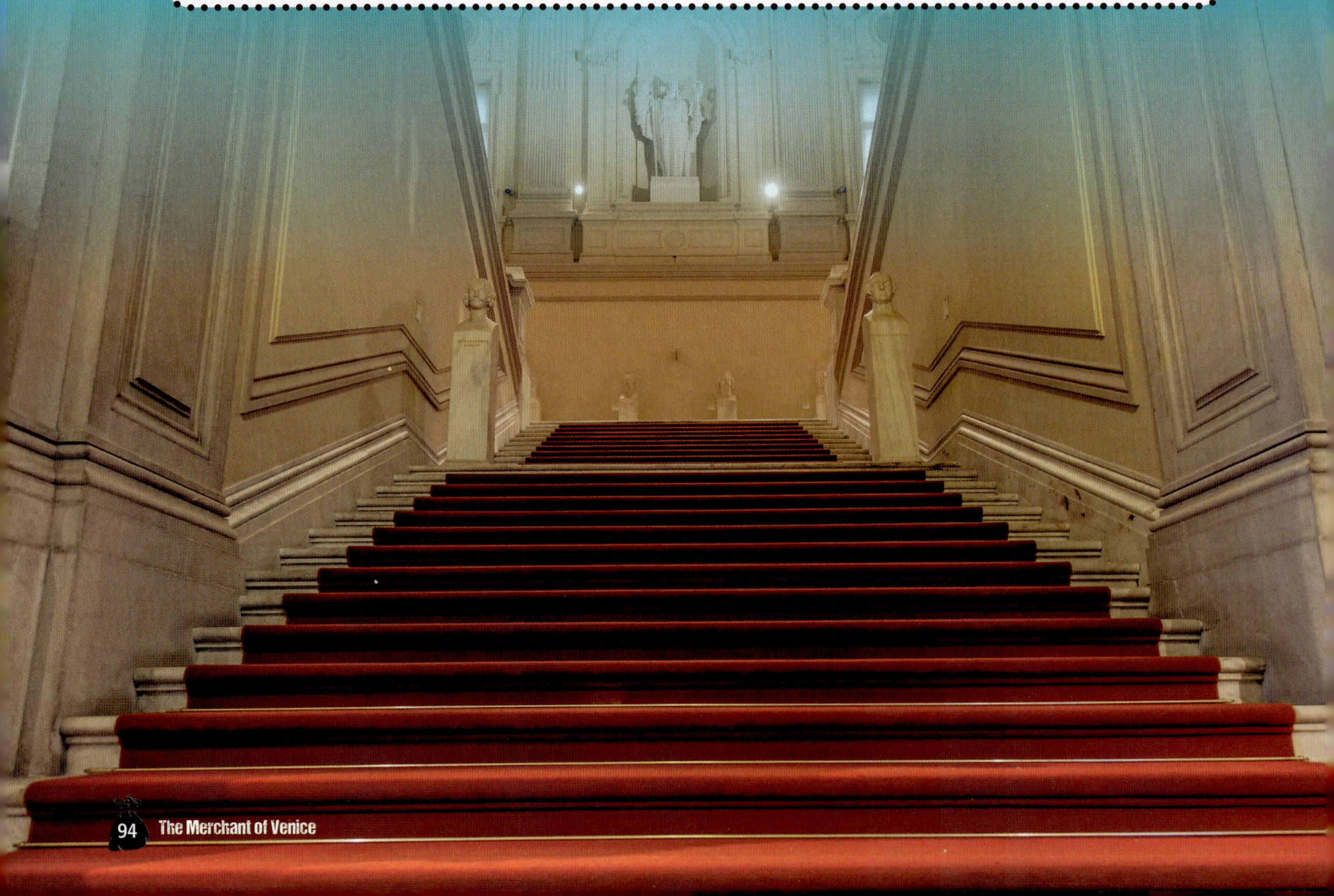

Enter NERISSA with a Servitor.

NERISSA

Quick, quick, I pray thee, draw the curtain straight.[1]
The Prince of Arragon hath ta'en his oath,
And comes to his election presently.[2]

1. *straight:* immediately
2. *And comes ... presently:* is coming to make his choice immediately

Flourish of cornets. Enter the PRINCE OF ARRAGON, his train and PORTIA.

PORTIA

Behold, there stand the caskets, noble Prince.
If you choose that wherein I am contained,
Straight shall our nuptial rites be solemnized.[3]
But if you fail, without more speech, my lord,
You must be gone from hence[4] immediately.

3. *Straight ... solemnized:* Our marriage will be performed immediately.
4. *hence:* here

ARRAGON

I am enjoined[5] by oath to observe[6] three things:
First, never to unfold[7] to anyone
Which casket 'twas I chose. Next, if I fail
Of the right casket, never in my life
To woo a maid in way of marriage. Lastly,
If I do fail in fortune of my choice,
Immediately to leave you and be gone.

5. *enjoined:* bound/instructed
6. *observe:* adhere to/respect
7. *unfold:* reveal

PORTIA

To these injunctions[8] everyone doth swear
That comes to hazard[9] for my worthless self.

8. *injunctions:* conditions
9. *hazard:* gamble/participate in the lottery

ARRAGON

And so have I addressed[10] me. Fortune now
To my heart's hope! Gold, silver, and base lead.
'Who chooseth me must give and hazard all he hath.'
You shall[11] look fairer ere[12] I give or hazard.
What says the golden chest? Ha, let me see.
'Who chooseth me shall gain what many men desire.'
'What many men desire'—that 'many' may be meant
By[13] the fool multitude, that choose by show,[14]
Not learning more than the fond[15] eye doth teach,

10. *addressed:* prepared
11. *shall:* must
12. *ere:* before
13. *By:* For
14. *show:* appearances
15. *fond:* foolish

Which pries[16] not to th'interior, but, like the martlet,[17]
Builds in the weather[18] on the outward wall
Even in the force and road of casualty.[19]
I will not choose what many men desire,
Because I will not jump[20] with common spirits[21]
And rank me with the barbarous multitudes.[22]
Why then, to thee, thou silver treasure-house.
Tell me once more what title thou dost bear.[23]
'Who chooseth me shall get as much as he deserves'—
And well said too, for who shall go about
To cozen[24] fortune and be honourable
Without the stamp of merit?[25] Let none[26] presume
To wear an undeservèd dignity.
O, that estates, degrees and offices
Were not derived corruptly, and that clear honour
Were purchased[27] by the merit of the wearer![28]
How many then should cover[29] that stand bare,[30]
How many be commanded that command?
How much low peasantry would then be gleaned[31]
From the true seed of honour, and how much honour
Picked from the chaff and ruin of the times
To be new varnished?[32] Well, but to my choice.
'Who chooseth me shall get as much as he deserves.'
I will assume desert.[33] Give me a key for this,
And instantly unlock my fortunes here.

[*He opens the silver casket.*]

16. *pries:* looks
17. *martlet:* swallow
18. *weather:* open air
19. *on the … casualty:* where his house is vulnerable to danger
20. *jump:* agree
21. *common spirits:* people
22. *barbarous multitudes:* ignorant common people
23. *bear:* say/carry
24. *cozen:* cheat
25. *for who … merit?: The Prince is saying that it would be wrong to cheat fate to get something that you did not deserve.*
26. *none:* no one
27. *purchased:* acquired
28. *O, that … wearer!:* If only people got property, titles and positions based on merit, not corruption.
29. *cover:* wear hats
30. *stand bare:* bareheaded *(servants had to take off their hats before their masters/superiors)*
31. *gleaned:* separated
32. *How much … varnished?:* If the world was based on merit, you would see people who now appear honourable becoming peasants and people who are cast aside as socially inferior would shine with honour and nobility.
33. *I will assume desert:* I am claiming success.

PORTIA

Too long a pause for that which you find there.

ARRAGON

What's here? The portrait of a blinking idiot
Presenting me a schedule.[34] I will read it.
How much unlike art thou to Portia!
How much unlike my hopes and my deservings!
'Who chooseth me shall have as much as he deserves.'
Did I deserve no more than a fool's head?
Is that my prize? Are my deserts no better?[35]

PORTIA

To offend and judge, are distinct offices,
And of opposèd natures.[36]

ARRAGON

What is here?

[*He reads the schedule.*]

'The fire seven times tried[37] this;
Seven times tried that judgement is,
That did never choose amiss.[38]
Some there be that shadows kiss;
Such have but a shadow's bliss.[39]
There be fools alive, iwis,[40]
Silvered o'er;[41] and so was this.
Take what wife you will to bed,
I will ever be your head.
So be gone; you are sped.'[42]
Still more fool I shall appear

By the time I linger here.[43]
With one fool's head I came to woo,
But I go away with two.
Sweet, adieu.[44] I'll keep my oath,
Patiently to bear my wroth.[45]

Exeunt Arragon and train.

PLOT POINT

This is a real moment of suspense for Portia as there is now a fifty-fifty chance that the Prince will open the correct casket (seeing as she already knows the gold one doesn't contain her picture and the Prince of Arragon is about to open the silver one). When he delays after opening it, Portia knows that he has been unsuccessful.

34. *schedule:* written scroll

35. *Are my … better?:* Do I deserve no better than this?

36. *To offend … natures:* To judge and to make a mistake are two very different things.

37. *tried:* purified

38. *Seven times tried … amiss: The scroll is saying that the silver used to make its casket has been purified seven times. It suggests that careful judgement – the kind that never makes a mistake – is also a slow process that needs time and effort.*
39. *Some there … bliss:* There are some people who love fantasy and illusion, but they do not experience real happiness.
40. *iwis:* in truth/certainly
41. *Silvered o'er:* with silver *(grey)* hair *(and so appear to have wisdom)*

42. *sped:* finished

43. *Sill more … here:* The longer I stay, the more foolish I'll seem.

44. *adieu:* goodbye

45. *wroth:* grief

SPOTLIGHT ON … IMAGERY

Portia uses the image of the moth drawn to the flame (line 78) to represent the suitors who have come to Belmont to woo her. Do you think this is an effective image?

46. *deliberate:* careful
47. *The ancient … destiny:* The old saying is true: you can't choose when you'll die or who you'll marry.

PLOT POINT

Notice the change in mood here when Portia's servant informs her of the arrival of a suitor from Venice. Nerissa hopes it is Bassanio. Thus the scene ends on an uplifting note.

48. *alighted:* landed/arrived
49. *regreets:* greetings
50. *Yet:* Until now
51. *likely:* suitable
52. *costly:* lavish
53. *fore-spurrer:* messenger

PLOT POINT

Note that, at this point in the play, Portia and the audience now know that the winning casket is the lead one. This heightens the drama in the play: will Bassanio be lucky enough to choose the right casket?

54. *anon:* soon say
55. *kin to thee:* relation of yours
56. *high-day wit:* language reserved for special occasions *(like holidays)*
57. *post:* messenger
58. *Lord Love:* Cupid

PORTIA

Thus hath the candle singed the moth.
O, these deliberate[46] fools! When they do choose,
They have the wisdom by their wit to lose.

NERISSA

The ancient saying is no heresy:
Hanging and wiving goes by destiny.[47]

PORTIA

Come, draw the curtain, Nerissa.

Enter a Servant.

SERVANT

Where is my lady?

PORTIA

Here. What would my lord?

SERVANT

Madam, there is alighted[48] at your gate
A young Venetian, one that comes before
To signify th'approaching of his lord,
From whom he bringeth sensible regreets,[49]
To wit, besides commends and courteous breath,
Gifts of rich value. Yet[50] I have not seen
So likely[51] an ambassador of love.
A day in April never came so sweet
To show how costly[52] summer was at hand
As this fore-spurrer[53] comes before his lord.

PORTIA

No more, I pray thee, I am half afeard
Thou wilt say anon[54] he is some kin to thee,[55]
Thou spend'st such high-day wit[56] in praising him.
Come, come, Nerissa, for I long to see
Quick Cupid's post[57] that comes so mannerly.

NERISSA

Bassanio, Lord Love,[58] if thy will it be!

Exeunt.

OVERVIEW OF ACT 2, SCENE 9

- This is the second major casket scene. This time the Prince of Arragon (from Spain) is due to make his choice. The Prince enters with his '**train**' (**entourage/staff**) yet Portia enters alone. Does this suggest that Portia is becoming tired of the casket lottery?
- The Prince of Arragon appears, like his name suggests, arrogant and self-important, and he is convinced that he is deserving of Portia.
- Before making his choice, Portia reminds him of the conditions of the oath and the consequences of his choice. The Prince of Arragon cannot reveal his choice of casket to anyone, can never marry anyone else in the future and must leave Belmont immediately if he does not choose the correct casket.
- As the Prince of Arragon proceeds to make his selection, he immediately dismisses the lead casket, saying that it would have to look more attractive to make him risk so much:

  You shall look fairer ere I give or hazard. (line 21)
- Next, he considers the gold casket, but also rejects it, claiming that it is the obvious choice for the 'barbarous multitudes' (common people) (line 32) who only judge on what they see on the outside.
- Coming to the silver casket, which reads 'Who chooseth me shall get as much as he deserves' (line 35), he **laments** (regrets) the fact that not everyone in the world gets what they deserve and claims that there are many people who have 'undeservèd dignity' (line 39). He is very **self-assured** (confident) and has no doubt that he deserves to win Portia:

  I will assume desert. (line 50)
- As he unlocks his fortunes, Portia comments that it is 'Too long a pause for that which you find there' (line 52). It is obvious that he has been unsuccessful.
- Inside the casket, he is greeted with 'The portrait of a blinking idiot presenting [him with] a schedule' (lines 53–54). The Prince of Arragon is utterly **incredulous** (in disbelief):

  Did I deserve no more than a fool's head?
  Is that my prize? Are my deserts no better? (lines 58–59)
- After reading the scroll, which essentially accuses him of being foolish, he comments:

  With one fool's head I came to woo,
  But I go away with two. (lines 74–75)
- He decides to leave immediately and vows to keep his oath. Perhaps the Prince of Arragon has learnt a lesson. As he says himself, not everyone gets what they deserve.
- Portia's comment that 'Thus hath the candle singed the moth' (line 78) is significant. Each 'moth' or suitor has been attracted to the 'candle' which represents Portia, but each has been 'singed' or burnt by their foolishness and self-importance.
- The scene ends with the news of a Venetian messenger coming to announce the arrival of his master. Portia's servant comments that:

  A day in April never came so sweet
  To show how costly summer was at hand (lines 92–93)
- This creates a **buoyant** (positive/uplifting) mood of anticipation after the dismal experience of witnessing the performance of the two previous suitors. Nerissa is hopeful it is Bassanio:

  Bassanio, Lord Love, if thy will it be! (line 100)
- The **tension** is heightened at the end of this scene as we are now aware that the winning casket is the lead one and we are hopeful that Bassanio will choose it.

REVIEWING

1. Explain the **three** conditions of the oath that each suitor must swear.
2. Why does the Prince of Arragon reject (a) the lead casket and (b) the gold casket?
3. What is the Prince of Arragon's main reason for choosing the silver casket?
4. How does he react to what he finds inside the silver casket?
5. At the end of the scene, what news does the servant bring?

CREATING

Interior Monologue

What is an interior monologue?

An interior monologue is a piece of writing expressing a character's inner thoughts.

Write an interior monologue (in modern English) for **Portia**. Record her private thoughts as this scene unfolds. The interior monologue should be approximately 150 words.

REFLECTING

1. Reflecting on the Caskets P

Turn to **page 35** of your portfolio to record your response to the Prince of Arragon choosing the silver casket.

2. Character File P

Turn to **page 126** of your portfolio to write a brief note about how **Portia** comes across in this scene. Use a quote if possible.

LOOKING BACK AT ACT 2

1. Overview P

Pair Activity

With your partner, turn to **page 4** of your portfolio to write **one sentence or phrase** in the box for each scene in Act 2. This sentence or phrase should **sum up the main action** in that scene.

2. Quotes Quiz P

Turn to **page 36** of your portfolio to review the important quotes for Act 2.

3. Individual Assignment – Choose one of the following activities:

(a) Themes: Discuss the theme of **false appearances** in this act.

(b) Creating: You are a reporter for *The Belmont Herald*, a daily newspaper. You have been asked to interview either the Prince of Morocco **OR** the Prince of Arragon for your newspaper. Write the interview **questions** and the **answers** to be published in the newspaper.

P **(c) What If...?:** What if Jessica and Lorenzo had mobile phones and had been texting each other prior to her escape? Turn to **page 38** of your portfolio to write their conversation. Feel free to use 'textspeak' if it makes it more realistic.

LINKING TO THE EXAM

Key Moments P

In the exam, you might be asked to write about a key moment of the play. Turn to **page 39** of your portfolio to complete a Junior Cycle English question on this topic.

ACT 3

In this act, the theme of **love** and **marriage** and the **bond** theme are very much interlinked. We learn that Antonio's ships are lost at sea which creates an **ominous** (gloomy) sense of **foreboding** (fear/worry) at the start of the act.

When Bassanio arrives at Belmont to chance his luck with the caskets, it is clear that Portia favours him. However, their joy is short-lived as news of Antonio's losses is confirmed and his death seems **inevitable** (unavoidable). Bassanio leaves the **idyllic** (perfect) paradise of Belmont to return to Venice to help Antonio.

Meanwhile, Portia and Nerissa have devised a plan to go to Venice in disguise to help out.

ACT 3, SCENE 1

Setting: Venice. A street.

In this **scene** you will:

- **Explore** Shylock's speech.
- **Reflect** on Shylock's character.

Action – What Happens?

At the start of this scene, Salerio confirms the news that one of Antonio's vessels has been shipwrecked. Solanio and Salerio meet Shylock who accuses them of knowing about his daughter's plan to escape. Solanio and Salerio mock and jeer at Shylock. Shylock responds by asserting his dignity as a human being and a Jew.

Later, **Tubal**, a Jew, informs Shylock that efforts to find Jessica and retrieve his stolen gold have proved fruitless. Tubal informs Shylock that he has heard news that a second ship of Antonio's has run aground. This news makes Shylock hopeful that he can now get revenge on Antonio.

Useful Words

usurer – a money-lender who charges very high rates of interest

mart – marketplace (or stock exchange)

Enter SOLANIO and SALERIO.

SOLANIO

Now, what news on the Rialto?

SALERIO

Why, yet it lives there unchecked[1] that Antonio hath a ship of rich lading[2] wrecked on the narrow seas—the Goodwins, I think they call the place—a very dangerous flat, and fatal, where the carcasses of many a tall ship lie buried, as they say, if my gossip Report[3] be an honest woman of her word.

1. *unchecked:* it is undisputed
2. *rich landing:* rich cargo

PLOT POINT

The Goodwins, or Goodwin Sands, is a 10-mile-long sandbank off the British coast near Kent, where many ships were wrecked.

3. *Report:* Rumour *Salerio is personifying 'Report' or 'Rumour' as a gossiping lady.*

SOLANIO

I would she were as lying a gossip in that as ever knapped[4] ginger or made her neighbours believe she wept for the death of a third husband.[5] But it is true, without any slips of prolixity[6] or crossing the plain highway of talk, that the good Antonio, the honest Antonio—O that I had a title good enough to keep his name company—

4. *knapped:* nibbled
5. *I would … husband: Solanio is wishing that the report of Antonio's ship is a lie, like someone eating ginger to conceal the smell of alcohol, or a woman crying over the death of her third husband.*
6. *slips of prolixity:* over-the-top lies

SALERIO

Come, the full stop.[7]

7. *Come, the full stop:* Finish your point.

SOLANIO

Ha, what sayest thou? Why, the end[8] is, he hath lost a ship.

8. *end:* point

SALERIO

I would[9] it might prove the end of his losses.

9. *would:* wish

SOLANIO

Let me say 'amen' betimes,[10] lest[11] the devil cross[12] my prayer, for here he comes in the likeness[13] of a Jew.

10. *betimes:* quickly
11. *lest:* in case
12. *cross:* ruins
13. *likeness:* shape/body

Enter SHYLOCK.

How now, Shylock, what news among the merchants?

SHYLOCK

You knew, none so well, none so well as you, of my daughter's flight.[14]

14. *flight:* escape

SALERIO

That's certain. I for my part knew the tailor that made the wings she flew withal.[15]

SOLANIO

And Shylock for his own part knew the bird was fledged,[16] and then it is the complexion[17] of them all to leave the dam.[18]

SHYLOCK

She is damned for it.

SALERIO

That's certain, if the devil may be her judge.

SHYLOCK

My own flesh and blood to rebel![19]

SOLANIO

Out upon it, old carrion, rebels it at these years?[20]

SHYLOCK

I say my daughter is my flesh and my blood.

SALERIO

There is more difference between thy flesh and hers than between jet[21] and ivory; more between your bloods than there is between red wine and Rhenish.[22] But tell us, do you hear whether Antonio have had any loss at sea or no?

SHYLOCK

There I have another bad match.[23] A bankrupt, a prodigal,[24] who dare scarce show his head on the Rialto; a beggar that was used to come so smug upon the mart.[25] Let him look to his bond. He was wont to[26] call me usurer:[27] let him look to his bond. He was wont to lend money for a[28] Christian courtesy:[29] let him look to his bond.

15. ***withal:*** with

PLOT POINT

Shylock accuses Solanio and Salerio of knowing about his daughter's elopement or 'flight' in advance. They tease him, using the image of a bird flying the nest. Salerio jokes that he knew the tailor who made Jessica's wings, while Solanio tells Shylock that it was time for Jessica to leave the the nest.

16. ***was fledged:*** ready to fly *(has her feathers)*
17. ***complexion:*** nature
18. ***dam:*** mother *(i.e. fly the nest)*

LOOKING AT LANGUAGE

Pun: Shylock uses a pun (a play on words) on the word 'dam' to suggest that his daughter Jessica will be 'damned' for eloping.

19. ***My own … rebel!:*** *Shylock means 'his own child,' but Solanio interprets this to mean Shylock's sexual urges.*

20. ***Out upon … years?:*** *Solanio is pretending that he is shocked that Shylock has sexual urges at his old age.*

21. ***jet:*** *black mineral*

22. ***Rhenish:*** strong white wine from Germany

23. ***bad match:*** bad deal

24. ***prodigal:*** spendthrift/waster

25. ***mart:*** stock exchange
26. ***He was wont to:*** He used to
27. ***usurer:*** *a money-lender who charges very high rates of interest*
28. ***for a:*** out of
29. ***Christian courtesy:*** interest free

LOOKING AT LANGUAGE

Repetition: Shylock repeats 'Let him look to his bond' three times here. What is the effect of this repetition, in your opinion?

30. *forfeit:* breaks the contract *(i.e. is unable to repay the loan)*

SALERIO

Why, I am sure if he forfeit[30] thou wilt not take his flesh. What's that good for?

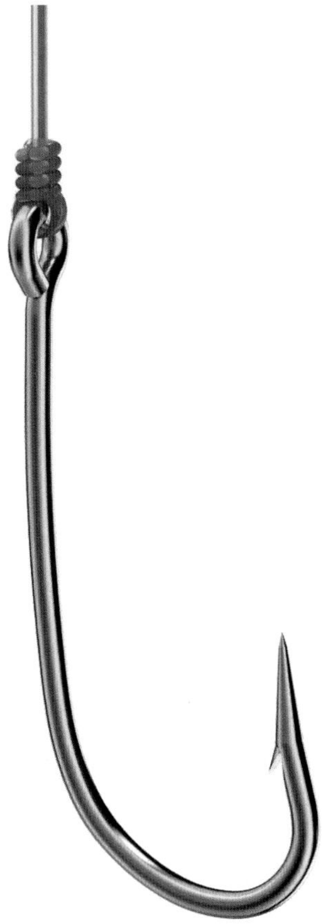

31. *To bait fish withal:* To use as fish bait.
32. *hindered me half a million:* prevented me making half a million ducats
33. *scorned my nation:* ridiculed the Jewish nation
34. *thwarted:* ruined
35. *Hath:* Has
36. *dimensions:* bodily form
37. *revenge:* seek revenge
38. *what is his humility?:* how does he respond?

SHYLOCK

To bait fish withal.[31] If it will feed nothing else, it will feed my revenge. He hath disgraced me, and hindered me half a million;[32] laughed at my losses, mocked at my gains, scorned my nation,[33] thwarted[34] my bargains, cooled my friends, heated mine enemies, and what's his reason?—I am a Jew. Hath[35] not a Jew eyes? Hath not a Jew hands, organs, dimensions,[36] senses, affections, passions; fed with the same food, hurt with the same weapons, subject to the same diseases, healed by the same means, warmed and cooled by the same winter and summer as a Christian is? If you prick us, do we not bleed? If you tickle us, do we not laugh? If you poison us, do we not die? And if you wrong us, shall we not revenge?[37] If we are like you in the rest, we will resemble you in that. If a Jew wrong a Christian, what is his humility?[38] Revenge. If a Christian wrong a Jew, what should his sufferance be by Christian example?[39] Why, revenge. The villainy you teach me I will execute, and it shall go hard but I will better the instruction.[40]

Enter a SERVANT.

SERVANT
Gentlemen, my master Antonio is at his house and desires to speak with you both.

SALERIO
We have been up and down to seek him.

Enter TUBAL.

SOLANIO
Here comes another of the tribe.[41] A third cannot be matched[42] unless the devil himself turn Jew.

Exeunt SOLANIO, SALERIO and Servant.

SHYLOCK
How now, Tubal? What news from Genoa? Hast thou found my daughter?

TUBAL
I often came where I did hear of her, but cannot find her.

SHYLOCK
Why, there, there, there, there. A diamond gone cost me two thousand ducats in Frankfurt. The curse never fell upon our nation till now—I never felt it till now. Two thousand ducats in that and other precious, precious jewels. I would[43] my daughter were dead at my foot and the jewels in her ear! Would she were hearsed[44] at my foot, and the ducats in her coffin! No news of them? Why, so. And I know not what's spent in the search. Why thou, loss upon loss: the thief gone with so much, and so much to find the thief, and no satisfaction, no revenge, nor no ill luck stirring but what lights[45] o' my shoulders,[46] no sighs but o' my breathing, no tears but o' my shedding.

39. *If a Christian … example?: Shylock is considering the most appropriate way for a Jewish person to respond to a wrong caused by a Christian, using Christian standards.*
40. *The villainy … instruction: Shylock is saying that he will learn from the bad example Christians have shown him and go even further with his revenge.*

41. *another of the tribe:* another Jew
42. *matched:* found to match them

43. *would:* wish
44. *hearsed:* dead in a coffin

45. *lights:* lands
46. *nor no … shoulders:* and no one has bad luck except me

TUBAL

Yes, other men have ill luck too. Antonio, as I heard in Genoa—

SHYLOCK

What, what, what? Ill luck, ill luck?

TUBAL

Hath an argosy cast away[47] coming from Tripolis.

SHYLOCK

I thank God, I thank God. Is it true, is it true?

TUBAL

I spoke with some of the sailors that escaped the wreck.

SHYLOCK

I thank thee, good Tubal. Good news, good news! Ha, ha—heard in Genoa?

TUBAL

Your daughter spent in Genoa, as I heard, one night fourscore[48] ducats.

SHYLOCK

Thou stick'st a dagger in me. I shall never see my gold again. Fourscore ducats at a sitting? Fourscore ducats?

TUBAL

There came divers[49] of Antonio's creditors in my company to Venice that swear he cannot choose but break.[50]

SHYLOCK

I am very glad of it. I'll plague[51] him, I'll torture him. I am glad of it.

TUBAL

One of them showed me a ring that he had of your daughter for a[52] monkey.

47. *an argosy cast away:* a large ship wrecked

48. *fourscore:* eighty

49. *divers:* many

50. *break:* become bankrupt

51. *plague:* hound

52. *for a:* in exchange for a

53. ***turquoise:*** turquoise ring
54. ***Leah:*** *possibly Shylock's late wife and Jessica's mother*
55. ***undone:*** finished
56. ***fee:*** hire
57. ***Bespeak:*** Employ
58. ***him:*** Antonio
59. ***I can … will:*** I could charge whatever rates of interest I wish.

SHYLOCK

Out upon her! Thou torturest me, Tubal. It was my turquoise.[53] I had it of Leah[54] when I was a bachelor. I would not have given it for a wilderness of monkeys.

TUBAL

But Antonio is certainly undone.[55]

SHYLOCK

Nay, that's true, that's very true. Go, Tubal, fee[56] me an officer. Bespeak[57] him a fortnight before. I will have the heart of him[58] if he forfeit, for were he out of Venice I can make what merchandise I will.[59] Go, Tubal, and meet me at our synagogue; go, good Tubal; at our synagogue, Tubal.

'One of them showed me a ring that he had of your daughter for a monkey.'

(Tubal, lines 105–106)

OVERVIEW OF ACT 3, SCENE 1

- In this scene, we get a deeper insight into **Shylock's character**.
- At the start of the scene, it has been confirmed that one of Antonio's ships has been wrecked and at the end of the scene we learn that another has also been destroyed.
- Solanio and Salerio meet Shylock and ridicule him over his daughter's escape. Shylock accuses Salerio and Solanio of knowing about Jessica's plan to leave. Shylock is **incensed** (angry) that she has fled:

  My own flesh and blood to rebel! (line 31)

- Salerio tells Shylock that his daughter is not like him:

  There is more difference between thy flesh and hers
  than between jet and ivory (lines 34–35)

- Salerio asks Shylock if he has heard anything about Antonio's 'loss at sea' (line 38) to which Shylock replies: 'There I have another bad match' (line 39). He warns: 'Let him [Antonio] look to his bond' (line 42), a phrase which is repeated three times and becomes increasingly threatening each time.
- Salerio asks Shylock what good Antonio's flesh would be if Antonio were unable to keep the terms of the bond. In response, Shylock makes a powerful speech **asserting** (declaring/stating) his dignity as a Jew and as a human being. Through Shylock's powerful speech, Shakespeare is presenting a more vulnerable and human side to Shylock's character. The speech, which is structured on a series of related **rhetorical questions**, has the effect of **eliciting** (drawing) sympathy from the audience:

  If you prick us, do we not bleed?
  If you tickle us, do we not laugh? If you poison
  us, do we not die? (lines 59–61)

- Shylock feels that, as a Jew, he has been treated with **contempt** (hatred) and disrespect. In his speech he calls on Christians to see Jews as equals. At the end of his speech, Shylock becomes increasingly bitter towards Christians whom he accuses of having double standards. He vows that he will practise the lessons in revenge that he has learnt from Christians:

  If a Christian
  wrong a Jew, what should his sufferance be by
  Christian example? Why, revenge. The villainy you
  teach me I will execute, and it shall go hard but I
  will better the instruction. (lines 64–68)

- Solanio and Salerio leave to see Antonio at his house. As they leave, Tubal, a Jew, arrives to inform Shylock of the latest news regarding his runaway daughter.
- Tubal tells Shylock that he did not find his daughter, though he often came close. Shylock **laments** (regrets) the amount of money spent on trying to get his daughter back and reflects on his financial losses. Shylock makes an outrageous statement wishing that his daughter were dead and he had his jewels back:

  I would my
  daughter were dead at my foot and the jewels in her ear!
  Would she were hearsed at my foot, and the ducats in
  her coffin! (lines 80–83)

- Tubal informs Shylock of the losses his daughter is **incurring** (running up), spending 'in one night fourscore ducats' (lines 96–97) in Genoa and exchanging a precious ring for a monkey. Shylock is particularly **incensed** at this revelation, believing this ring to be his 'turquoise' (line 108), a precious ring he associates with Leah, who we assume is his late wife.

- However, there is some **solace** (hope) for Shylock when he learns of Antonio's extensive losses. Tubal tells him that another of Antonio's ships has been wrecked coming from Tripolis and many of Antonio's creditors 'swear he cannot choose but break' (line 102), meaning that it is almost certain that Antonio will become bankrupt. Shylock is **elated** (overjoyed) as, if he eliminates Antonio, he can make up for his (Shylock's) losses by charging more interest:

  > *I will have the heart of him if he forfeit, for were*
  > *he out of Venice I can make what merchandise I*
  > *will.* (lines 113–115)

- It seems that, by the end of the scene, any sympathy we may have felt for Shylock during his speech rapidly diminishes, as he appears **callous** (cruel) and **vindictive** (nasty) in planning the death of Antonio.

REVIEWING

1. What news has been confirmed on the Rialto?
2. What did Shylock accuse Solanio and Salerio of knowing?
3. Shylock repeats the phrase 'let him look to his bond' three times when he mentions Antonio. What three reasons does he have for giving Antonio this warning?
4. How does Shylock respond when Salerio asks what good Antonio's flesh would be to him?
5. Re-read lines 77–87. Discuss whether you feel any sympathy for Shylock in this part of the scene.
6. What news did Tubal learn in Genoa about (a) Antonio's ships and (b) Shylock's daughter?
7. At the end of the scene, Shylock sees another benefit of eliminating Antonio. What is this?

EXPLORING

Shylock's 'To bait fish withal' Speech

Pair Activity

This is one of the most famous speeches in the play and Shylock makes use of rhetorical questions to plead his case.

What Is a Rhetorical Question?

A rhetorical question is a question that makes a statement and does not require a direct response from the listener. An example would be *'Hath not a Jew eyes?'* (lines 53–54)

Rhetorical questions have the effect of persuading an audience and convincing them of your opinion. It is a very effective technique used in making speeches.

In pairs, read the speech (lines 48–68). Change speaker at each question mark.

Next, turn to **page 42** of your portfolio to complete the written exercise on this speech.

CREATING

1. Image Review

Examine the image on page 111 of Tubal and Shylock. Choose **two quotes** from the scene (one from Tubal and one from Shylock) that you think best suit this image.

2. Shipwreck in Tripolis

Pair Activity

Tubal informs us that he spoke to one of the sailors who survived the shipwreck in Tripolis. Write out the conversation they might have had and perform it together.

REFLECTING

Character File P

Overall, do you think Shylock is presented as more a **villain** or a **victim** in this scene? Turn to **page 135** of your portfolio and write your response to **Shylock** in this scene. Use quotations where possible to support your points.

ACT 3, SCENE 2

Setting: Belmont. A room in Portia's house.

In this **scene** you will:

- Explore Bassanio and Portia's **language**.
- Reflect on the **characters** of Bassanio and Portia.

Action – What Happens?

This is the **climax** of the love scene. Bassanio has come to try his luck with the caskets. It is clear that Portia favours Bassanio above all other suitors and she looks on nervously as he makes his choice. Gratiano has his own surprising revelation to make in this scene too!

Later in the scene, Lorenzo, Jessica and Salerio arrive with news of Antonio's devastating losses. A letter from Antonio to Bassanio changes the mood of the scene completely. At the end of the scene, Bassanio returns to Venice immediately to try to assist Antonio.

Useful Words

tarry – wait/delay

oration – speech

rack – an instrument of torture

bereft – deprived

Enter BASSANIO, PORTIA, GRATIANO, NERISSA and Attendants.

PORTIA

I pray you tarry.[1] Pause a day or two
Before you hazard, for in choosing[2] wrong
I lose your company. Therefore forbear[3] a while.
There's something tells me—but it is not love—
I would not lose you; and you know yourself
Hate counsels not in such a quality.[4]
But lest[5] you should not understand me well—
And yet a maiden hath no tongue but thought[6]—
I would detain[7] you here some month or two
Before you venture[8] for me. I could teach you
How to choose right, but then I am forsworn.[9]
So will I never be;[10] so may you miss me.[11]
But if you do,[12] you'll make me wish a sin,
That I had been forsworn.[13] Beshrew[14] your eyes,
They have o'erlooked[15] me and divided me.[16]
One half of me is yours, the other half yours—
Mine[17] own, I would say, but if mine, then yours,
And so all yours.[18] O, these naughty[19] times
Puts bars between the owners and their rights;[20]

CHARACTER NOTE

When you have read Portia's opening speech, consider what change(s) you notice in her. What aspects of her character are revealed?

1. *tarry:* wait/delay a little longer
2. *for in choosing:* if you choose
3. *forebear:* be patient
4. *Hate counsels … quality: Portia is hinting to Bassanio that she is telling him that she would not like to lose him because she likes him.*
5. *lest:* in case
6. *a maiden … thought:* ladies are not expected to express/speak their thoughts
7. *detain:* keep
8. *venture:* take your chance/gamble
9. *forsworn:* forbidden to by oath
10. *So will I never be:* I will never break my promise
11. *so may you miss me:* you may lose me
12. *if you do:* if you do lose
13. *But if … forsworn:* You'll make me wish that I had broken my promise and revealed the correct casket to you.
14. *Beshrew:* Curse
15. *o'erlooked:* bewitched/enchanted
16. *divided me:* caused me to become conflicted
17. *Mine:* My
18. *One half … all yours: Portia is saying that all of her belongs to Bassanio.*
19. *naughty:* wicked
20. *Puts bars … rights:* We are prevented from having what we own.

21. *And so, ... not I:* If it turns out like this let fortune pay for it, not me.
22. *piece:* extend
23. *eke:* increase
24. *To stay ... election:* To delay you from choosing.
25. *I live upon the rack:* I am in torture.
26. *treason:* crime of betrayal
27. *mistrust:* uncertainty
28. *fear:* doubt
29. *amity:* friendship
30. *There may ... love: Bassanio is saying that treason and love do not go together in the same way that snow and fire do not go together.*
31. *rack: an instrument of torture*
32. *enforcèd:* forced
33. *life:* that I will live

SHAKESPEARE'S WORLD

The rack referred to by Bassanio was an Elizabethan instrument of torture used for people guilty of crimes including treason. A person's hands and feet were tied to ropes attached to the corners of the rack, which were then pulled in opposite directions. This would lead to dislocated hips, knees and shoulders, causing excruciating pain. What do you think Bassanio is trying to say by referring to the rack here? Notice how both Portia and Bassanio develop this idea of the rack throughout their conversation (lines 24–38).

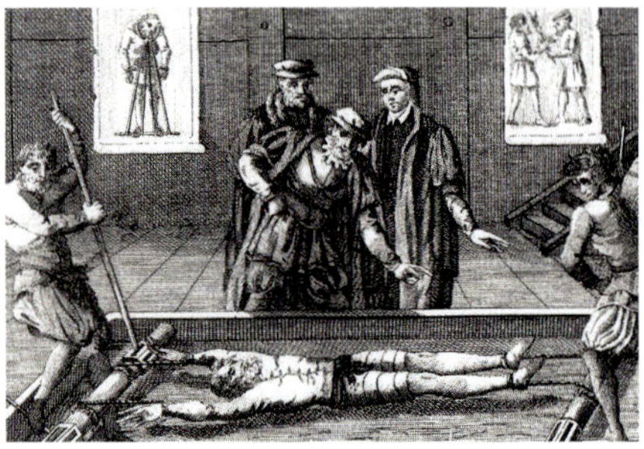

34. *sum:* extent
35. *deliverance:* release/freedom
36. *aloof:* well back

And so, though yours, not yours. Prove it so,
Let fortune go to hell for it, not I.[21]
I speak too long; but 'tis to piece[22] the time,
To eke[23] it, and to draw it out in length
To stay you from election.[24]

BASSANIO

Let me choose,
For as I am, I live upon the rack.[25]

PORTIA

Upon the rack, Bassanio? Then confess
What treason[26] there is mingled with your love.

BASSANIO

None but that ugly treason of mistrust,[27]
Which makes me fear[28] th'enjoying of my love.
There may as well be amity[29] and life
'Tween snow and fire, as treason and my love.[30]

PORTIA

Ay, but I fear you speak upon the rack,[31]
Where men enforcèd[32] do speak anything.

BASSANIO

Promise me life[33] and I'll confess the truth.

PORTIA

Well then, confess and live.

BASSANIO

'Confess and love'
Had been the very sum[34] of my confession.
O happy torment, when my torturer
Doth teach me answers for deliverance![35]
But let me to my fortune and the caskets.

PORTIA

Away then. I am locked in one of them.
If you do love me, you will find me out.
Nerissa and the rest, stand all aloof.[36]

Let music sound while he doth make his choice.
Then if he lose he makes a swan-like end,
Fading in music.[37] That the comparison
May stand more proper, my eye shall be the stream
And watery deathbed for him.[38] He may win,
And what is music then? Then music is
Even as the flourish[39] when true subjects bow
To a new-crownèd monarch. Such it is
As are those dulcet[40] sounds in break of day
That creep into the dreaming bridegroom's ear
And summon him to marriage.[41] Now he goes,
With no less presence,[42] but with much more love
Than young Alcides[43] when he did redeem
The virgin tribute paid by howling Troy
To the sea-monster.[44] I stand for sacrifice.
The rest aloof are the Dardanian wives,[45]
With bleared visages[46] come forth to view
The issue of th'exploit.[47] Go, Hercules!
Live thou,[48] I live. With much much more dismay
I view the fight than thou that mak'st the fray.[49 50]

Music, whilst BASSANIO comments on the caskets to himself.

[SONG.]
Tell me where is fancy[51] bred,
Or[52] in the heart, or in the head?
How begot,[53] how nourishèd?[54]
    Reply, reply.
It is engendered[55] in the eyes,
With gazing fed;[56] and fancy dies
In the cradle[57] where it lies.
Let us all ring fancy's knell.[58]
I'll begin it: ding, dong, bell.
    Ding, dong, bell.

BASSANIO

So may the outward shows be least themselves:[59]
The world is still deceived with ornament.[60]
In law, what plea so tainted and corrupt
But, being seasoned[61] with a gracious voice,

37. ***Let music … end:*** *The swan was thought to sing once, just before its death.*
38. ***my eye …him:*** My tears will create the stream for the dying swan.
39. ***flourish:*** fanfare of trumpets
40. ***dulcet:*** sweet
41. ***As are … marriage:*** *Portia is referring to the tradition of playing music under the bridegroom's window on the morning of his wedding.*
42. ***presence:*** dignity
43. ***Alcides:*** Hercules
44. ***Now he … sea-monster:*** *Portia is referring to when Hercules saved the Trojan princess Hesione who was being sacrificed to a sea-monster. Hercules did this to gain the reward and not because he loved her.*
45. ***Dardanian wives:*** women of Troy
46. ***bleared visages:*** weeping faces
47. ***The issue of th'exploit:*** The outcome of the event.
48. ***Live thou:*** If you live
49. ***fray:*** fight
50. ***With much … fray:*** I am more nervous/terrified watching the fight than the person fighting is. *In other words, Portia is much more nervous watching Bassanio making his choice than he is.*
51. ***fancy:*** infatuation
52. ***Or:*** Whether
53. ***How begot:*** it started
54. ***how nourishèd:*** it continued
55. ***engendered:*** created
56. ***gazing fed:*** sustained by looking
57. ***cradle:*** eyes
58. ***knell:*** funeral bell

PLOT POINT

Portia is bending the rules by playing this song for Bassanio as he prepares to make his choice. She gives him a very specific clue with a rhyme at the start of the song. What is the clue? (Hint: Think about the material of the correct casket.) Do you think Portia is right to give Bassanio hints? Why?

59. ***So may … themselves:*** *The message of this song is that infatuation (or love based purely on appearances) does not last. This is taken as a clue by Bassanio not to judge on appearances.*
60. ***ornament:*** trappings/appearances
61. ***seasoned:*** made attractive

62. ***Obscures:*** Hides

63. ***In religion … ornament?:*** In religion, a serious clergyman may quote scripture to defend errors/sins.
64. ***vice:*** misconduct/sin
65. ***There is … parts:*** Even things that are totally evil can appear good on the outside.

66. ***wear yet:*** still wear

67. ***How many … milk?:*** *The liver was considered a symbol of bravery and a white liver was seen as a sign of cowardice. Bassanio is saying men who look brave on the outside (who wear beards like Hercules and Mars) are often cowardly on the inside.*
68. ***excrement:*** external sign *(i.e. beard)*
69. ***To render them redoubted:*** To make them appear frightening
70. ***Look on … weight:*** *Skin-lightening products and wigs were very fashionable in Elizabethan England and were sold by the weight.*
71. ***Making the … it:*** Making those who wear most of it seem superficial or shallow.
72. ***crispèd:*** curly
73. ***Which maketh … wind:*** that playfully bounce in the wind
74. ***fairness:*** beauty
75. ***second head:*** a wig
76. ***sepulchre:*** tomb
77. ***Thus:*** Therefore/So
78. ***guilèd:*** treacherous

79. ***Indian beauty:*** dark-skinned

80. ***Midas:*** King Midas *Everything Midas touched turned to gold, even his food.*
81. ***common drudge:*** servant *Silver is described as a servant because it was the most common metal from which coins were made.*
82. ***Which rather … aught:*** Which appears more off-putting than promising
83. ***eloquence:*** fine appearance

SPOTLIGHT ON … STAGECRAFT

Portia's Aside

How would you imagine Portia delivers these lines on stage without the other characters overhearing what she says? Can you sum up in one sentence what Portia is feeling here?

84. ***As:*** Such as
85. ***rash-embraced:*** spontaneous/sudden
86. ***Allay thy ecstasy:*** Tone down your excitement
87. ***scant this excess:*** lessen *(or control)* this excessive emotion/excitement
88. ***surfeit:*** will become ill with too much happiness

Obscures[62] the show of evil? In religion,
What damnèd error but some sober brow
Will bless it and approve it with a text,
Hiding the grossness with fair ornament?[63]
There is no vice[64] so simple but assumes
Some mark of virtue on his outward parts.[65]
How many cowards whose hearts are all as false
As stairs of sand, wear yet[66] upon their chins
The beards of Hercules and frowning Mars,
Who, inward searched, have livers white as milk?[67]
And these assume but valour's excrement[68]
To render them redoubted.[69] Look on beauty,
And you shall see 'tis purchased by the weight,[70]
Which therein works a miracle in nature,
Making them lightest that wear most of it.[71]
So are those crispèd[72] snaky golden locks
Which maketh such wanton gambols with the wind[73]
Upon supposèd fairness,[74] often known
To be the dowry of a second head,[75]
The skull that bred them in the sepulchre.[76]
Thus[77] ornament is but the guilèd[78] shore
To a most dangerous sea, the beauteous scarf
Veiling an Indian beauty;[79] in a word,
The seeming truth which cunning times put on
To entrap the wisest. Therefore, thou gaudy gold,
Hard food for Midas,[80] I will none of thee.
Nor none of thee, thou pale and common drudge[81]
'Tween man and man. But thou, thou meagre lead,
Which rather threaten'st than dost promise aught,[82]
Thy paleness moves me more than eloquence,[83]
And here choose I. Joy be the consequence!

PORTIA

[*aside*] How all the other passions fleet to air,
As[84] doubtful thoughts, and rash-embraced[85] despair,
And shudd'ring fear, and green-eyed jealousy!
O love, be moderate! Allay thy ecstasy,[86]
In measure rain thy joy, scant this excess.[87]
I feel too much thy blessing: make it less,
For fear I surfeit.[88]

BASSANIO

What find I here?

[*Opening the leaden casket.*]

Fair Portia's counterfeit.[89] What demi-god[90]
Hath come so near creation?[91] Move these eyes?[92]
Or whether, riding on the balls of mine,
Seem they in motion?[93] Here are severed lips
Parted with sugar breath. So sweet a bar
Should sunder[94] such sweet friends.[95] Here in her hairs
The painter plays the spider, and hath woven
A golden mesh t'entrap the hearts of men
Faster than gnats[96] in cobwebs. But her eyes—
How could he see to do them? Having made one,
Methinks[97] it should have power to steal both his[98]
And leave itself unfurnished.[99] Yet look how far
The substance[100] of my praise doth wrong this shadow[101]
In underprizing[102] it, so far this shadow
Doth limp behind the substance. Here's the scroll,
The continent[103] and summary of my fortune.

[*Reads.*]

'You that choose not by the view[104]
Chance as fair[105] and choose as true.
Since this fortune falls to you,
Be content and seek no new.
If you be well pleased with this,
And hold your fortune for your bliss,
Turn you where your lady is,
And claim her with a loving kiss.'

A gentle scroll. Fair lady, by your leave,
I come by note[106] to give and to receive,
Like one of two contending in a prize,[107]
That thinks he hath done well in people's eyes,
Hearing applause and universal shout,
Giddy in spirit, still gazing in a doubt
Whether those peals[108] of praise be his or no.
So, thrice-fair lady, stand I even so,
As doubtful whether what I see be true,
Until confirmed, signed, ratified by you.[109]

89. *counterfeit:* image/likeness
90. *demi-god:* gifted painter
91. *Hath come … creation?:* Came so close to imitating reality?
92. *Move these eyes?:* Are these eyes *(of the painting)* moving?
93. *Or whether, …motion?:* Or it is just the movement of my own eyes that makes them seem to be moving?
94. *sunder:* Keep apart
95. *So sweet … sweet friends:* The breath *('sweet bar')* that separates Portia's lips *('sweet friends')*.
96. *gnats:* small flies
97. *Methinks:* I think
98. *his:* his eyes
99. *And leave itself unfurnished:* And leave one incomplete *(without the other eye)*.
100. *substance:* real thing *(i.e. Portia)*
101. *shadow:* imitation *(i.e. the portrait)*
102. *underprizing:* understating
103. *continent:* container
104. *by the view:* by appearance
105. *You that … fair:* Those who do not make choices based on appearances deserve good luck
106. *by note:* at the instructions of the note
107. *contending in a prize:* competing in a contest
108. *peals:* shouts
109. *As doubtful … you:* I won't believe it is true until you confirm it.

PORTIA

You see me, lord Bassanio, where I stand,
Such as I am. Though for myself alone
I would not be ambitious in my wish
To wish myself much better, yet for you
I would be trebled twenty times myself,
A thousand times more fair, ten thousand times more rich,
That only to stand high in your account,
I might in virtues, beauties, livings,[110] friends,
Exceed account.[111] But the full sum of me
Is sum of something, which, to term in gross,[112]
Is an unlessoned girl, unschooled, unpractisèd,[113]
Happy[114] in this, she is not yet so old
But she may learn; happier than this,[115]
She is not bred[116] so dull but she can learn;
Happiest of all[117] is that her gentle spirit
Commits itself to yours to be directed
As from her lord, her governor, her king.
Myself and what is mine to you and yours
Is now converted.[118] But[119] now I was the lord
Of this fair mansion, master of my servants,
Queen o'er myself: and even now, but now,
This house, these servants, and this same myself
Are yours, my lord's. I give them with this ring,
Which when you part from, lose, or give away,
Let it presage[120] the ruin of your love,
And be my vantage to exclaim on you.[121]

BASSANIO

Madam, you have bereft[122] me of all words.
Only my blood speaks to you in my veins,
And there is such confusion in my powers[123]
As after some oration[124] fairly spoke
By a belovèd prince, there doth appear
Among the buzzing pleasèd multitude,[125]
Where every something being blent together
Turns to a wild[126] of nothing save of joy,
Expressed and not expressed. But when this ring
Parts from this finger, then parts life from hence.[127]
O, then be bold to say[128] Bassanio's dead!

110. *livings:* possessions
111. *Though for … account: Portia is saying that she wishes she were better, richer and more beautiful to impress Bassanio.*
112. *to terms in gross:* to describe fully
113. *Is an … unpractisèd:* I am uneducated, untrained and inexperienced
114. *Happy:* Fortunate
115. *happier than this:* more fortunate
116. *She is not bred:* She has not been raised/reared
117. *Happiest of all:* Most fortunate
118. *converted:* transferred
119. *But:* Just

CHARACTER NOTE

Notice the change in Portia's character here. She is saying that she wishes to be better and more worthy of Bassanio. How is this different to the Portia we have seen previously?

120. *presage:* signify
121. *And be … you:* And be my excuse to give out to you.
122. *bereft:* deprived
123. *powers:* faculties/mind
124. *oration:* speech
125. *multitude:* crowd
126. *wild:* chaos
127. *hence:* here
128. *bold to say:* say confidently

PLOT POINT

Bassanio says he cannot fully articulate how he feels as he is overwhelmed with emotion. He compares this sensation to the positive, uplifting feeling of joy a crowd might experience after hearing their beloved prince speak. Portia gives Bassanio a ring which he promises never to part with until he dies. This ring is an important symbol of their love.

NERISSA

My lord and lady, it is now our time
That have stood by and seen our wishes prosper
To cry 'Good joy, good joy, my lord and lady!'

GRATIANO

My lord Bassanio, and my gentle lady,
I wish you all the joy that you can wish,
For I am sure you can wish none from me.[129]
And when your honours mean to solemnize
The bargain of your faith,[130] I do beseech[131] you
Even at that time I may be married too.

BASSANIO

With all my heart, so[132] thou canst get a wife.

GRATIANO

I thank your lordship, you have got me one.
My eyes, my lord, can look as swift as yours.
You saw the mistress, I beheld the maid.[133]
You loved, I loved; for intermission[134]
No more pertains to me, my lord, than you.
Your fortune stood upon the caskets there,
And so did mine too, as the matter falls;[135]
For wooing here until I sweat again,[136]
And swearing till my very roof[137] was dry
With oaths of love, at last—if promise last[138]—
I got a promise of this fair one here
To have her love, provided that your fortune
Achieved[139] her mistress.

PORTIA

Is this true, Nerissa?

NERISSA

Madam, it is, so you stand pleased withal.[140]

BASSANIO

And do you, Gratiano, mean good faith?

GRATIANO

Yes, faith, my lord.

129. *For I … me:* I am sure you do not need my good wishes.

130. *And when … faith:* When you celebrate your marriage

131. *beseech:* ask/beg

132. *so:* if

133. *the maid:* Nerissa

134. *intermission:* delay *(Like you, I have not delayed in finding myself a wife.)*

135. *as the matter falls:* as it happens

136. *again:* repeatedly

137. *roof: roof of his mouth*

138. *if promise last: if Nerissa keeps her promise to marry Gratiano*

139. *Achieved:* Attained

PLOT POINT

Gratiano reveals that Nerissa agreed to marry him on the condition that Bassanio chose the correct casket.

140. *so you … withal:* but only if you approve

BASSANIO

Our feast shall be much honoured in your marriage.

GRATIANO

We'll play with them the first boy[141] for a thousand ducats.

NERISSA

What, and stake down?[142]

GRATIANO

No, we shall ne'er win at that sport and stake down.
But who comes here? Lorenzo and his infidel![143]
What, and my old Venetian friend Salerio!

Enter LORENZO, JESSICA and SALERIO, a Messenger from Venice.

BASSANIO

Lorenzo and Salerio, welcome hither,
If that the youth of my new interest here
Have power[144] to bid you welcome. By your leave,
I bid my very friends and countrymen,
Sweet Portia, welcome.

PORTIA

So do I, my lord.
They are entirely welcome.

LORENZO

I thank your honour. For my part, my lord,
My purpose was not to have seen you here,
But meeting with Salerio by the way
He did entreat me, past all saying nay
To come with him along.[145]

SALERIO

I did, my lord,
And I have reason for it. Signor Antonio
Commends him to you.[146]

[He gives BASSANIO a letter.]

141. ***the first boy:*** who has the first boy

142. ***What, and stake down?:*** Shall we bet now?

143. ***infidel:*** unbeliever *(i.e. Jessica)*

144. ***Have power:*** Gives me the right

145. ***He did … along:*** He asked me to go with him and wouldn't take no for an answer.

146. ***Commends him to you:*** Sends his greetings to you.

BASSANIO

Ere[147] I ope his letter
I pray you tell me how my good friend doth.

SALERIO

Not sick, my lord, unless it be in mind;[148]
Nor well, unless in mind: his letter there
Will show you his estate.[149]

GRATIANO

Nerissa, cheer yon stranger.[150] Bid her welcome.
Your hand, Salerio. What's the news from Venice?
How doth that royal[151] merchant good Antonio?
I know he will be glad of our success.
We are the Jasons; we have won the fleece.[152]

SALERIO

I would[153] you had won the fleece[154] that he hath lost.

PORTIA

There are some shrewd[155] contents in yon same paper
That steals the colour from Bassanio's cheek.
Some dear friend dead, else nothing in the world
Could turn so much the constitution
Of any constant man.[156] What, worse and worse?
With leave, Bassanio, I am half yourself,
And I must freely have the half of anything
That this same paper brings you.[157]

BASSANIO

O sweet Portia,
Here are a few of the unpleasant'st words
That ever blotted paper! Gentle lady,
When I did first impart my love to you
I freely told you all the wealth I had
Ran in my veins: I was a gentleman;
And then I told you true; and yet, dear lady,
Rating myself at nothing, you shall see
How much I was a braggart.[158] When I told you
My state[159] was nothing, I should then have told you
That I was worse than nothing, for indeed
I have engaged[160] myself to a dear friend,

147. *Ere:* Before

148. *Not sick, … mind:* not physically sick

149. *estate:* condition

150. *Nerissa, … stranger: Nerissa is being asked to welcome Jessica.*

151. *royal:* princely

152. *We are … fleece: This reminds us of the myth of Jason from Act 1. Gratiano is saying that he and Bassanio are like Jason as they have successfully won their prize.*

153. *would:* wish

154. *fleece: This sounds like the 'fleets' of ships that Antonio has lost.*

155. *shewd:* evil

156. *There are … man:* It must be news that some dear friend has died as nothing else could alter the appearance of such a solid man.

157. *With leave, … you: Portia is saying that now that she is to marry Bassanio, she must share in his troubles.*

CHARACTER NOTE

Bassanio shows genuine concern for Antonio when he reads his letter. He is forthcoming with the truth, revealing to Portia that he is indebted to Antonio as he has no wealth himself. There is sincerity in Bassanio's words here. Has your impression of him changed?

158. *Rating myself … braggart:* When I counted myself as nothing, I was being boastful.

159. *state:* wealth

160. *engaged:* indebted

Engaged my friend to his mere[161] enemy,
To feed my means. Here is a letter, lady,
The paper as the body of my friend,[162]
And every word in it a gaping wound
Issuing life-blood. But is it true, Salerio?
Have all his ventures failed? What, not one hit?[163]
From Tripolis, from Mexico, and England,
From Lisbon, Barbary and India,
And not one vessel 'scape the dreadful touch
Of merchant-marring rocks?[164]

SALERIO

Not one, my lord.
Besides, it should[165] appear, that if he had
The present[166] money to discharge[167] the Jew
He would not take it. Never did I know
A creature that did bear the shape of man
So keen[168] and greedy to confound[169] a man.
He plies[170] the Duke at morning and at night,
And doth impeach the freedom of the state
If they deny him justice.[171] Twenty merchants,
The Duke himself, and the magnificoes[172]
Of greatest port,[173] have all persuaded[174] with him,
But none can drive him from the envious[175] plea
Of forfeiture, of justice and his bond.

161. ***mere:*** utter

162. ***The paper … friend:*** *Bassanio compares the letter from Antonio to Antonio's body and Antonio's words to blood dripping from his wounds.*

163. ***hit:*** successful venture

164. ***merchant-marring rocks:*** rocks that destroy merchants' vessels/ships

165. ***should:*** would

166. ***present:*** ready

167. ***discharge:*** pay

168. ***keen:*** eager

169. ***confound:*** destroy

170. ***plies:*** addresses

171. ***And doth … justice:*** *Shylock claims that Venice would be discredited if he is not given justice.*

172. ***magnificoes:*** important people in Venice

173. ***port:*** dignity

174. ***persuaded:*** argued/pleaded

175. ***envious:*** spiteful/malicious

PLOT POINT

Notice that just as the casket plot has reached its climax with the expected marriage of Bassanio and Portia, news comes from Venice to threaten the couple's happiness. The bond plot has not yet been resolved. Bassanio receives a letter from Antonio informing him that all his ships have been wrecked. Salerio adds that despite many people pleading with Shylock, nothing can dissuade Shylock from having his justice and 'his bond'.

176. *deny not:* do not prevent it

JESSICA

When I was with him I have heard him swear
To Tubal and to Chus, his countrymen,
That he would rather have Antonio's flesh
Than twenty times the value of the sum
That he did owe him; and I know, my lord,
If law, authority and power deny not,[176]
It will go hard with poor Antonio.

PORTIA

Is it your dear friend that is thus in trouble?

BASSANIO

The dearest friend to me, the kindest man,
The best-conditioned[177] and unwearied spirit
In doing courtesies,[178] and one in whom
The ancient Roman honour more appears
Than any that draws breath in Italy.

177. *best-conditioned:* best-natured

178. *The best-conditioned … courtesies:* a man who never tires of doing a favour

PORTIA

What sum owes he the Jew?

BASSANIO

For me, three thousand ducats.

PORTIA

What, no more?
Pay him six thousand, and deface[179] the bond.
Double six thousand, and then treble that,
Before a friend of this description
Shall lose a hair through Bassanio's fault.
First go with me to church and call me wife,
And then away to Venice to your friend;
For never shall you lie by Portia's side
With an unquiet[180] soul. You shall have gold
To pay the petty debt twenty times over.
When it is paid, bring your true friend along.
My maid Nerissa and myself meantime
Will live as maids and widows. Come, away,
For you shall hence upon your wedding day.
Bid your friends welcome, show a merry cheer.[181]
Since you are dear[182] bought, I will love you dear.[183]
But let me hear the letter of your friend.

179. *deface:* destroy

PLOT POINT

Portia immediately offers to pay the bond. She is determined that Bassanio should never experience guilt about the debt he owes to Antonio, advising they get married immediately before Bassanio returns to Venice to discharge the debt.

180. *unquiet:* troubled

181. *cheer:* countenance/face

182. *dear:* expensively
183. *dear:* dearly

BASSANIO

[*Reads.*] 'Sweet Bassanio, my ships have all miscarried,[184] my creditors grow cruel, my estate is very low, my bond to the Jew is forfeit, and since in paying it, it is impossible I should live, all debts are cleared between you and I, if I might but see you at my death. Notwithstanding, use your pleasure.[185] If your love do not persuade you to come, let not my letter.'

184. ***miscarried:*** been destroyed

185. ***use your pleasure:*** do as you think best

PORTIA

O love! Dispatch[186] all business, and be gone.

186. ***Dispatch:*** Quickly deal with

BASSANIO

Since I have your good leave[187] to go away
I will make haste,[188] but till I come again,
No bed shall e'er be guilty of my stay,
Nor rest be interposer 'twixt us twain.[189]

187. ***good leave:*** permission/blessing

188. ***haste:*** hurry

189. ***Since I … twain:*** *Bassanio is saying that he will not rest until he sees Portia again.*

Exeunt.

OVERVIEW OF ACT 3, SCENE 2

KEY SCENE OF LOVE

Part 1 (lines 1–185) – Bassanio makes his selection.

- This is the **climax** of the **theme of love and marriage** in the play. The hero Bassanio has arrived to make his choice. From the outset, it is clear that Portia favours Bassanio and she makes no effort to conceal this fact. She asks Bassanio to delay making his choice as he will have to leave immediately if he chooses incorrectly and she will lose him forever:

  I would detain you here some month or two
  Before you venture for me. (lines 9–10)

- Portia also suggests that she would be willing to reveal the correct casket to Bassanio, only that she has made a promise to her dead father not to. She admits that she has been enchanted by Bassanio and this is the source of her **inner conflict**:

  Beshrew your eyes,
  They have o'erlooked me and divided me. (lines 14–15)

  Portia is 'divided' between remaining loyal to her father's wishes and revealing the casket to Bassanio so that she never has to lose him.

- Bassanio, however, would rather make his choice immediately, claiming he is in torture and cannot bear to wait any longer:

  Let me choose,
  For as I am, I live upon the rack. (lines 24–25)

  This exchange between Portia and Bassanio adds tension and suspense to the scene. Next, Portia and Bassanio engage in some playful **banter** (conversation) which helps to ease the tension somewhat.

- Portia directs Bassanio to the caskets to make his choice. She gives instructions for music to be played, saying that if the outcome is sad, the music will be like Bassanio's swansong and her tears will create a stream. If he is successful, however, the music will be like a fanfare celebrating his win.
- Consider the first three lines of the song:

  Tell me where is fancy bred,
  Or in the heart, or in the head?
  How begot, how nourishèd? (lines 63–65)

  Is it a coincidence that the last word of the first three lines of Portia's song all rhyme with 'lead'? Is Bassanio getting a clue after all?

- Before he chooses, Portia compares Bassanio to Hercules who went to save the Trojan princess Hesione who was being sacrificed to a sea-monster. Unlike Hercules, who undertook this epic quest for reward (Hesione's father gave Hercules horses as a reward), Bassanio is undertaking his challenge for love. Portia can hardly bear to look at Bassanio as he is making his choice, commenting:

  With much much more dismay
  I view the fight than thou that mak'st the fray. (lines 61–62)

  This suggests the sense of anxiety and terror that she feels in looking helplessly on.

- It is immediately clear from his words that Bassanio is going to choose the lead casket:

  So may the outward shows be least themselves:
  The world is still deceived with ornament. (lines 73–74)

- Bassanio is not drawn to the gold casket. He proceeds to give examples of where we see false appearances in life, mentioning how in law a case well argued can cover over an evil crime – 'the show of evil' (line 77). In religion, the Bible can be used to justify a sin, while people who look brave on the outside with 'The beards of Hercules and frowning Mars' (line 85) may in reality have 'livers white as milk' (line 86). The next example of false appearances that Bassanio mentions relates to beauty and how women use cosmetics and fake hair (wigs) to create a false appearance. Bassanio, however, is not to be fooled by false appearances and so rejects the 'gaudy gold' (line 101) casket.
- Bassanio quickly dismisses the silver one too, claiming that silver is the 'pale and common drudge 'Tween man and man' (lines 103–104).
- As he approaches the 'meagre lead' (line 104) casket, Portia finds it hard to control her emotions – 'O love, be moderate! Allay thy ecstasy' (line 111). Bassanio's success is certain.
- Bassanio opens the lead casket and meditates on Portia's portrait. His language here becomes **hyperbolic** (exaggerated and over-the-top) as he observes how the painter, whom he calls a 'demi-god' (line 115), created such a realistic image of Portia:

  But her eyes—
  How could he see to do them? Having made one,
  Methinks it should have power to steal both his
  And leave itself unfurnished. (lines 123–126)

- He reads the scroll which congratulates him on not choosing by appearance and directs him to Portia to 'claim her with a loving kiss' (line 138). Bassanio is very **deferential** (respectful) and somewhat unsure of himself as he approaches Portia:

  So, thrice-fair lady, stand I even so,
  As doubtful whether what I see be true,
  Until confirmed, signed, ratified by you. (lines 146–148)

Portia's Character

- There is a **noticeable change** in Portia's character in this scene. Previously, Portia appeared to be a strong, opinionated person, but in this scene she is quite humble and **subservient** (obedient/submissive). When Bassanio chooses the lead casket, Portia seems modest, almost insecure:

  You see me, lord Bassanio, where I stand,
  Such as I am. Though for myself alone
  I would not be ambitious in my wish
  To wish myself much better, yet for you
  I would be trebled twenty times myself (lines 149–153)

  Portia wants to be better than she is to please Bassanio. She claims that she is 'an unlessoned girl, unschooled, unpractisèd' (line 159) who is willing to learn from Bassanio.

- As Portia transfers all her property and wealth to Bassanio, she gives him a ring as a token of her love. She warns:

  I give them [all she has] with this ring,
  Which when you part from, lose, or give away,
  Let it presage the ruin of your love (lines 171–173)

- Bassanio is quick to reassure her that the only way he would lose the ring is through death:

  But when this ring
  Parts from this finger, then parts life from hence.
  O, then be bold to say Bassanio's dead! (lines 183–185)

- These words are **ominous** (menacing/threatening) as the audience is now aware of just how important it is for Bassanio to keep the ring safe. The ring is of huge symbolic significance as it represents the love between Portia and Bassanio.

Part 2 (lines 186–217) – Gratiano and Nerissa declare their intention to marry.

- No sooner have Portia and Bassanio exchanged vows of love, than Gratiano reveals the surprising request that he be married at the same time as Portia and Bassanio. Bassanio thinks that he is not being serious and comments:

  With all my heart, so thou canst get a wife. (line 195)

- Bassanio expresses surprise that Gratiano has secured a wife so quickly. Gratiano says:

  You saw the mistress, I beheld the maid.
  You loved, I loved (lines 198–199)

- The revelation that Gratiano has courted and proposed to Nerissa in that short period of time surprises everyone – especially the audience. Nerissa had one condition however: Bassanio had to choose the correct casket.
- Bassanio tells Gratiano that he would be honoured to share their wedding day – 'Our feast shall be much honoured in your marriage' (line 212). As they are joking about who will have the first boy, Lorenzo, Jessica and Salerio enter unexpectedly.
- Gratiano greets Lorenzo and Salerio by name, but only refers to Jessica as Lorenzo's 'infidel' (line 216), which is quite disrespectful. Bassanio and Portia also welcome them heartily.

Part 3 (lines 218–326) – The arrival of Lorenzo, Jessica and Salerio with news of Antonio's losses.

- Lorenzo reveals that he had no intention of coming to Belmont, but he met Salerio who convinced him to accompany him. Salerio sends greetings from Antonio and hands Bassanio a letter from him. As Bassanio is opening the letter, Gratiano jokes that Antonio will be glad of their success – 'We are the Jasons; we have won the fleece' (line 240).
- The **mood** of the entire play changes now from **comedy** to **tragedy** as Bassanio **peruses** (reads) the letter. Portia notices the dramatic change the letter has had on Bassanio's **countenance** (face) and assumes the letter must contain news of someone's death:

  There are some shrewd contents in yon same paper
  That steals the colour from Bassanio's cheek. (lines 242–243)

- Portia pleads with Bassanio to share the news with her. Bassanio informs Portia that he misrepresented himself when he said he had nothing. In fact, he claims, he was:

  worse than nothing, for indeed
  I have engaged myself to a dear friend,
  Engaged my friend to his mere enemy,
  To feed my means. (lines 259–262)

- Salerio confirms the contents of Antonio's letter – that all his vessels (ships) have been destroyed at sea. No one could have predicted such catastrophic losses and now, Salerio informs us, Shylock is intent on **exacting** (demanding) the penalty as per the bond and it seems that no one can stop him:

  But none can drive him from the envious plea
  Of forfeiture, of justice and his bond. (lines 281–282)

- Portia is quick to suggest some kind of solution, offering to pay whatever amount it takes to 'deface the bond' (line 298). She acknowledges that Bassanio must leave quickly, but not before he marries her:

  First go with me to church and call me wife,
  And then away to Venice to your friend (lines 302–303)

  When she reads the letter, Portia urges Bassanio to leave without delay (after they get married). At the end of the scene, Bassanio tells Portia that he will not rest until he sees her again.
- The scene is full of **tension** and **foreboding** (anxiety/unease) as we learn that nothing will persuade Shylock to show mercy. Bassanio must leave the **fairy-tale world of Belmont** and face **the real world of Venice** where his dear friend Antonio could lose his life because of him.

THEMES

- The themes of **love and marriage**, **money** and **false appearances** are evident in this scene.
- This scene is the **climax** of the **theme of love and marriage** in the play as Bassanio chooses the correct casket and wins Portia's hand in marriage. The theme is also shown through the relationship between Gratiano and Nerissa, reminding us that love is a universal theme and not just for the wealthy!
- The **theme of false appearances** is apparent when Bassanio is choosing a casket and outlines the many examples of how the world is deceived by outward appearances.
- The lovers' happiness is short-lived which reminds us how, in this play, the **theme of money** is also linked to the **theme of love**. Antonio guaranteed the loan from Shylock to send Bassanio on his quest for love. Unfortunately, all of Antonio's ships have become wrecked and Shylock is demanding that the terms of his bond be upheld.

REVIEWING

1. Explain why Portia wants Bassanio to delay before making his choice.
2. Why does Bassanio want to make his choice immediately?
3. Explain why Portia decides to play music while Bassanio is making his choice. Give **two** reasons.
4. Do you think that Bassanio is affected by the music? Explain your answer.
5. What does Portia give Bassanio as a gift and what warning does she give with it?
6. What is Bassanio's reply?
7. What surprising news does Gratiano reveal?
8. What news does Antonio's letter contain?
9. How does Portia react when she reads the letter?

EXPLORING

1. Bassanio Makes His Choice P

Pair Activity

(a) Turn to **page 44** of your portfolio to complete the grid on Bassanio's language.

(b) Do you agree with Bassanio that people are still deceived by **false appearances**? Discuss this with your partner. Turn to **page 45** of your portfolio to write down **three examples** of where people are deceived by false appearances.

2. Bassanio and Portia's Language – Hyperbole P

Bassanio and Portia both use hyperbole in their language to each other. Turn to **page 46** of your portfolio to complete the tasks on hyperbole.

CREATING

1. Songs – The Love Soundtrack

In this scene, Portia chooses a meaningful song with a **subliminal** (hidden) message to help Bassanio make his choice. What **four** songs would you choose to reflect Bassanio and Portia's relationship in this scene? Explain your **reason** for choosing each song.

For example, think of a song that suggests the love Portia and Bassanio feel for each other; a song to communicate Portia's desire to make Bassanio stay; a song that suggests Portia's feeling of unworthiness; and a song for when the couple say goodbye but not for long.

2. Bassanio's Letter to Antonio P

Write Bassanio's response to Antonio's letter. Turn to **page 47** of your portfolio to help you.

REFLECTING

1. Reflecting on Jessica

What does Jessica say about her father in this scene? Does this surprise you? Why do you think she says this?

2. Reflecting on Shylock and Antonio P

Even though neither Shylock nor Antonio appear in this scene, we hear a lot about them. Find two quotes for each character and say what impression of the character this creates. Turn to **page 48** of your portfolio to help you.

3. Character File P

Both Bassanio and Portia feature prominently in this scene. Write your impression of both for this scene in your portfolio. Turn to **page 120** for **Bassanio** and **page 127** for **Portia** to record your responses.

4. My Reflection on Act 3, Scene 2 P

(a) Turn to **page 49** of your portfolio to record your response to Bassanio choosing the lead casket.

(b) Next, complete the **scene reflection** on **page 50** of your portfolio.

ACT 3, SCENE 3

Setting: Venice. A street.

In this **scene** you will:

- **Read** Shylock's words aloud.
- Reflect on the characters of **Antonio** and **Shylock**.
- **Predict the outcome** of the bond theme.

Action – What Happens?

In this brief scene, we are back in Venice where Shylock is demanding justice. He is unwilling to hear Antonio's pleas for mercy and says that nothing will stand in the way of him getting justice (i.e. taking Antonio's life). By the end of the scene, Antonio is **resigned to** (accepts) his fate.

Useful Words

intercessor – someone who pleads for people
dull-eyed – gullible/easily fooled
impeach – discredit
cur – dog
bootless – hopeless
commodity – trade

ACT 3, SCENE 3

Enter SHYLOCK, SOLANIO, ANTONIO and Jailer.

SHYLOCK

Jailer, look to him.[1] Tell not me of mercy.
This is the fool that lent out money gratis.[2]
Jailer, look to him.

1. *look to him:* watch him
2. *gratis:* interest-free

ANTONIO

Hear me yet, good Shylock.

SHYLOCK

I'll have my bond. Speak not against my bond.
I have sworn an oath that I will have my bond.
Thou called'st me dog before thou hadst a cause,
But since I am a dog, beware my fangs.
The Duke shall grant me justice. I do wonder,
Thou naughty[3] jailer, that thou art so fond[4]
To come abroad[5] with him at his request.

3. *naughty:* worthless
4. *fond:* foolish
5. *abroad:* outside

LOOKING AT LANGUAGE

Repetition: Notice how Shylock uses repetition in this scene (particularly in lines 12–17). What effect does this repetition have? How might the audience's opinion of Shylock be influenced by his words in this scene?

ANTONIO

I pray thee hear me speak.

SHYLOCK

I'll have my bond. I will not hear thee speak.
I'll have my bond, and therefore speak no more.
I'll not be made a soft and dull-eyed[6] fool
To shake the head, relent, and sigh, and yield[7]
To Christian intercessors.[8] Follow not.
I'll have no speaking. I will have my bond.

Exit.

6. *dull-eyed:* gullible/easily fooled
7. *yield:* give in
8. *intercessors: people who plead for others*

SPOTLIGHT ON … IMAGERY

Notice the imagery of the dog that is used in this scene (lines 5–7 and 18–19). Discuss how Shylock's use of the image of the dog differs from Solanio's.

SOLANIO

It is the most impenetrable cur[9]
That ever kept[10] with men.

9. *impenetrable cur:* heartless dog
10. *kept:* lived

ANTONIO

Let him alone.
I'll follow him no more with bootless[11] prayers.
He seeks my life. His reason well I know:

11. *bootless:* hopeless

I oft delivered from his forfeitures
Many that have at times made moan to me,[12]
Therefore he hates me.

SOLANIO

I am sure the Duke
Will never grant this forfeiture to hold.[13]

ANTONIO

The Duke cannot deny the course of law,[14]
For the commodity[15] that strangers have
With us in Venice, if it be denied,
Will much impeach[16] the justice of his state,
Since that the trade and profit of the city
Consisteth of all nations.[17] Therefore go.
These griefs and losses have so bated[18] me
That I shall hardly spare a pound of flesh
Tomorrow to my bloody creditor.
Well, jailer, on. Pray God Bassanio come
To see me pay his debt, and then I care not.

Exeunt.

12. *I oft … me:* I often helped people out who pleaded with me that they could not repay their debt to him.
13. *this forfeiture to hold:* this penalty to stand
14. *The Duke … law:* The Duke cannot prevent the course of law *(interfere with legal proceedings)*.
15. trade
16. *impeach:* discredit/bring it into disrepute
17. *For the … nations:* If we don't respect the legal contracts of foreigners who trade with us in Venice, then we will bring dishonour to Venice and damage its trading reputation.
18. *bated:* diminished/made me lose weight

OVERVIEW OF ACT 3, SCENE 3

- The action of this short scene brings us back to Venice and makes us aware of the **danger** Antonio now faces. Shylock has come with a jailer to capture Antonio. He is completely unwilling to listen to Antonio and constantly insists on his bond:

  I'll have my bond. Speak not against my bond.
  I have sworn an oath that I will have my bond. (lines 4–5)

- It is clear from what Shylock says that it is not just about the bond. He has a **vendetta** (an ongoing bitter dispute) against Antonio because of Antonio's over-generous lending practices and he is now determined to get his revenge:

  Jailer, look to him. Tell not me of mercy.
  This is the fool that lent out money gratis. (lines 1–2)

- Shylock is completely merciless in this scene and truly emerges as a **vindictive** (vengeful) villain:

  Thou called'st me dog before thou hadst a cause,
  But since I am a dog, beware my fangs. (lines 6–7)

- He appears so hard and merciless that Solanio remarks that Shylock 'is the most impenetrable cur that ever kept with men' (lines 18–19).

- Antonio is becoming increasingly **resigned** to his bloody fate and comments that 'I'll follow him no more with bootless prayers' (line 20). Solanio is optimistic that the Duke of Venice will **intercede** (negotiate) on Antonio's behalf, but Antonio is more realistic, acknowledging that there is little the Duke can do when the law is clearly on Shylock's side.
- By the end of the scene, we are aware that Antonio is weary and resigned to his fate:

  These griefs and losses have so bated me
  That I shall hardly spare a pound of flesh
  Tomorrow to my bloody creditor. (lines 32–34)

- Antonio's one wish before he dies is to see Bassanio. There is a huge contrast in this scene between the **unrelenting** (merciless/determined) villain, Shylock, and the **stoical** (patient/uncomplaining) victim, Antonio.

REVIEWING

1. Why does Shylock refuse to listen to Antonio?
2. What do you think Solanio means in lines 18 and 19?
3. Why does Antonio think Shylock hates him so much?
4. Why is the Duke unable to help Antonio?
5. How have all of Antonio's losses and recent bad experiences affected him?
6. What is Antonio's final wish before he dies?

ORAL LANGUAGE

Shylock's 'I'll have my bond' Speech

Pair Activity

With your partner, look back over lines 4–17 where Shylock is insisting on his bond.

(a) Perform the speech. One person should play the part of Antonio and one person should play the part of Shylock. The person who is playing Antonio should close their eyes while Shylock speaks his lines to him/her. Consider the **tone of voice** you are using. Are there words you would emphasise?

(b) Swap roles and repeat.

(c) Discuss together the effect of Shylock's words on you.

REFLECTING

Character File P

Turn to the Character File section of your portfolio to record your response to **(a) Shylock** (**page 136**) and **(b) Antonio** (**page 114**) in this scene. Use quotations where possible to support your points.

PREDICTING

How Will It End? P

The future certainly looks bleak for Antonio. How do you think the play will end? Will Shylock get his pound of flesh? Will Bassanio return on time? Turn to **page 51** of your portfolio to write down your ideas.

ACT 3, SCENE 4

Setting: Belmont. A room in Portia's house.

In this **scene** you will:

- Reflect on the character of **Portia**.
- Write a **diary entry** for Jessica or a **letter** to Portia's cousin, Doctor Bellario.

Action – What Happens?

In this scene, we are back in Belmont where Portia asks Lorenzo and Jessica to be in charge while she leaves. She tells them that she and Nerissa are going to a monastery until Bassanio returns. However, we soon learn that Portia is making plans for her and Nerissa to go to Venice disguised as men. She instructs her servant, Balthasar, to borrow notes and clothing from her cousin, Doctor Bellario, who is a lawyer in Padua. She asks Balthasar to return quickly and meet her at the ferry where she and Nerissa will leave for Venice.

Useful Words

conceit – understanding
amity – friendship
traject – ferry
lineaments – features/characteristics
bosom lover – intimate friend
accoutered – dressed

ACT 3, SCENE 4

Enter PORTIA, NERISSA, LORENZO, JESSICA and BALTHASAR, a man of Portia's.

LORENZO [*to PORTIA*]

Madam, although I speak it in your presence,
You have a noble and a true conceit
Of godlike amity,[1] which appears most strongly
In bearing thus the absence of your lord.
But if you knew to whom you show this honour,
How true a gentleman you send relief,
How dear a lover[2] of my lord your husband,
I know you would be prouder of the work
Than customary bounty can enforce you.[3]

PORTIA

I never did repent for doing good,
Nor shall not now; for in companions
That do converse and waste[4] the time together,
Whose souls do bear an equal yoke of love,
There must be needs a like proportion
Of lineaments, of manners, and of spirit,[5]
Which makes me think that this Antonio,
Being the bosom lover[6] of my lord,
Must needs be like my lord. If it be so,
How little is the cost I have bestowed
In purchasing the semblance of my soul
From out the state of hellish cruelty.[7]
This comes too near the praising of myself,
Therefore no more of it. Hear other things:
Lorenzo, I commit into your hands
The husbandry and manage[8] of my house
Until my lord's return.[9] For mine own part,
I have toward heaven breathed a secret vow
To live in prayer and contemplation,
Only attended by Nerissa here,
Until her husband and my lord's return.
There is a monastery two miles off,
And there will we abide.[10] I do desire you
Not to deny this imposition,[11]
The which my love and some necessity
Now lays upon you.

1. *You have ... amity:* You have a very good understanding of true friendship.
2. *lover:* friend
3. *Than customary ... you:* Than you would normally be for doing a kind deed.
4. *waste:* spend
5. *There must ... spirit:* Friends who spend time together must share similar characteristics.
6. *bosom lover:* intimate friend
7. *How little ... cruelty:* What a small price to pay to save someone who resembles my soul-mate.
8. *husbandry and manage:* care and management
9. *Lorenzo, ... return: Portia is putting Lorenzo and Jessica in charge of her house while she and Bassanio are gone.*
10. *abide:* stay
11. *deny this imposition:* decline this favour

LORENZO

Madam, with all my heart,
I shall obey you in all fair[12] commands.

PORTIA

My people do already know my mind,
And will acknowledge[13] you and Jessica
In place of Lord Bassanio and myself.
So fare you well till we shall meet again.

LORENZO

Fair thoughts and happy hours attend on you!

JESSICA

I wish your ladyship all heart's content.

PORTIA

I thank you for your wish, and am well pleased
To wish it back on you. Fare you well, Jessica.

Exeunt JESSICA and LORENZO.

Now, Balthasar,
As I have ever found thee honest-true,
So let me find thee still. Take this same letter,
And use thou all th'endeavour of a man
In speed to Padua.[14] See thou render[15] this
Into my cousin's hand, Doctor Bellario,
And look what notes and garments[16] he doth give thee,
Bring them, I pray thee, with imagined speed[17]
Unto the traject,[18] to the common[19] ferry
Which trades[20] to Venice. Waste no time in words,
But get thee gone. I shall be there before thee.

BALTHASAR

Madam, I go with all convenient[21] speed.

Exit.

12. ***fair:*** reasonable

13. ***acknowledge:*** recognise

PLOT POINT

Portia instructs her servant Balthasar to deliver a letter to her cousin, Doctor Bellario, in Padua and bring any items (notes or clothing) that Bellario sends her in return to Venice.

14. ***And use … Padua:*** Use all the speed that is humanly possible to go to Padua.
15. ***render:*** deliver
16. ***garments:*** clothing
17. ***with imagined speed:*** with the fastest speed imaginable
18. ***traject:*** ferry
19. ***common:*** public
20. ***trades:*** crosses
21. ***convenient:*** necessary

ACT 3, SCENE 4

PLOT POINT

Portia reveals her plan to Nerissa. They will see their husbands sooner than they think. Portia and Nerissa will disguise themselves as men, behave like men and travel to Venice. Note that by dressing up in this way, Portia and Nerissa are putting on false appearances.

PORTIA

Come on, Nerissa. I have work in hand
That you yet know not of. We'll see our husbands
Before they think of us.

NERISSA

Shall they see us?

PORTIA

They shall, Nerissa, but in such a habit[22]
That they shall think we are accomplishèd
With that we lack.[23] I'll hold thee any wager,[24]
When we are both accoutered[25] like young men,
I'll prove the prettier[26] fellow of the two,
And wear my dagger with the braver grace,
And speak between the change of man and boy
With a reed[27] voice, and turn two mincing[28] steps
Into a manly stride, and speak of frays[29]
Like a fine bragging youth, and tell quaint[30] lies
How honourable ladies sought my love,
Which I denying, they fell sick and died.
I could not do withal.[31] Then I'll repent,
And wish for all that, that I had not killed them;
And twenty of these puny[32] lies I'll tell,
That men shall swear I have discontinued school
Above a twelvemonth.[33] I have within my mind

22. *habit:* clothing

23. *That they ... lack:* That they will think we are men.
24. *I'll hold ... wager:* I will bet you anything
25. *accoutered:* dressed
26. *prettier:* more handsome

27. *reed:* squeaky
28. *mincing:* dainty/elegant
29. *frays:* fights/brawls

30. *quaint:* elaborate

31. *I could ... withal:* I could not help it.

32. *puny:* pathetic

33. *That men ... twelvemonth:* that I have left school over a year ago

A thousand raw tricks of these bragging Jacks[34]
Which I will practise.

NERISSA

Why, shall we turn to men?[35]

PORTIA

Fie, what a question's that
If thou wert near a lewd interpreter![36]
But come, I'll tell thee all my whole device[37]
When I am in my coach, which stays[38] for us
At the park gate; and therefore haste away,
For we must measure[39] twenty miles today.

Exeunt.

34. ***bragging Jacks:*** boastful young men
35. ***turn to men:*** turn into men
36. ***Fie, ... interpreter!:*** That would be a very rude thing to say. *Portia is deliberately misinterpreting Nerissa, pretending that Nerissa is being rude when she said 'turn to' as this had a sexual meaning.*
37. ***device:*** plan
38. ***stays:*** is waiting
39. ***measure:*** travel

OVERVIEW OF ACT 3, SCENE 4

- Lorenzo **commends** (praises) Portia on showing great generosity of spirit for helping Antonio. He assures Portia that if she knew Antonio, 'How true a gentleman you send relief' (line 6), she would be extraordinarily proud of herself. Portia replies that she has never regretted doing a favour and she will not regret it now:

  I never did repent for doing good,
  Nor shall not now (lines 10–11)
- She imagines that as Antonio and Bassanio are such close friends, they must resemble each other and be similar in terms 'Of lineaments, of manners, and of spirit' (line 15). Portia dismisses her part in helping Antonio, showing a certain **modesty** (humility) in her nature:

  This comes too near the praising of myself,
  Therefore no more of it. (lines 22–23)
- Next, Portia tells Lorenzo that she and Nerissa have decided to go to a monastery and 'live in prayer and contemplation' (line 28) until Bassanio returns. Portia asks Lorenzo and Jessica to take charge of the running of her house. Lorenzo agrees to her request.
- When Lorenzo and Jessica leave, Portia asks her loyal servant, Balthasar, to deliver a letter as quickly as he possibly can to her cousin who lives in Padua. The letter asks for assistance in the form of 'notes and garments' (line 51) or legal documents and clothing that Portia wishes to use in Venice. She asks Balthasar to bring these items to the ferry where she will cross to Venice.
- Portia now reveals the plan to Nerissa. They will disguise themselves as men and, she jokes, put on 'a reed voice' (line 67) and walk in a 'manly stride' (line 68). She jests that she will boast and brag about all the ladies who have pined to death over 'him'. Portia wants to leave immediately; her coach is waiting to take them away and they must leave without delay.

THEMES

The **theme of false appearances** features in this scene as Portia and Nerissa are going to disguise their true appearances and, as we shall see, present themselves as male lawyers. In this case, however, we see a positive aspect of the theme of false appearances as Portia will use her false appearance or disguise to help Antonio.

REVIEWING

1. How does Portia respond when Lorenzo compliments her for helping Antonio?
2. What favour does Portia ask of Lorenzo and Jessica?
3. Where does Portia tell Lorenzo that she and Nerissa are going?
4. What instructions does Portia give Balthasar?
5. What is Portia's plan?

CREATING

Complete either **task A** or **task B** below:

Task A – Jessica's Diary P

In this scene, Portia has finally acknowledged Jessica and has put Jessica and Lorenzo in charge of her house. Turn to **page 52** of your portfolio to record Jessica's thoughts and feelings on the events that have happened since she left her father's house in her diary.

Task B – Portia's Letter to Doctor Bellario P

Turn to **page 53** of your portfolio to write Portia's urgent letter to her cousin, Doctor Bellario. (Look back over lines 49 to 55 to help you.)

REFLECTING

Character File P

Turn to the Character File section of your portfolio to record your response to **Portia** on **page 128**. Use quotations where possible to support your points.

ACT 3, SCENE 5

Setting: Belmont. A room in Portia's house.

In this **scene** you will:

- Reflect on the **relationship** between Jessica and Lorenzo.
- Discuss the **positive and negative aspects** of this scene.

Action – What Happens?

This scene appears somewhat out of sync with the rest of the play. Launcelot and Jessica engage in light-hearted banter. Launcelot continues to twist words and misinterpret meanings. Lorenzo becomes a little frustrated with Launcelot when he deliberately misconstrues (misinterprets) Lorenzo's instructions for dinner. When Lorenzo asks Jessica her opinion of Portia, she is full of high praise for her, saying that she has no equal on earth.

Useful Words

tricksy – ambiguous/having more than one possible meaning

stomachs – appetites

meet – proper

fellow – equal

Enter LAUNCELOT and JESSICA.

LAUNCELOT

Yes, truly; for look you, the sins of the father are to be laid upon the children,[1] therefore I promise you I fear[2] you. I was always plain[3] with you, and so now I speak my agitation[4] of the matter, therefore be o' good cheer, for truly I think you are damned. There is but one hope in it that can do you any good, and that is but a kind of bastard hope, neither.

1. ***the sins … children:*** children will inherit their father's sins
2. ***fear:*** fear for
3. ***plain:*** honest
4. ***agitation:*** *Launcelot means to say 'cogitation,' meaning his 'thoughts,' instead of 'agitation.'*

JESSICA

And what hope is that, I pray thee?

LAUNCELOT

Marry, you may partly hope that your father got you not,[5] that you are not the Jew's daughter.

5. ***that your … not:*** that your father is not your real father

JESSICA

That were a kind of bastard[6] hope indeed. So[7] the sins of my mother should be visited upon me.

6. ***bastard:*** illegitimate
7. ***So:*** Therefore

LAUNCELOT

Truly then, I fear you are damned both by father and mother. Thus, when I shun Scylla your father, I fall into Charybdis your mother. Well, you are gone[8] both ways.[9]

8. ***gone:*** doomed
9. ***Thus, … ways:*** *In mythology, Scylla was a sea-monster and Charybdis was a dangerous whirlpool. The meaning here is that Jessica is doubly damned by her parents.*

JESSICA

I shall be saved by my husband. He hath made me a Christian.

LAUNCELOT

Truly, the more to blame he! We were Christians enough before, e'en as many as could well live one by another. This making of Christians will raise the price of hogs. If we grow all to be pork-eaters we shall not shortly have a rasher on the coals for money.[10]

10. ***This making … money:*** *Launcelot is saying that if Jews convert to Christianity there will be more people eating pork, which will cause such an increase in the price of pork that it would be impossible to buy.*

Enter LORENZO.

JESSICA

I'll tell my husband, Launcelot, what you say. Here he comes.

LORENZO

I shall grow jealous of you shortly, Launcelot, if you thus get my wife into corners.[11]

JESSICA

Nay, you need not fear us, Lorenzo. Launcelot and I are out.[12] He tells me flatly there's no mercy for me in heaven because I am a Jew's daughter, and he says you are no good member of the commonwealth,[13] for in converting Jews to Christians you raise the price of pork.

11. *if you … corners:* if you keep having secret chats with my wife
12. *out:* arguing
13. *commonwealth:* society/the Venetian state

LORENZO

I shall answer that[14] better to the commonwealth than you can the getting up of the Negro's belly. The Moor is with child by you, Launcelot.[15]

LAUNCELOT

It is much that the Moor should be more than reason,[16] but if she be less than an honest woman, she is indeed more than I took her for.[17]

LORENZO

How every fool can play upon the word! I think the best grace of wit will shortly turn into silence, and discourse grow commendable in none only but parrots.[18] Go in, sirrah, bid them prepare for dinner.

LAUNCELOT

That is done, sir. They have all stomachs.[19]

LORENZO

Goodly Lord, what a wit-snapper[20] are you! Then bid them prepare dinner.

LAUNCELOT

That is done too, sir; only 'cover'[21] is the word.

LORENZO

Will you cover then, sir?

LAUNCELOT

Not so, sir, neither. I know my duty.[22]

LORENZO

Yet more quarrelling with occasion![23] Wilt thou show the whole wealth of thy wit in an instant? I pray thee understand a plain man in his plain meaning. Go to thy fellows; bid them cover the table, serve in the meat, and we will come in to dinner.

14. ***I shall answer that:*** I will explain

15. ***The Moor ... Launcelot:*** *Launcelot is apparently responsible for an African servant of Portia's household becoming pregnant.*

16. ***It is ... reason:*** It's unfortunate that there's more of the Moor than there should be. *This is a pun on 'Moor.'*

17. ***but if ... for:*** *Launcelot is saying that even if she is not an honest woman, he still thinks she is more respectable than he first thought.*

18. ***How every ... parrots:*** *Lorenzo is growing tired of Launcelot's excessive wordplay and suggests that soon intelligent men will have to be silent and leave the talking to parrots.*

19. ***stomachs:*** appetites *Lorenzo is instructing Launcelot to tell the servants to get dinner ready, whereas Launcelot pretends he means tell them to get ready to eat dinner.*

20. ***wit-snapper:*** a person who makes sharp comments

21. ***'cover':*** to set the table *Again, Launcelot deliberately misinterprets 'cover' to mean put on one's hat.*

22. ***Not so, ... duty:*** *It was customary for people who were socially inferior to take off their hats as a mark of respect to their social superiors. This causes Launcelot to say he will not put on his hat, as he knows his 'duty' or social position.*

23. ***Yet more ... occasion!:*** Still finding an opportunity to play with words!

PLOT POINT

Lorenzo is by this point exasperated with Launcelot's incessant wordplay and repeats his simple instructions (lines 49–50). What is your opinion of Launcelot in this scene: humorous and providing light relief, or annoying and irksome?

LAUNCELOT

For the table,[24] sir, it shall be served in. For the meat, sir, it shall be covered. For your coming in to dinner, sir, why, let it be as humours and conceits shall govern.[25]

Exit.

LORENZO

O dear discretion, how his words are suited![26]
The fool hath planted in his memory
An army of good words, and I do know
A many fools that stand in better place,
Garnished[27] like him, that for a tricksy[28] word
Defy the matter.[29] How cheer'st thou, Jessica?[30]
And now, good sweet, say thy opinion:
How dost thou like the Lord Bassanio's wife?

JESSICA

Past all expressing. It is very meet[31]
The Lord Bassanio live an upright[32] life,
For, having such a blessing in his lady,
He finds the joys of heaven here on earth,
And if on earth he do not merit it,
In reason he should never come to heaven.
Why, if two gods should play some heavenly match
And on the wager lay two earthly women,
And Portia one, there must be something else
Pawn'd[33] with the other; for the poor rude world
Hath not her fellow.[34][35]

LORENZO

Even such a husband
Hast thou of me as she is for a wife.[36]

JESSICA

Nay, but ask my opinion too of that!

LORENZO

I will anon.[37] First let us go to dinner.

24. ***the table:*** the meal *Launcelot is misinterpreting Lorenzo's words to set the actual table, which can be interpreted as the 'food' or 'meal'.*
25. ***as humours … govern:*** as you wish
26. ***how his … suited!:*** how he never stops playing on words!
27. ***Garnished:*** Dressed
28. ***tricksy:*** *ambiguous/a word with more than one possible meaning*
29. ***Defy the matter:*** Refuse to talk sense
30. ***How cheer'st thou, Jessica?:*** How are you, Jessica?
31. ***meet:*** proper/appropriate
32. ***upright:*** upstanding/good
33. ***Pawn'd:*** Wagered/Pledged
34. ***fellow:*** equal
35. ***Why, if … fellow:*** If two gods were betting and one had wagered Portia, the other god would have to wager something else for she has no equal. *This is a roundabout way of saying that Portia is beyond compare.*
36. ***Even such … wife:*** *Lorenzo jokes that he is as good a husband as Portia is a wife.*
37. ***anon:*** soon

JESSICA

Nay, let me praise you while I have a stomach.[38]

LORENZO

No, pray thee, let it serve for table-talk.[39]
Then, howsome'er thou speak'st, 'mong other things
I shall digest it.[40]

JESSICA

Well, I'll set you forth.[41]

Exeunt.

38. ***while I … stomach:*** while I'm in the mood *(with 'stomach' meaning both 'appetite' and 'mood/inclination')*
39. ***table-talk:*** dinner conversation
40. ***Then, howsome'er … it:*** And whatever you would like to say about that as well as about other topics I will listen to you.
41. ***I'll set you forth:*** I will praise you.

OVERVIEW OF ACT 3, SCENE 5

- This light-hearted scene seems to provide some **respite** (a short break) for the audience before the next scene. We are still in the **idyllic** (perfect/ideal), romantic fairy-tale world of Belmont where Lorenzo and Jessica have been left in charge of Portia's estate.
- At the start of this scene Launcelot is teasing Jessica. He tells her that she will be damned because she is the daughter of a Jew. Jessica cleverly states that since she is now the wife of a Christian, and has converted to Christianity, she will be saved:

  I shall be saved by my husband. He hath made me a
  Christian. (lines 15–16)

- Lorenzo arrives and jokes that he will become jealous of Launcelot's secret chats with his wife. Launcelot continues to use his **characteristic** (typical) puns and **malapropisms** (incorrect use of a word in place of a word that sounds similar) in his language. Lorenzo reveals that Launcelot has made one of Portia's servants (an African woman) pregnant. In his typical **blasé** (casual) fashion, Launcelot shrugs it off and makes **disparaging** (insulting) remarks about her.
- When Lorenzo instructs Launcelot to tell the servants to prepare dinner, there **ensues** (follows) a comic scene of wordplay where Launcelot continually and deliberately misinterprets Lorenzo's words for **comical** effect.
- When Launcelot leaves, we gain a brief insight into the **relationship** between Jessica and Lorenzo. It seems that Jessica and Lorenzo are quite content together.
- Lorenzo asks Jessica her opinion of Portia, to which she replies that Portia is beyond compare. She lavishes praise on Portia using **religious imagery**, suggesting how divine and unique Portia is. She claims that Bassanio has 'such a blessing in his lady, He finds the joys of heaven here on earth' (lines 65–66). She also declares that there is no one on earth equal to Portia – 'for the poor rude world hath not her fellow' (lines 72–73).
- Lorenzo playfully insists that he is as good a husband as Portia is a wife:

  Even such a husband
  Hast thou of me as she is for a wife. (lines 73–74)

- The scene ends with Jessica and Lorenzo engaging in light-hearted banter as they leave for dinner.

Villa Foscari, near Venice, which supposedly was Shakespeare's inspiration for Belmont.

REVIEWING

1. How is Jessica doomed, according to Launcelot?
2. What reply does Jessica give to this?
3. What information does Lorenzo reveal about Launcelot's relationship with one of Portia's African servants?
4. How does Launcelot respond to this news?
5. What is Jessica's opinion of Portia?

EXPLORING

Director's Notebook – Keep or Cut? P

Pair Activity

If you were the director of this play, would you keep this scene or cut it? Look back over it and discuss the arguments **for and against** keeping it. Write your response on **page 54** of your portfolio.

REFLECTING

Lorenzo and Jessica's Relationship P

What is your opinion of the relationship between Jessica and Lorenzo based on what you have seen so far? Turn to **page 54** of your portfolio to record your response.

LOOKING BACK AT ACT 3

1. Overview P

Pair Activity

With your partner, turn to **page 4** of your portfolio to write **one sentence or phrase** in the box for each scene in Act 3. This sentence or phrase should **sum up the main action** in that scene.

2. Quotes Quiz P

Turn to **page 55** of your portfolio to review the **important quotes** for Act 3.

3. Individual Assignment – Choose one of the following activities:

(a) **Themes**: Discuss the theme of **love and marriage** in this act.

(b) **Setting**: Compare and contrast the world of **Belmont** and the world of **Venice**.

P **(c)** **What If...?**: What if the scene with Shylock, Antonio and the Jailer in **Act 3**, **Scene 3** was reported on **Twitter** as breaking news? Imagine you are an **onlooker** witnessing the scene and **tweet the main action** as it unfolds. Turn to **page 58** of your portfolio to write your tweets in modern English.

A good tweet:

- Is short and to the point (less than 280 characters).
- Is clearly written.
- Attracts readers' attention by asking a question or revealing interesting news/facts.
- Uses a hashtag (#) in front of a key word or an important topic.

LINKING TO THE EXAM

Writing About Characters and Key Moments P

In the exam, you might be asked to write about characters that you liked or disliked.

Turn to **pages 59–62** of your portfolio to examine a question about characters that you liked or disliked and key moments that feature these characters.

ACT 4

This act, which contains one very long scene and one very short scene, is mainly concerned with the themes of **justice** and **mercy** as Antonio and Shylock go to court to resolve their dispute. The **Trial Scene** (Act 4, Scene 1) is full of tension and suspense as Portia, disguised as a lawyer named 'Balthasar', pleads with Shylock to show mercy. When all her efforts to persuade Shylock fail, there is a faint glimmer of hope as Portia finds a compelling **legal loophole** (flaw or glitch in the legal case) with which to challenge Shylock's case.

ACT 4, SCENE 1

Setting: Venice. A court of justice.

In this **scene** you will:

- Explore **Portia's speech**.
- Examine Antonio's use of **imagery**.
- Consider the **role** each character played in the scene.
- **Produce a scene** in groups.

Action – What Happens?

This scene is the climax of the bond theme in the play. Shylock remains unrelenting (not giving way) despite the Duke's best efforts to persuade him to show mercy to Antonio. The case is to be presided over (conducted/overseen) by Portia, disguised as 'Balthasar', a learned judge, who has come on the recommendation of Doctor Bellario.

Portia appeals to Shylock to take up to three times the amount of money he is owed. Shylock refuses. Portia finds a legal loophole (flaw or glitch in the legal case) that eases the tension of the scene and Antonio is saved. Shylock is punished for his **malice** and **vindictiveness (bitterness)**.

Useful Words

adversary – enemy	**temporal** – earthly	**obdurate** – stubborn
render – provide/give	**envy** – spite/malice	**balance** – weighing scales
bosom – chest	**currish** – dog-like/bad-tempered	**tarry** – wait

Enter the DUKE, the Magnificoes, ANTONIO, BASSANIO, GRATIANO, SALERIO and others.

DUKE

What, is Antonio here?

ANTONIO

Ready, so please your grace.

DUKE

I am sorry for thee. Thou art come to answer
A stony adversary,[1] an inhuman wretch
Uncapable of pity, void and empty
From any dram[2] of mercy.

ANTONIO

I have heard
Your grace hath ta'en great pains to qualify
His rigorous course,[3] but since he stands obdurate,[4]
And that no lawful means can carry me
Out of his envy's reach,[5] I do oppose
My patience to his fury, and am armed[6]
To suffer with a quietness of spirit
The very tyranny[7] and rage of his.[8]

DUKE

Go one,[9] and call the Jew into the court.

SALERIO

He is ready at the door. He comes, my lord.

Enter SHYLOCK.

DUKE

Make room, and let him stand before our[10] face.
Shylock, the world thinks—and I think so too—
That thou but lead'st this fashion of thy malice
To the last hour of act, and then 'tis thought
Thou'lt show thy mercy and remorse more strange
Than is thy strange apparent cruelty,[11]
And where thou now exacts the penalty—
Which is a pound of this poor merchant's flesh—

1. *adversary:* enemy
2. *dram:* trace
3. *hath ta'en ... course:* has made a great effort to soften Shylock's harsh course of action
4. *obdurate:* stubborn
5. *can carry ... reach:* can save me from his malice/spite
6. *armed:* prepared
7. *tyranny:* cruelty
8. *My patience ... his:* I am prepared to endure his cruelty patiently.
9. *Go one:* Someone go
10. *our:* my

PLOT POINT

The Duke gives Shylock the opportunity to show mercy to Antonio, claiming that even the most hard-hearted people couldn't help but feel sorry for Antonio's misfortune.

11. *Shylock, ...cruelty:* Everybody thinks (and I think so too) that you will keep up this pretence of malice until the last minute and then you will do something even more extraordinary by showing mercy and compassion.

Thou wilt not only loose the forfeiture,[12]
But, touched with human gentleness and love,
Forgive a moiety[13] of the principal,[14]
Glancing an eye of pity on his losses,
That have of late so huddled[15] on his back
Enough to press a royal merchant down
And pluck commiseration of his state
From brassy bosoms and rough hearts of flint,[16]
From stubborn Turks and Tartars[17] never trained
To offices of tender courtesy.[18]
We all expect a gentle answer, Jew.

SHYLOCK

I have possessed[19] your grace of what I purpose,
And by our holy Sabbath have I sworn
To have the due and forfeit[20] of my bond.
If you deny it, let the danger[21] light
Upon your charter[22] and your city's freedom.[23]
You'll ask me why I rather choose to have
A weight of carrion flesh[24] than to receive
Three thousand ducats. I'll not answer that,
But say it is my humour.[25] Is it answered?[26]
What if my house be troubled with a rat,
And I be pleased to give ten thousand ducats
To have it baned?[27] What, are you answered yet?
Some men there are love not a gaping pig,[28]
Some that are mad if they behold a cat,
And others, when the bagpipe sings i'th' nose,[29]
Cannot contain their urine; for affection,[30]
Mistress of passion, sways it to the mood
Of what it likes or loathes.[31] Now for your answer:
As there is no firm reason to be rendered
Why he[32] cannot abide a gaping pig,
Why he[33] a harmless necessary cat,
Why he[34] a woollen bagpipe, but of force
Must yield to such inevitable shame
As to offend himself being offended,[35]
So can I give no reason, nor I will not,
More than a lodged[36] hate and a certain loathing[37]
I bear Antonio, that I follow thus
A losing suit[38] against him. Are you answered?

12. *loose the forfeiture:* give up the penalty
13. *moiety:* portion
14. *principal:* original sum of money borrowed
15. *huddled:* piled
16. *pluck commiseration ... flint:* draw pity from the most notoriously hard-hearted people
17. *stubborn Turks and Tartars:* *Turks and Tartars were considered heathens.*
18. *never trained ... courtesy:* unfamiliar with such acts of compassion or tenderness

PLOT POINT

Shylock is determined to stick to the bond, claiming that denying his rights would bring the city of Venice into disrepute.

19. *possessed:* informed
20. *forfeit:* penalty which is due
21. *danger:* damage
22. *charter:* *a city's rights and privileges*
23. *If you ... freedom:* If you deny me my bond the rights and freedom of the city could be endangered.
24. *carrion flesh:* dead meat
25. *humour:* mood
26. *Is it answered?:* Does that answer your question?
27. *baned:* poisoned
28. *gaping pig:* roasted hog/pig
29. *sings ... nose:* releases its nasal sound
30. *affection:* our impulses
31. *for affection ... loathes:* We all have things that we like or dislike. *(Our impulses make us like or dislike something according to our mood.)*
32. *he:* one man
33. *he:* another man
34. *he:* another yet
35. *Must yield ... offended:* He can't help offending others because he himself has been offended
36. *lodged:* deep
37. *a certain loathing:* a particular hatred
38. *losing suit:* unprofitable case

BASSANIO

This is no answer, thou unfeeling man,
To excuse the current of thy cruelty.[39]

39. *the current of thy cruelty:* cruel feelings running through you

SHYLOCK

I am not bound[40] to please thee with my answers.

40. *bound:* obliged

BASSANIO

Do all men kill the things they do not love?

SHYLOCK

Hates any man the thing he would not kill?[41]

41. *Hates any ... kill?:* What man wouldn't kill the thing he hates?

PLOT POINT

Shylock is insisting on his bond. His justification is simply that he feels like it. He cites examples of unusual things that annoy people, such as seeing a hog roasting, a cat or the noise of the bagpipes. According to Shylock, there is no accounting for people's moods or impulses. He says he has no other reason to insist on his bond, only his deep hatred for Antonio.

BASSANIO

Every offence is not a hate at first.[42]

SHYLOCK

What, wouldst thou have a serpent sting thee twice?

ANTONIO

I pray you think you question with the Jew.[43]
You may as well go stand upon the beach
And bid the main flood bate his usual height;[44]
You may as well use question with the wolf
Why he hath made the ewe bleat for the lamb;[45]
You may as well forbid the mountain pines
To wag[46] their high tops and to make no noise
When they are fretten[47] with the gusts of heaven,
You may as well do anything most hard
As seek to soften that—than which what's harder?—
His Jewish heart. Therefore, I do beseech you,[48]
Make no more offers, use no farther means,
But with all brief and plain conveniency[49]
Let me have judgement and the Jew his will.

BASSANIO

[*to SHYLOCK*] For thy three thousand ducats here is six.

SHYLOCK

If every ducat in six thousand ducats
Were in six parts, and every part a ducat,
I would not draw[50] them. I would have my bond.

DUKE

How shalt thou hope for mercy, rend'ring[51] none?[52]

SHYLOCK

What judgement shall I dread, doing no wrong?
You have among you many a purchased slave,
Which, like your asses and your dogs and mules,
You use in abject[53] and in slavish parts[54]
Because you bought them. Shall I say to you,
'Let them be free, marry them to your heirs?
Why sweat they under burdens?[55] Let their beds

42. *Every offence ... first:* Not all insults cause hatred at first.

SPOTLIGHT ON ... IMAGERY

Antonio's Use of Imagery: Antonio says that there is no point arguing with Shylock. He claims that you may as well attempt impossible things as try to get Shylock to relent.

P Turn to **page 63** of your portfolio to complete the tasks on Antonio's use of imagery.

43. *I pray ... Jew:* Please remember that you are arguing with the Jew.
44. *bid the ... height:* ask the high tide to reduce its usual height
45. *as well ... lamb:* or ask the wolf why it made the mother sheep cry at the loss of her lamb
46. *wag:* sway
47. *fretten:* disturbed/blown about
48. *I do beseech you:* I beg you
49. *brief and plain conveniency:* speed and efficiency
50. *draw:* take
51. *rend'ring:* showing/giving
52. *How shalt ... none?:* How can you hope for mercy for yourself when you show none?
53. *abject:* awful
54. *parts:* roles
55. *Why sweat ... burdens?:* Why are they working so hard?

Be made as soft as yours, and let their palates
Be seasoned with such viands?'[56] You will answer
'The slaves are ours.' So do I answer you.
The pound of flesh which I demand of him
Is dearly bought. 'Tis mine and I will have it.
If you deny me, fie[57] upon your law:
There is no force in the decrees of Venice.[58]
I stand for judgement. Answer: shall I have it?

DUKE

Upon my power I may dismiss this court[59]
Unless Bellario, a learnèd doctor
Whom I have sent for to determine[60] this,
Come here today.

SALERIO

My lord, here stays without[61]
A messenger with letters from the doctor,
New come[62] from Padua.

DUKE

Bring us the letters. Call the messenger.

BASSANIO

Good cheer, Antonio. What, man, courage yet!
The Jew shall have my flesh, blood, bones and all
Ere[63] thou shalt lose for me one drop of blood.

ANTONIO

I am a tainted wether of the flock,
Meetest for death.[64] The weakest kind of fruit
Drops earliest to the ground; and so let me.
You cannot better be employed, Bassanio,
Than to live still and write mine epitaph.[65]

Enter NERISSA (disguised as a lawyer's clerk).

DUKE

Came you from Padua, from Bellario?

56. *let their ... viands?:* let them eat the same food as you eat

57. *fie:* shame

58. *There is ... Venice:* There is no power in the laws of Venice.

59. *Upon my ... court:* I have the power to dismiss this court.

60. *determine:* decide

61. *stays without:* waits outside

62. *New come:* Who has just arrived

63. *Ere:* Before

64. *I am ... death:* I am the weak ram of the flock most suitable for slaughter.

65. *You cannot ... epitaph:* There is no better use for you, Bassanio, than to live on and remember me after I'm dead. *An epitaph is a short text, usually on a headstone, about someone who has died.*

CHARACTER NOTE

What is your opinion of Antonio? Consider the two images he gives of himself. Do you feel sorry for him, or do you think that he is a little self-pitying?

NERISSA

From both, my lord. [*Presenting letter.*] Bellario greets your grace.

BASSANIO

Why dost thou whet thy knife so earnestly?[66]

66. *Why dost ... earnestly?:* Why are you sharpening your knife so eagerly?

SHYLOCK

To cut the forfeiture from that bankrupt there.

GRATIANO

Not on thy sole[67] but on thy soul, harsh Jew,
Thou mak'st thy knife keen.[68] But no metal can,
No, not the hangman's axe, bear half the keenness
Of thy sharp envy.[69] Can no prayers pierce thee?

67. *Not on thy sole:* *Shylock is sharpening the knife on the sole of his shoe.*
68. *keen:* sharp
69. *envy:* malice/spite

SHYLOCK

No, none that thou hast wit[70] enough to make.

70. *wit:* intelligence

GRATIANO

O, be thou damned, inexecrable[71] dog,
And for thy life[72] let justice be accused!
Thou almost mak'st me waver in my faith

71. *inexecrable:* hateful
72. *And for thy life:* And for allowing you to live

73. *Pythagoras: Pythagoras was a Greek philosopher who believed that the soul was immortal and could pass into the bodies of different animals after death.*

74. *trunks:* bodies
75. *currish:* dog-like/bad-tempered

76. *gallows:* the place where people were hanged
77. *fell:* evil
78. *unhallowed dam:* unholy mother

79. *Infused:* Implanted
80. *Thy currish ... thee:* Your soul was once the soul of a wolf hanged for killing a human being which entered your body before you were born. *Elizabethans put animals on trial and hanged animals that were convicted of committing crimes!*

81. *Till thou ... loud:* Unless your words can invalidate this contract, you are wasting your breath shouting at me.

82. *Repair thy ... ruin:* Be quiet or you will do some permanent damage to your mind.

83. *He attendeth ... by:* He is waiting nearby.

PLOT POINT

The young doctor is Portia in disguise as Doctor Balthasar coming to assist the court.

84. *conduct:* escort

85. *in loving visitation:* having a friendly visit

86. *cause in controversy:* matter in dispute

87. *turned o'er:* perused/read

88. *He is ... opinion:* He has been given my opinion on the case.
89. *bettered with:* enhanced by
90. *the greatness ... commend:* the greatness of which I cannot recommend highly enough
91. *importunity:* request
92. *comes with him ... stead:* In answer to your request, I have sent Balthasar as my replacement.

To hold opinion with Pythagoras[73]
That souls of animals infuse themselves
Into the trunks[74] of men. Thy currish[75] spirit
Governed a wolf, who, hanged for human slaughter,
Even from the gallows[76] did his fell[77] soul fleet,
And, whilst thou lay'st in thy unhallowed dam,[78]
Infused[79] itself in thee;[80] for thy desires
Are wolvish, bloody, starved and ravenous.

SHYLOCK

Till thou canst rail the seal from off my bond
Thou but offend'st thy lungs to speak so loud.[81]
Repair thy wit, good youth, or it will fall
To cureless ruin.[82] I stand here for law.

DUKE

This letter from Bellario doth commend
A young and learnèd doctor to our court.
Where is he?

NERISSA

He attendeth here hard by,[83]
To know your answer, whether you'll admit him.

DUKE

With all my heart. Some three or four of you
Go give him courteous conduct[84] to this place.
Meantime the court shall hear Bellario's letter.
[*Reads.*]

'Your grace shall understand that at the receipt of your letter I am very sick, but in the instant that your messenger came, in loving visitation[85] was with me a young doctor of Rome; his name is Balthasar. I acquainted him with the cause in controversy[86] between the Jew and Antonio the merchant. We turned o'er[87] many books together. He is furnished with my opinion[88] which, bettered with[89] his own learning—the greatness whereof I cannot enough commend[90]—comes with him at my importunity[91] to fill up your grace's request in my stead.[92] I beseech you let his lack of years be no impediment to let him lack a reverend estimation, for I never knew so young a body with so old a head.[93] I leave him to your gracious acceptance, whose trial shall better publish his commendation.'[94]

93. *I beseech ... head:* Please don't underestimate him or show him less respect because of his youth as I never saw someone so young to be so wise.

94. *whose trial ... commendation:* he will prove himself performing his role

DUKE

You hear the learn'd Bellario, what he writes;
And here, I take it, is the doctor come.

Enter PORTIA (disguised as DOCTOR BALTHASAR, followed by official).

Give me your hand. Come you from old Bellario?

PORTIA

I did, my lord.

DUKE

You are welcome. Take your place.
Are you acquainted with the difference
That holds this present question in the court?[95]

95. *Are you ... court?:* Are you familiar with the dispute that is being tried in the court?

PORTIA

I am informèd throughly[96] of the cause.[97]
Which is the merchant here, and which the Jew?

96. *throughly:* thoroughly
97. *cause:* case

DUKE

Antonio and old Shylock, both stand forth.

PORTIA

Is your name Shylock?

SHYLOCK

Shylock is my name.

PORTIA

Of a strange nature is the suit you follow,
Yet in such rule that the Venetian law
Cannot impugn you as you do proceed.[98]

98. *Of a strange ... proceed:* Even though your case is unusual, Venetian law cannot stop you from proceeding with it.

[*to ANTONIO*] You stand within his danger, do you not?

ANTONIO

Ay, so he says.

PORTIA

Do you confess the bond?[99]

ANTONIO

I do.

PORTIA

Then must the Jew be merciful.

SHYLOCK

On what compulsion must I?[100] Tell me that.

PORTIA

The quality of mercy is not strained.[101]
It droppeth as the gentle rain from heaven
Upon the place beneath.[102] It is twice blest;
It blesseth him that gives and him that takes.[103]
'Tis mightiest in the mightiest.[104] It becomes
The thronèd monarch better than his crown.[105]
His sceptre shows the force of temporal power,
The attribute to awe and majesty,
Wherein doth sit the dread and fear of kings;[106]
But mercy is above this sceptred sway.[107]
It is enthronèd in the hearts of kings;
It is an attribute to God himself,[108]
And earthly power doth then show likest God's
When mercy seasons justice.[109] Therefore, Jew,
Though justice be thy plea, consider this:
That in the course of justice none of us
Should[110] see salvation. We do pray for mercy,
And that same prayer doth teach us all to render[111]
The deeds of mercy. I have spoke thus much
To mitigate the justice of thy plea,[112]
Which if thou follow, this strict court of Venice
Must needs give sentence 'gainst the merchant there.

99. *Do you ... bond?:* Do you acknowledge the contract/agreement?

100. *On what ... I?:* Who can make me *(show mercy)*?

101. *strained:* forced *No one can force a person to show mercy.*

102. *It droppeth ... beneath:* It falls naturally, like rain from heaven.
103. *It is ... takes:* It has a double advantage, as it blesses the person who gives it as well as the person who receives it.
104. *'Tis mightiest in the mightiest:* Mercy is strongest when it is shown by powerful people.
105. *It becomes ... crown:* Mercy suits a king better than his own crown.

106. *His sceptre ... kings:* The king's sceptre is a symbol of his earthly power and inspires awe and fear from subjects.
107. *But mercy ... sway:* Mercy is higher than this earthly power.

108. *It is ... himself:* It is a quality of God himself.

109. *And earthly ... justice:* And earthly power then resembles divine power when mercy is a feature of justice.
110. *Should:* Would
111. *render:* show
112. *I have ... plea:* I have spoken this to convince you to soften your demand for justice

SPOTLIGHT ON ...

PORTIA'S MONOLOGUE

In her monologue, Portia argues that mercy is a noble attribute that benefits everyone, the giver as well as the receiver. It is a divine quality that elevates a king and is more powerful than symbols of kingship such as the crown or sceptre.

SHYLOCK

My deeds upon my head![113] I crave the law,
The penalty and forfeit of my bond.

PORTIA

Is he not able to discharge[114] the money?

BASSANIO

Yes, here I tender[115] it for him in the court,
Yea, twice the sum. If that will not suffice,
I will be bound to pay it ten times o'er
On forfeit of my hands, my head, my heart.
If this will not suffice, it must appear
That malice bears down truth.[116] And I beseech you,
Wrest once the law to your authority.[117]
To do a great right, do a little wrong,
And curb this cruel devil of his will.[118]

PORTIA

It must not be. There is no power in Venice
Can alter a decree establishèd.[119]
'Twill be recorded for a precedent,
And many an error by the same example
Will rush into the state. It cannot be.[120]

SHYLOCK

A Daniel[121] come to judgement, yea, a Daniel!
O wise young judge, how I do honour thee!

PORTIA

I pray you let me look upon the bond.

SHYLOCK

Here 'tis, most reverend doctor, here it is.

PORTIA

Shylock, there's thrice[122] thy money offered thee.

SHYLOCK

An oath, an oath, I have an oath in heaven.
Shall I lay perjury upon my soul?[123]
No, not for Venice.

113. *My deeds ... head!:* I take full responsibility for my actions!

114. *discharge:* pay

115. *tender:* offer

116. *If this ... truth:* If that's not enough, then it appears that malice triumphs over justice.

117. *And I ... authority:* I beg you to use your power to bend the law.

118. *And curb ... will:* And prevent this cruel devil getting his way.

PLOT POINT

Shylock is now being offered three times the original amount of the loan. How much is this? There appears to be an inconsistency here with the amount Bassanio has just offered in line 208. Can you give an explanation as to why the amount being offered by Portia is three times the original amount?

119. *a decree establishèd:* an established law

120. *It must ... be: Portia is saying that she cannot make an exception in this case as it will set a bad precedent/example for the future.*

121. *Daniel: Daniel was a wise young judge in the Bible.*

122. *thrice:* three times

LOOKING AT LANGUAGE

Repetition: Shylock repeats the word 'oath' three times in line 226. What effect do you think this has?

123. *An oath, ... soul?: As Shylock took an oath in drawing up the bond, he would be committing perjury (lying) if he backs down now.*

124. *tenor:* terms of the bond

125. *exposition:* explanation

126. *There is ... me:* Nothing anyone can say will persuade me to change my mind.

127. *bosom:* chest

128. *For the ... bond:* The law fully supports the penalty which is due.

PORTIA

Why, this bond is forfeit,
And lawfully by this the Jew may claim
A pound of flesh, to be by him cut off
Nearest the merchant's heart. [*to SHYLOCK*] Be merciful.
Take thrice thy money. Bid me tear the bond.

SHYLOCK

When it is paid according to the tenor.[124]
It doth appear you are a worthy judge.
You know the law. Your exposition[125]
Hath been most sound. I charge you by the law
Whereof you are a well-deserving pillar,
Proceed to judgement. By my soul I swear
There is no power in the tongue of man
To alter me.[126] I stay here on my bond.

ANTONIO

Most heartily I do beseech the court
To give the judgement.

PORTIA

Why then, thus it is:
You must prepare your bosom[127] for his knife—

SHYLOCK

O noble judge, O excellent young man!

PORTIA

For the intent and purpose of the law
Hath full relation to the penalty
Which here appeareth due upon the bond.[128]

SHYLOCK

'Tis very true. O wise and upright judge!
How much more elder art thou than thy looks!

PORTIA

Therefore lay bare your bosom.

SHYLOCK

Ay, his breast.
So says the bond, doth it not, noble judge?
'Nearest his heart'—those are the very words.

PORTIA

It is so. Are there balance[129] here to weigh
The flesh?

SHYLOCK

I have them ready.

PORTIA

Have by some surgeon, Shylock, on your charge,
To stop his wounds, lest he do bleed to death.[130]

SHYLOCK

Is it so nominated[131] in the bond?

129. *balance:* weighing scales

130. *Have by ... death:* Have a doctor on hand at your own expense to stop the blood in case he bleeds to death.

131. *nominated:* stated

CHARACTER NOTE

Shylock questions if he is obliged by law to have a doctor ready to help Antonio in case he bleeds to death. What does this reveal about Shylock? How might the audience react to this statement by Shylock?

PORTIA

It is not so expressed, but what of that?
'Twere good you do so much for charity.

SHYLOCK

I cannot find it. 'Tis not in the bond.[132]

PORTIA

You, merchant, have you anything to say?

ANTONIO

But little. I am armed and well prepared.
Give me your hand, Bassanio; fare you well.
Grieve not that I am fall'n to this for you,
For herein Fortune shows herself more kind
Than is her custom; it is still her use
To let the wretched man outlive his wealth,
To view with hollow eye and wrinkled brow
An age of poverty,[133] from which ling'ring penance
Of such misery doth she cut me off.
Commend me to your honourable wife.
Tell her the process[134] of Antonio's end.
Say how I loved you, speak me fair[135] in death,
And when the tale is told, bid her be judge
Whether Bassanio had not once a love.
Repent but you that[136] you shall lose your friend,
And he repents not[137] that he pays your debt;
For if the Jew do cut but deep enough,
I'll pay it instantly[138] with all my heart.[139]

BASSANIO

Antonio, I am married to a wife
Which is as dear to me as life itself,
But life itself, my wife, and all the world
Are not with me esteemed above thy life.
I would lose all, ay, sacrifice them all
Here to this devil, to deliver[140] you.

PORTIA

Your wife would give you little thanks for that
If she were by to hear you make the offer.

132. ***'Tis not ... bond:*** *Shylock is sticking rigidly to the exact terms of the bond.*

133. ***Grieve not ... poverty:*** Don't be sad Bassanio that this has happened to me because of you. This time, Fortune is showing kindness as the unhappy man would normally live on in poverty.

134. ***process:*** tale

135. ***speak me fair:*** speak well of me

LOOKING AT LANGUAGE

Irony: Re-read line 274. How might this line spoken by Antonio be considered ironic?

136. ***Repent but you that:*** Be sad only because

137. ***he repents not:*** he doesn't regret

138. ***instantly:*** immediately

139. ***with all my heart:*** *Antonio is literally going to the pay the debt 'with all his heart' as the pound of flesh is to be taken from close to his heart.*

SPOTLIGHT ON ...

DRAMATIC IRONY

Dramatic irony occurs when the audience or characters on stage know something that other characters do not. Can you find at least two examples of dramatic irony in this scene?

140. ***deliver:*** save

GRATIANO

I have a wife who, I protest, I love.
I would[141] she were in heaven so she could
Entreat[142] some power to change this currish[143] Jew.

141. *I would:* I wish that

142. *Entreat:* Ask

143. *currish:* dog-like/bad-tempered

NERISSA

'Tis well you offer it behind her back;
The wish would make else an unquiet house.

SHYLOCK

These be the Christian husbands. I have a daughter;
Would any of the stock of Barrabas[144]
Had been her husband rather than a Christian!
We trifle time:[145] I pray thee pursue sentence.

144. *Barrabas:* a descendant of Barrabas *Barrabas was a Jewish thief who Pontius Pilate pardoned instead of Jesus.*

145. *We trifle time:* We are wasting time

PORTIA

A pound of that same merchant's flesh is thine.[146]
The court awards it, and the law doth give it.

146. *thine:* yours

SHYLOCK

Most rightful judge!

PLOT POINT

Shylock is thrilled that the wise judge is following the bond to the letter of the law.

PORTIA

And you must cut this flesh from off his breast.
The law allows it, and the court awards it.

SHYLOCK

Most learnèd judge! A sentence: come, prepare!

147. *Tarry:* Wait

148. *jot:* drop

149. *expressly:* specifically

PLOT POINT

Portia (as Doctor Balthasar) continues to take the language of the bond literally. In this case, she has found a loophole which offers a glimmer of hope that Antonio will be spared. The 'pound of flesh' must be taken without spilling a drop of blood. If Shylock spills one drop of Antonio's blood, he must forfeit everything he owns to the state of Venice.

150. *confiscate unto:* will be confiscated (taken) by

PORTIA

Tarry[147] a little. There is something else.
This bond doth give thee here no jot[148] of blood.
The words expressly[149] are 'a pound of flesh'.
Take then thy bond. Take thou thy pound of flesh,
But in the cutting it, if thou dost shed
One drop of Christian blood, thy lands and goods
Are by the laws of Venice confiscate
Unto[150] the state of Venice.

GRATIANO

O upright judge!
Mark, Jew! O learnèd judge!

SHYLOCK

Is that the law?

151. *act:* the written legal document that contains the law

152. *urgest:* demand

PORTIA

Thyself shalt see the act;[151]
For as thou urgest[152] justice, be assured
Thou shalt have justice more than thou desir'st.

GRATIANO

O learnèd judge! Mark, Jew—a learnèd judge!

SHYLOCK

I take this offer, then. Pay the bond thrice,
And let the Christian go.

BASSANIO

Here is the money.

153. *Soft:* Hold on

PLOT POINT

Shylock is now willing to take three times the amount of the original loan, but Portia insists he should only get his original amount.

PORTIA

Soft,[153] the Jew shall have all justice. Soft, no haste.
He shall have nothing but the penalty.

GRATIANO

O Jew, an upright judge, a learnèd judge!

PORTIA

Therefore prepare thee to cut off the flesh.
Shed thou no blood, nor cut thou less nor more
But just a pound of flesh. If thou tak'st more
Or less than a just pound, be it but so much
As makes it light or heavy in the substance
Or the division of the twentieth part
Of one poor scruple[154]—nay, if the scale do turn
But in the estimation of a hair,[155]
Thou diest, and all thy goods are confiscate.[156]

GRATIANO

A second Daniel, a Daniel, Jew!
Now, infidel, I have you on the hip.[157]

PORTIA

Why doth the Jew pause? Take thy forfeiture.[158]

SHYLOCK

Give me my principal,[159] and let me go.

BASSANIO

I have it ready for thee. Here it is.

PORTIA

He hath refused it in the open court.[160]
He shall have merely justice and his bond.

GRATIANO

A Daniel, still say I, a second Daniel!
I thank thee, Jew, for teaching me that word.

SHYLOCK

Shall I not have barely my principal?

PORTIA

Thou shalt have nothing but the forfeiture
To be so taken at thy peril, Jew.

SHYLOCK

Why then, the devil give him good of it![161]
I'll stay no longer question.

154. *the division ... scruple:* even if it's just a tiny fraction

155. *in the estimation of a hair:* by a hair's breadth

156. *confiscate:* seized/taken

157. *Now, ... hip:* We have you now, unbeliever!

158. *forfeiture:* penalty

159. *principal:* original sum of the loan

PLOT POINT

Notice how Shylock simply wants his original sum now. However, Portia informs him that as he refused the original amount in open court, he can now only take his 'pound of flesh', but must do so at his own risk.

160. *open court:* publicly

LOOKING AT LANGUAGE

What do you notice about Gratiano's use of language here? Look at lines 316, 321 and 338.

161. *the devil ... it!:* He's welcome to it!

PORTIA

Tarry, Jew.
The law hath yet another hold on you.
It is enacted[162] in the laws of Venice,
If it be proved against an alien[163]
That by direct or indirect attempts
He seek the life of any citizen,
The party 'gainst the which he doth contrive[164]
Shall seize one half his goods; the other half
Comes to the privy coffer[165] of the state,
And the offender's life lies in the mercy
Of the Duke only, 'gainst all other voice[166]—
In which predicament I say thou stand'st,
For it appears by manifest proceeding[167]
That indirectly and directly too,
Thou hast contrived[168] against the very life
Of the defendant, and thou hast incurred
The danger formerly by me rehearsed.[169]
Down,[170] therefore, and beg mercy of the Duke.

GRATIANO

Beg that thou mayst have leave to hang thyself—
And yet, thy wealth being forfeit to the state,
Thou hast not left the value of a cord.[171]
Therefore thou must be hanged at the state's charge.[172]

DUKE

That thou shalt see the difference of our spirit,
I pardon thee thy life before thou ask it.
For half thy wealth, it is Antonio's.
The other half comes to the general[173] state,
Which humbleness may drive unto a fine.[174]

PORTIA

Ay, for the state, not for Antonio.[175]

SHYLOCK

Nay, take my life and all, pardon not that.
You take my house when you do take the prop
That doth sustain my house;[176] you take my life
When you do take the means whereby I live.

162. *enacted:* stated
163. *alien:* foreigner
164. *The party ... contrive:* The person whom he has plotted against
165. *privy coffer:* the Duke's personal fortune
166. *'gainst all other voice:* without appeal
167. *For it ... proceeding:* it appears by all your public actions
168. *contrived:* plotted
169. *hast incurred ... rehearsed:* made yourself open to the penalty that I previously described
170. *Down:* Kneel down

PLOT POINT

Portia does not allow Shylock to leave at this point – she wants to punish him further. She claims that the demand for a pound of flesh is tantamount to plotting to kill a Venetian citizen, which carries a severe penalty: the 'victim', in this case Antonio, must receive half of the perpetrator's (Shylock's) goods and the other half must be surrendered to the Duke of Venice. The Duke also has the power to sentence the perpetrator to death.

171. *Thou hast ... cord:* You don't even have the price of a rope left.
172. *charge:* expense

PLOT POINT

The Duke himself is now showing that all-important 'quality of mercy' that Portia spoke about earlier and so pardons Shylock's life before he is asked to.

173. *general:* whole
174. *Which humbleness ... fine:* *The Duke is saying that he will act with humility and will not take half of Shylock's goods, but rather impose a fine instead.*
175. *Ay, ... Antonio:* *Portia is saying that the Duke may impose a fine instead of taking the state's share, but Antonio will still get his half of Shylock's wealth.*

SPOTLIGHT ON ... SHYLOCK

Do you feel any sympathy for Shylock at this point? How might you advise the actor playing Shylock to deliver lines 372–375? Think about the tone of voice the actor should use here.

176. *You take ... house:* You destroy my house when you take my means of supporting it *(i.e. his money)*.

PORTIA

What mercy can you render[177] him, Antonio?

GRATIANO

A halter gratis.[178] Nothing else, for God's sake.

ANTONIO

So please my lord the Duke and all the court
To quit the fine for one half of his goods,[179]
I am content, so he will let me have
The other half in use,[180] to render it,
Upon his death, unto the gentleman
That lately stole his daughter.[181]
Two things provided more: that for this favour
He presently[182] become a Christian;
The other, that he do record a gift,
Here in the court of all he dies possessed
Unto his son Lorenzo and his daughter.[183]

DUKE

He shall do this, or else I do recant[184]
The pardon that I late[185] pronouncèd here.

PORTIA

Art thou contented, Jew? What dost thou say?

SHYLOCK

I am content.

PORTIA

Clerk, draw a deed of gift.

SHYLOCK

I pray you give me leave to go from hence.[186]
I am not well. Send the deed after me,
And I will sign it.

DUKE

Get thee gone, but do it.

177. *render:* show

178. *A halter gratis:* A hangman's rope for free.

179. *So please ... goods:* If you, noble Duke, will cancel the fine for one half of Shylock's goods

180. *The other half in use:* to invest the other half

181. *unto the ... daughter:* *Antonio is talking about Lorenzo (who married Shylock's daughter Jessica).*

182. *presently:* immediately

PLOT POINT

Antonio asks for the fine to be dropped. He stipulates that Lorenzo should inherit his half of Shylock's fortune and requests that Shylock become a Christian and sign a deed in court leaving all of his wealth to Jessica and Lorenzo after his death. Shylock must accept, or the Duke will reverse his pardon.

183. *The other, ... daughter:* *Antonio's second request is that Shylock sign a deed to leave everything he owns to Lorenzo and Jessica when he dies.*

184. *recant:* withdraw/take back

185. *late:* just

186. *hence:* here

GRATIANO

In christening shalt thou have two godfathers:
Had I been judge, thou shouldst have had ten more,
To bring thee to the gallows, not the font.[187]

Exit SHYLOCK.

DUKE

Sir, I entreat[188] you home with me to dinner.

PORTIA

I humbly do desire your grace of pardon.
I must away[189] this night toward Padua,
And it is meet I presently set forth.[190]

DUKE

I am sorry that your leisure serves you not.[191]
Antonio, gratify this gentleman,
For in my mind you are much bound[192] to him.

Exit DUKE and his train.

BASSANIO

Most worthy gentleman, I and my friend
Have by your wisdom been this day acquitted
Of grievous penalties,[193] in lieu whereof
Three thousand ducats due unto the Jew
We freely cope your courteous pains withal.[194]

ANTONIO

And stand indebted over and above
In love and service to you evermore.

PORTIA

He is well paid that is well satisfied,
And I, delivering[195] you, am satisfied,
And therein do account myself well paid.
My mind was never yet more mercenary.[196]
I pray you know me when we meet again.
I wish you well; and so I take my leave.

187. *Had I ... front: Gratiano is saying that if he were the judge, there would have been a full jury (of twelve men) who would condemn Shylock to death by hanging ('the gallows') rather than allow him to become a Christian ('the [baptismal] font').*

188. *entreat:* invite

189. *away:* leave

190. *it is ... forth:* I must leave immediately.

191. *I am ... not:* I am sorry that you don't have the time.

192. *bound:* obliged

193. *Most worthy ... penalties:* Your wisdom has released us from a deadly penalty.

194. *in lieu ... withal:* and as a payment for your great efforts we offer you 3,000 ducats

195. *delivering:* saving/releasing

196. *My mind ... mercenary:* I have never been interested in money.

BASSANIO

Dear sir, of force I must attempt you further.[197]
Take some remembrance[198] of us as a tribute,
Not as a fee. Grant me two things, I pray you:
Not to deny me, and to pardon me.[199]

PORTIA

You press me far, and therefore I will yield.[200]
[*to ANTONIO*] Give me your gloves,
I'll wear them for your sake.
[*to BASSANIO*] And, for your love,
I'll take this ring from you.
Do not draw back your hand. I'll take no more,
And you in love shall not deny me this.

BASSANIO

This ring, good sir? Alas, it is a trifle.[201]
I will not shame myself to give you this.

PORTIA

I will have nothing else, but only this;
And now methinks I have a mind to it.[202]

BASSANIO

There's more depends on this[203] than on the value.
The dearest ring in Venice will I give you,
And find it out by proclamation,[204]
Only for this, I pray you pardon me.

PORTIA

I see, sir, you are liberal in offers.
You taught me first to beg, and now methinks
You teach me how a beggar should be answered.[205]

BASSANIO

Good sir, this ring was given me by my wife,
And when she put it on she made me vow
That I should neither sell, nor give, nor lose it.

197. *I must attempt you further:* I must insist

198. *remembrance:* token of remembrance

199. *pardon me:* pardon my insistence

200. *You press ... yield:* You are very insistent, so I will give in.

201. *Alas, ... trifle:* it's just a trinket/it's nothing

202. *And now ... it:* Now I think I really want it.

203. *There's more ... this:* There's more involved here than just value.

204. *proclamation:* public announcement

205. *I see, ... answered:* You are very generous in your offers! First you make me ask for something, like a beggar. Then you treat me like a beggar by refusing me.

206. *That 'scuse ... gifts:* That's an excuse many men use to avoid giving gifts.
207. *An if:* If
208. *hold out enemy:* stay angry with you

PORTIA

That 'scuse serves many men to save their gifts.[206]
An if[207] your wife be not a madwoman,
And know how well I have deserved this ring,
She would not hold out enemy[208] for ever
For giving it to me. Well, peace be with you!

Exeunt PORTIA and NERISSA.

209. *commandement:* instructions

ANTONIO

My lord Bassanio, let him have the ring.
Let his deservings and my love withal
Be valued 'gainst your wife's commandement.[209]

BASSANIO

Go, Gratiano, run and overtake him.
Give him the ring, and bring him, if thou canst,
Unto Antonio's house. Away, make haste.

Exit GRATIANO.

210. *thither:* go there

Come, you and I will thither[210] presently,
And in the morning early will we both
Fly toward Belmont. Come, Antonio.

Exeunt.

OVERVIEW OF ACT 4, SCENE 1

KEY SCENE – THE TRIAL SCENE

This is the **climax** of the bond theme. Shylock is demanding justice in the court which is being **presided over** (conducted) by the Duke and Portia, disguised as a lawyer called 'Balthasar'. Shylock's reluctance to take anything other than the penalty of the pound of flesh means that Antonio's life now hangs in the balance.

Part 1 (lines 1–166) – The Duke pleads with Shylock to show mercy to Antonio.

- As the action opens on this **dramatic climax scene**, it is clear that the Duke has great sympathy for Antonio:

  Thou art come to answer
  A stony adversary, an inhuman wretch
  Uncapable of pity, void and empty
  From any dram of mercy. (lines 2–5)

- Although the Duke recognises that Shylock is a dangerous and deadly enemy, he is unable to protect Antonio from him. Shylock is demanding his penalty and threatens to discredit the laws of Venice if he does not get it:

  If you deny it, let the danger light
  Upon your charter and your city's freedom. (lines 37–38)

- It is clear that Shylock is motivated by revenge. He despises Antonio intensely and now he has a seemingly valid legal reason to **eliminate** (get rid of) him. When asked by the Duke why he wants Antonio's flesh he replies:

  So can I give no reason, nor I will not,
  More than a lodged hate and a certain loathing
  I bear Antonio, that I follow thus
  A losing suit against him. Are you answered? (lines 58–61)

- This 'lodged hate' and 'loathing' **stems** from the fact that Antonio lends out money interest-free and loses Shylock valuable business. Antonio realises that there is no point arguing any further with Shylock and asks his friends to **desist** (stop):

  You may as well do anything most hard
  As seek to soften that—than which what's harder?—
  His Jewish heart. (lines 77–79)

- Next, Bassanio offers Shylock double the amount of the loan (6,000 ducats). Shylock refuses, saying 'I would have my bond' (line 86).
- The Duke tells Shylock that in order to get mercy, one should show it. However, Shylock simply shrugs this off saying, 'What judgement shall I dread, doing no wrong?' (line 88).
- Shylock claims that many Venetians have 'many a purchased slave' (line 89) whom they mistreat. He argues that if he were to question those people about their slaves, he would be told, 'The slaves are ours' (line 97). Shylock links this idea to the pound of flesh, which he feels belongs to him:

  The pound of flesh which I demand of him
  Is dearly bought. 'Tis mine and I will have it. (lines 98–99)

- The Duke is informed that a messenger has come from Doctor Bellario (a lawyer) and is waiting outside to see him. Bassanio tries to cheer Antonio up and shows true loyalty and friendship when he says:

  Good cheer, Antonio. What, man, courage yet!
  The Jew shall have my flesh, blood, bones and all
  Ere thou shalt lose for me one drop of blood. (lines 110–112)

- Nerissa enters, disguised as a judge's clerk, and gives a letter to the Duke from Doctor Bellario. Nerissa informs the Duke that a 'young and learnèd doctor' (line 143) has come to the court at the recommendation of Doctor Bellario.
- Nerissa gives the Duke a letter from Bellario which details how, due to illness, he is unable to judge the case. He is sending a young doctor called 'Balthasar' to take his place. This letter is an **ingenious** (clever) plan on the part of Portia. The letter recommends 'Balthasar' and **cautions** the Duke about judging 'Balthasar' on his youthful appearance:

  I beseech you let his lack of
  years be no impediment to let him lack a reverend
  estimation, for I never knew so young a body with so
  old a head. (lines 159–162)

This letter of introduction will make Portia's arrival at court much easier.

Part 2 (lines 167–302) – Portia, disguised as a learned doctor of law, leads the court proceedings with the help of Nerissa, disguised as his clerk.

- The audience is wondering what Portia will do to try to help Antonio. Tension is mounting as the trial begins.
- Portia urges Shylock to be merciful. In her famous 'the quality of mercy' speech (lines 182–203), Portia suggests that the quality of being merciful should not be forced or artificial. It should happen naturally, like rain falling from heaven. She **asserts** (claims) that being merciful is a double blessing, as it benefits the person who shows mercy as well as the person who receives it. Portia uses **religious** and **regal** (royal) imagery throughout her speech to highlight the nobility and importance of showing mercy. People who show mercy, she claims, are almost God-like.
- Portia's speech has little or no effect on Shylock. He is more determined than ever to have his bond. Shylock states that he will take responsibility for his own actions:

  My deeds upon my head! I crave the law,
  The penalty and forfeit of my bond. (lines 204–205)

- Bassanio, once again, offers to pay Shylock twice the bond and **implores** (begs) Portia to bend the law in this exceptional case:

  And I beseech you,
  Wrest once the law to your authority.
  To do a great right, do a little wrong,
  And curb this cruel devil of his will. (lines 212–215)

- When Portia **flatly** (firmly) rejects Bassanio's plea, saying it would set a bad example in Venice, Shylock is overjoyed calling her a 'Daniel' (line 221), or very wise judge.
- Portia now offers Shylock **three times** the amount of the bond:

  Be merciful.
  Take thrice thy money. Bid me tear the bond. (lines 231–232)

- Again, Shylock rejects this amount, informing Portia that 'There is no power in the tongue of man to alter [him]' (lines 239–240). Nothing, it seems, can change his mind.

- Antonio is anxious not to **prolong (**draw out) the case and asks Portia to give her judgement. Portia advises that Antonio 'must prepare [his] bosom for [Shylock's] knife' (line 243). Shylock is **elated** that he is going to have his way:

  O noble judge, O excellent young man! (line 244)

- Shylock's reaction to Portia's suggestion to get a doctor for Antonio is very interesting. Shylock's unwillingness to get a doctor, as it is not explicitly stated in the agreement, confirms our suspicion that Shylock doesn't just want his 'pound of flesh'. Shylock wants Antonio dead. If Shylock were simply interested in his 'pound of flesh', he should have no problem extracting it and then seeing to it that Antonio has a doctor nearby so that he does not bleed to death.
- Antonio is resigned to his fate as he says farewell to Bassanio:

  Commend me to your honourable wife.
  Tell her the process of Antonio's end.
  Say how I loved you (lines 271–273)

- This is a **poignant** (tender) moment in the play as we realise that Antonio is about to be sacrificed for his friend's debts. Antonio's passive acceptance of his fate contrasts with Shylock's active **vindictiveness** (bitterness) in the scene.

Part 3 (lines 303–398) – Shylock's fortune changes. There is hope for Antonio.

- Just as Shylock is preparing to take his penalty, Portia asks him to 'Tarry a little' (line 303). Here we see a remarkable change of fortune as Portia finds a **legal loophole** (flaw/glitch in the legal case) which prevents Shylock from taking his pound of flesh. Portia argues that, legally, Shylock is allowed to have the pound of flesh only and no blood must be spilt in the operation of taking the flesh:

  Take thou thy pound of flesh,
  But in the cutting it, if thou dost shed
  One drop of Christian blood, thy lands and goods
  Are by the laws of Venice confiscate
  Unto the state of Venice. (lines 306–310)

- As it is impossible for Shylock to proceed, he begins to back down. However, Portia does not show him mercy, warning him that he 'shalt have justice more than thou desir'st' (line 315).
- Gratiano, who has been teasing and taunting Shylock throughout, takes his opportunity to gloat using the very words that Shylock used:

  A second Daniel, a Daniel, Jew! (line 331)

- Shylock is now willing to take his money, but Portia refuses to give it as Shylock publicly 'refused it in the open court' (line 336).

  He shall have merely justice and his bond. (line 337)

- Just as Shylock is about to leave, Portia reveals that the law still has a 'hold' (line 345) on Shylock. It now emerges that by demanding his penalty Shylock was planning to kill a Venetian citizen and must therefore be punished.
- The Duke displays 'the difference of our spirit' (his Christian spirit) (line 366) by showing mercy to Shylock. He pardons his life and orders one half of Shylock's wealth to be given to Antonio and the other half to the state of Venice. He reduces the portion due to the state of Venice to a fine. However, instead of seeing this as an act of mercy, Shylock sees this as the worst form of punishment:

  you take my life
  When you do take the means whereby I live. (lines 374–375)

- It is now Antonio's turn to display mercy. He asks the Duke to cancel Shylock's fine and says that he will invest his half of Shylock's wealth on behalf of Jessica and Lorenzo. Antonio outlines two more conditions: that Shylock convert to Christianity and that he leave all his possessions to his daughter Jessica and son-in-law Lorenzo when he dies.
- Shylock has no choice but to agree to the terms, uttering a feeble 'I am content' (line 392). What a contrast to the powerful, vindictive character we witnessed at the start of this scene. Antonio's generosity of spirit forms a dramatic contrast with Shylock's lack of compassion in this scene.

Part 4 (lines 399–457) – Nerissa and Portia depart.

- After Shylock leaves, the Duke invites 'Balthasar' (Portia) to dinner, but Portia declines his invitation. Bassanio asks Portia to accept payment for saving Antonio's life. Portia refuses, saying that 'He is well paid that is well satisfied' (line 413), meaning that she is happy with a job well done and needs no further payment. However, Bassanio is very insistent:

  Dear sir, of force I must attempt you further.
  Take some remembrance of us as a tribute (lines 419–420)

- Bassanio soon regrets these words as Portia asks for the ring she gave him as payment. At first Bassanio refuses, telling her that 'more depends on this than on the value' (line 434), but after she leaves Antonio persuades him to part with it:

  Let his deservings and my love withal
  Be valued 'gainst your wife's commandement. (lines 450–451)

- The scene ends with Bassanio asking Gratiano to follow Portia and Nerissa with the ring.

REVIEWING

1. How would you describe Antonio's **mood** at the start of the scene?
2. Whose side is the Duke on? Explain your answer.
3. What reason does Shylock give for insisting on his bond?
4. Why does Antonio tell Bassanio to stop arguing with Shylock?
5. How does Shylock respond to Bassanio's offer of 6,000 ducats?
6. What point is Shylock trying to make by referring to slaves? How does he link this to his own situation?
7. What key information does the letter from Bellario contain?
8. How does the letter help Portia in court?
9. Bassanio asks Portia to 'do a great right, do a little wrong' (to bend the law) in relation to his case. Why does she reject this suggestion?
10. What does Shylock mean when he refers to 'Balthasar' as a 'Daniel'?
11. How does Shylock respond to Portia's offer of **three times** the bond?
12. How does Shylock react when Portia suggests that he has a doctor at the ready for Antonio? What does this tell you about Shylock's true intentions?
13. Portia sees a legal loophole in the contract. What is this loophole?
14. How does Portia respond when Bassanio offers Shylock the original sum of money ('the principal')?
15. Portia claims that Shylock is also guilty of another crime against a Venetian person. What is this crime and what is the usual punishment for this crime?
16. Describe the punishment that Shylock actually receives. Do you think that Shylock deserves the punishment he gets? Explain your answer.
17. In what way do **(a)** the Duke and **(b)** Antonio show mercy to Shylock?
18. Why do you think that Portia asks Bassanio for his ring as payment?

ORAL LANGUAGE

Portia's 'The quality of mercy' Speech P

Pair Activity

Read Portia's 'the quality of mercy' speech (lines 182–203) aloud in pairs, swapping at each semicolon (;) or full stop. Turn to **page 64** of your portfolio to complete the following activities:

(a) Read the speech a second time and note down all the words that have **religious associations** and all words that have **royal associations**. Discuss with your partner what effect this creates.

(b) In pairs, **paraphrase** (summarise) the main points of Portia's speech.

(c) Do you agree with Portia's arguments about **mercy**?

EXPLORING

Director's Notebook – Portia's Costume P

If you were the costume designer of this play, what costume would you design for Portia in this scene? Draw your design and write any costume notes on **page 66** of your portfolio.

REFLECTING

1. Reflect on the Characters' Roles in This Scene P

What role did each of the characters play in the Trial Scene?

Turn to **page 67** of your portfolio to outline:

- The character's **role** (what they did).
- The character's **words** (what they said/key quotes).
- Your **response** to the character.

Character File P

Using the information you have recorded for Question 1 above, update your character files for **(a) Shylock** (**page 137**), **(b) Portia** (**page 129**), **(c) Antonio** (**page 115**), **(d) Bassanio** (**page 121**) and **(e) Gratiano** (**page 138**) for this scene. You may wish to write more for some characters and include extra quotes where possible.

3. My Reflection on Act 4, Scene 1 P

Turn to **page 69** of your portfolio to record your response to the Trial Scene.

PROJECT

Producing and Presenting a Scene P

Group Activity

Imagine that you are one of the directors/producers of *The Merchant of Venice*. You are going to **stage the Trial Scene** to maximise the drama:

- In groups**, design**, **plan and prepare** for how you would produce this scene.
- Try to bring the scene to life as much as possible using **visual and sound effects**.
- You will make an **oral presentation** to the class when you have completed the project. (You could use a **PowerPoint**, **Prezi** (www.prezi.com) or **Popplet** (www.popplet.com) computer presentation if you wish, and/or models/posters to help with your presentation.)
- Each person in the group will be required to speak.

Turn to **pages 70–74** of your portfolio to help you with this task. When you have given your presentation to the class, complete your **reflection** on the project on **page 75** of your portfolio.

ACT 4, SCENE 2

Setting: Venice. A street

In this **scene** you will:

- Discuss the **importance of the rings** in the plot.

Action – What Happens?

In this very short scene, Portia and Nerissa are looking for Shylock's house so that he may sign the deed of gift (which means that after Shylock's death, Lorenzo and Jessica will inherit his wealth). Gratiano catches up with Portia and Nerissa and gives Portia the ring from Bassanio. Nerissa decides that she too will try to trick Gratiano into giving her the ring she gave him.

Useful Words

entreat – request

tarry – wait

Enter PORTIA and NERISSA.

PORTIA

Enquire the Jew's house out, give him this deed,[1]
And let him sign it. We'll away tonight
And be a day before our husbands home.
This deed will be well welcome to Lorenzo.

1. *Enquire ... deed:* *Portia is referring to the deed of gift. The deed of gift was mentioned in the last scene. It was written by Nerissa at Portia's request.*

Enter GRATIANO.

GRATIANO

Fair sir, you are well o'erta'en.[2]
My lord Bassanio upon more advice[3]
Hath sent you here this ring, and doth entreat[4]
Your company at dinner.

2. *Fair sir, ... o'erta'en:* I am delighted that I have caught up with you.
3. *upon more advice:* on further thought/on considering it further
4. *entreat:* request

PORTIA

That cannot be.
His ring I do accept most thankfully,
And so I pray you tell him. Furthermore,
I pray you show my youth old Shylock's house.

GRATIANO

That will I do.

NERISSA

Sir, I would speak with you.
[*aside to PORTIA*] I'll see if I can get my husband's ring
Which I did make him swear to keep for ever.

PORTIA

[*aside to NERISSA*] Thou mayst, I warrant.[5]
We shall have old[6] swearing
That they did give the rings away to men.
But we'll outface them,[7] and outswear them too.
[*aloud*] Away, make haste. Thou know'st where I will tarry.[8]

5. *warrant:* guarantee
6. *old:* lots of
7. *outface them:* stare them down
8. *Thou know'st ... tarry:* You know where I will be waiting.

NERISSA

Come, good sir, will you show me to this house?

Exeunt.

OVERVIEW OF ACT 4, SCENE 2

In this very short scene, Portia and Nerissa are looking for Shylock's house to deliver the deed for him to sign. Gratiano successfully catches up with them, gives Portia the ring from Bassanio and invites her to dinner. Portia declines the invitation to dinner and asks Gratiano for directions to Shylock's house.

Nerissa mischievously plots a way to make Gratiano give her the ring that she gave him. Nerissa and Portia are in a hurry to leave Venice that night so that they will be back in Belmont before their husbands return.

REVIEWING

1. Why are Portia and Nerissa looking for Shylock's house?
2. Read line 4 again. What do you think Portia might mean by this comment?
3. Why has Gratiano caught up with Portia and Nerissa?

ORAL LANGUAGE

Discuss the Importance of the Rings

Pair Activity

Portia claims the only payment she will accept is the ring that she gave to Bassanio, which he promised to keep until death. (Look back to Act 3, Scene 2 lines 183–184.) In pairs, discuss the following:

- Why do you think Portia insists on this payment?
- Why does Bassanio relent in the end?
- Do you think that Portia is being fair here? Is she showing mercy?
- Why you think Shakespeare has made the rings an important part of the storyline here? Is it just for comedy or does it have another function in the play?

REFLECTING

Character File P

Turn to **page 140** of your portfolio to discuss **Nerissa's** role in the play so far. Refer to her relationship with Portia and Gratiano, as well as her contribution to the Trial Scene.

LOOKING BACK AT ACT 4

1. Overview P

Pair Activity

With your partner, turn to **page 4** of your portfolio to write **one sentence or phrase** in the box for each scene in Act 4. This sentence or phrase should **sum up the main action** in that scene.

2. Quotes Quiz P

Turn to **page 76** of your portfolio to review the **important quotes** for Act 4.

3. Individual Assignment – Choose one of the following activities:

(a) **Court Reporter:** You are the **court reporter** sent by either (i) **a newspaper** or (ii) **a TV station** to cover the events in the Trial Scene. Write out a **summary/report** of the main events to be printed in the newspaper or to be delivered on camera. If you have access to a video camera, or a camera phone, you may record it for the class.

P **(b)** **Comic Strip:** Turn to **page 78** of your portfolio to create a comic strip summary of the Trial Scene.

(c) **Themes:** Write about the **themes of justice and mercy** in Act 4, Scene 1. In your piece, discuss whether you think justice has been done. Do you agree with the outcome of the trial? Do you think that Shylock gets what he deserves?

(d) **What If…?:** What if Portia did not find any legal loophole? Or what if her identity had been found out? Rewrite the scene so that it has a different outcome. Perform it aloud.

LINKING TO THE EXAM

Characters That Express Strong Views P

In your exam, you might be asked to reflect on how characters that express strong views heighten the drama. Turn to **page 80** of your portfolio to see tips on how to complete this type of question.

ACT 5

This act contains only one scene. Lorenzo and Jessica are enjoying the balmy night when Portia and Nerissa return from Venice. Not long after, Bassanio and Gratiano arrive back with Antonio.

This is a scene of light-hearted comedy with Portia and Nerissa questioning Bassanio and Gratiano about their precious rings. The play ends with harmony being restored in Belmont and the promise of new beginnings for the three newly married couples.

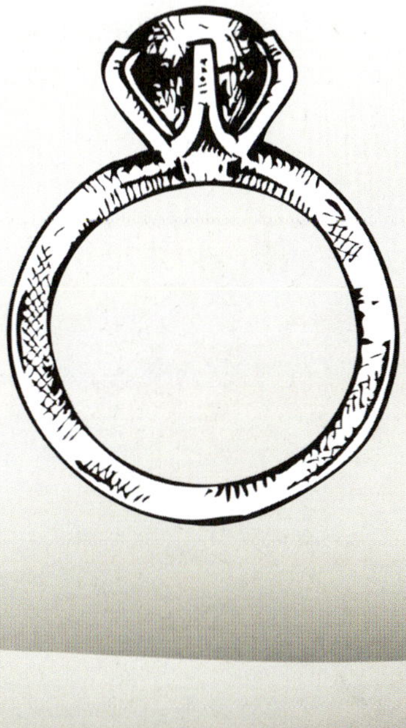

ACT 5, SCENE 1

Setting: Belmont. Avenue to Portia's house.

In this **scene** you will:

- Read part of **Portia and Bassanio's conversation** aloud.
- Illustrate your **favourite image** from the scene.
- Write the **letter** from Bellario revealing Portia and Nerissa's involvement in the trial.
- Reflect on whether this scene is a **good/suitable ending** for the play.

Action – What Happens?

This is the final scene of the play. The mood is serene (calm) and tranquil, with music playing and the couples being reunited. Lorenzo and Jessica are relaxing in Portia's garden in Belmont, looking at the night sky and listening to music as Portia and Nerissa arrive home. Soon Bassanio, Gratiano and Antonio arrive in Belmont and the ring plot reaches its conclusion with Nerissa and Portia's role in the court scene being revealed. Portia has positive news for Lorenzo, Jessica and Antonio which lifts their spirits at the close of the play.

Useful Words

amazed – confused

surety – guarantee

inter'gatory – question

cuckold – a man whose wife has been unfaithful

manna – food from heaven

sore – much

ACT 5, SCENE 1

Enter LORENZO and JESSICA.

LORENZO

The moon shines bright. In such a night as this,
When the sweet wind did gently kiss the trees
And they did make no noise—in such a night
Troilus, methinks,[1] mounted the Trojan walls
And sighed his soul toward the Grecian tents,
Where Cressid lay that night.[2]

JESSICA

In such a night
Did Thisbe[3] fearfully o'ertrip the dew
And saw the lion's shadow ere himself,
And ran dismayed away.

LORENZO

In such a night
Stood Dido[4] with a willow[5] in her hand
Upon the wild sea banks, and waft[6] her love
To come again to Carthage.

1. ***methinks:*** I think
2. ***Troilus, ... night:*** *Troilus was a prince from the city of Troy whose lover Cressid (Cressida) abandoned him for the Greek Diomedes.*
3. ***Thisbe:*** *Thisbe was frightened by a lion and ran away. Her lover Pyramus assumed she was dead and killed himself.*
4. ***Dido:*** Dido was the Queen of Carthage. She was abandoned by her lover, Aeneas.
5. ***willow:*** *A willow is a symbol of abandoned love.*
6. ***waft:*** waved to

JESSICA

In such a night
Medea[7] gathered the enchanted herbs
That did renew old Aeson.[8]

LORENZO

In such a night
Did Jessica steal from[9] the wealthy Jew,
And with an unthrift love[10] did run from Venice
As far as Belmont.

JESSICA

In such a night
Did young Lorenzo swear he loved her well,
Stealing her soul with many vows of faith,
And ne'er a true one.[11]

LORENZO

In such a night
Did pretty Jessica, like a little shrew,[12]
Slander[13] her love, and he forgave it her.

JESSICA

I would outnight you,[14] did nobody come.
But hark, I hear the footing[15] of a man.

Enter STEPHANO, a messenger.

LORENZO

Who comes so fast in silence of the night?

STEPHANO

A friend.

LORENZO

A friend—what friend? Your name, I pray you, friend?

STEPHANO

Stephano is my name, and I bring word
My mistress will before the break of day
Be here at Belmont. She doth stray about[16]

7. **Medea:** *Medea was deserted by her lover, Jason, whom she helped to win the golden fleece. She also helped Jason's father, Aeson.*
8. **Aeson:** *Jason's father*
9. **'steal from:** *Steal from' can mean 'stole money and jewels from' or 'escaped from'.*
10. **an unthrift love:** a spendthrift lover
11. **Stealing her ... one:** *Jessica is joking that Lorenzo's loving vows are false.*

LOOKING AT LANGUAGE

Repetition: By line 20, the phrase 'in such a night ...' has been spoken eight times by Lorenzo and Jessica. What is the effect of this repetition here, in your opinion?

12. **shrew:** *'Shrew' can mean 'a bad-tempered, assertive woman' or 'a small mouse-like animal'.*
13. **Slander:** Spoke badly about
14. **I would outnight you:** I would beat you at the game of 'In such a night'.
15. **footing:** footsteps

PLOT POINT

Jessica and Lorenzo are interrupted by Stephano, a messenger, who informs them that Portia and Nerissa are on their way back to Belmont.

16. **doth stray about:** goes out of her way

17. *holy crosses:* roadside shrines

18. *For happy wedlock hours:* For a happy marriage

By holy crosses,[17] where she kneels and prays
For happy wedlock hours.[18]

LORENZO

Who comes with her?

STEPHANO

None but a holy hermit and her maid.
I pray you, is my master yet returned?

LORENZO

He is not, nor we have not heard from him.
But go we in, I pray thee, Jessica,
And ceremoniously let us prepare[19]
Some welcome for the mistress of the house.

19. *ceremoniously let us prepare:* prepare in the appropriate manner

Enter LAUNCELOT.

LAUNCELOT

Sola, sola! Wo ha, ho! Sola, sola![20]

20. *Sola, ... sola!: Launcelot is imitating the sound of a messenger's horn.*

LORENZO

Who calls?

LAUNCELOT

Sola! Did you see Master Lorenzo?
Master Lorenzo, sola, sola!

LORENZO

Leave hollering,[21] man: here.

21. *Leave hollering:* Stop making that noise

LAUNCELOT

Sola! Where, where?

LORENZO

Here.

LAUNCELOT

Tell him there's a post[22] come from my master, with his horn full of good news. My master will be here ere[23] morning.

22. *post:* messenger

23. *ere:* before

Exit.

LORENZO

Sweet soul, let's in,[24] and there expect their coming.
And yet no matter. Why should we go in?
My friend Stephano, signify,[25] I pray you,
Within the house, your mistress is at hand,
And bring your music forth into the air.

Exit STEPHANO.

How sweet the moonlight sleeps upon this bank!
Here will we sit, and let the sounds of music
Creep in our ears. Soft stillness and the night
Become the touches of sweet harmony.[26]
Sit, Jessica. Look how the floor of heaven
Is thick inlaid with patens of bright gold.[27]
There's not the smallest orb which thou behold'st
But in his motion like an angel sings,
Still choiring to the young-eyed cherubins;[28]
Such harmony[29] is in immortal souls,
But whilst this muddy vesture of decay
Doth grossly close it in, we cannot hear it.[30]

Enter MUSICIANS.

Come, ho, and wake Diana[31] with a hymn.
With sweetest touches[32] pierce your mistress'[33] ear,
And draw her home with music.

[*Music.*]

JESSICA

I am never merry when I hear sweet[34] music.

LORENZO

The reason is your spirits are attentive,[35]
For do but note a wild and wanton[36] herd
Or race[37] of youthful and unhandled colts,[38]
Fetching mad bounds,[39] bellowing and neighing loud,
Which is the hot[40] condition of their blood,
If they but hear perchance[41] a trumpet sound,
Or any air[42] of music touch their ears,
You shall perceive them make a mutual stand,[43]
Their savage eyes turned[44] to a modest[45] gaze

24. ***let's in:*** let's go in
25. ***signify:*** announce
26. ***Soft stillness ... harmony:*** The stillness of the night makes the music sound sweeter.
27. ***Look how ... gold:*** Look how the night sky is richly decorated with discs/circles of gold.
28. ***There's not ... cherubins:*** Even the smallest sphere/planet that you can see is continually making music as it moves, singing for the angels of heaven.
29. ***harmony:*** *The 'music of the spheres' (musica universalis): this was the Elizabethan idea that the sun, moon and planets created harmonious, humming music as (it was thought) they revolved around the earth. They believed this harmony existed within the human body. They also believed that music had the power to affect the mood not only of humans but of animals.*
30. ***But whilst ... it:*** As our earthly bodies, which are subject to decay, enclose our souls, we are unable to hear this cosmic music.
31. ***Diana:*** *Diana was the goddess of the moon and of chastity (virginity).*
32. ***touches:*** notes
33. ***mistress':*** *Portia's*
34. ***sweet:*** melodious

PLOT POINT

Here, Lorenzo tells Jessica that she is more responsive to music than most people and claims that music has the power to calm even the wildest horses.

35. ***The reason ... attentive:*** You respond to music more than most.
36. ***wanton:*** playful/frisky
37. ***race:*** herd
38. ***colts:*** young untrained horses
39. ***Fetching mad bounds:*** jumping wildly
40. ***hot:*** passionate/wild
41. ***perchance:*** by chance/perhaps
42. ***air:*** sound or melody
43. ***You shall ... stand:*** You will notice them stop all together.
44. ***turned:*** transformed
45. ***modest:*** gentle

By the sweet power of music. Therefore the poet
Did feign that Orpheus drew trees, stones and floods;[46]
Since naught so stockish, hard and full of rage,
But music for the time doth change his nature.[47]
The man that hath no music in himself,
Nor is not moved with concord of sweet sounds,[48]
Is fit for treasons, stratagems, and spoils.[49]
The motions of his spirit are dull as night,
And his affections dark as Erebus.[50]
Let no such man be trusted. Mark[51] the music.

Enter PORTIA and NERISSA.

PORTIA
That light we see is burning in my hall.
How far that little candle throws his beams—
So shines a good deed in a naughty[52] world.

NERISSA
When the moon shone we did not see the candle.

PORTIA
So doth the greater glory dim the less.
A substitute[53] shines brightly as a king
Until a king be by, and then his state
Empties itself, as doth an inland brook
Into the main of waters.[54] Music, hark.

NERISSA
It is your music, madam, of the house.

PORTIA
Nothing is good, I see, without respect.[55]
Methinks[56] it sounds much sweeter than by day.

NERISSA
Silence bestows that virtue on it,[57] madam.

PORTIA
The crow doth sing as sweetly as the lark
When neither is attended,[58] and I think

46. ***Therefore the ... floods:*** *The poet Ovid pretended that Orpheus' music had the power to charm nature, making the trees and rocks follow him.*
47. ***Since naught ... nature:*** Since there is nothing so dull, hard and angry that music cannot change it for a time.
48. ***Nor is ... sounds:*** Or who is not moved by the harmony of sweet music
49. ***Is fit ... spoils:*** Is capable of betrayal, plots and plundering.
50. ***And his ... Erebus:*** His instincts are as dark as hell. *(Erebus was the Greek god of darkness.)*
51. ***Mark:*** Listen to

LOOKING AT LANGUAGE

Imagery: In lines 89–91, Portia marvels at how far the candle's light reaches in the darkness, comparing this light to a good deed in the wicked world. Why, in your opinion, does Portia make this comparison here?

52. ***naughty:*** wicked/evil
53. ***substitute:*** deputy
54. ***and then ... waters:*** and then his glory or power drains away, like a stream into an ocean
55. ***respect:*** context/comparison
56. ***Methinks:*** I think
57. ***Silence bestows ... it:*** The silence gives it that quality (enhances it).
58. ***attended:*** listened to

The nightingale, if she should sing by day,
When every goose is cackling, would be thought
No better a musician than the wren.
How many things by season seasoned are
To their right praise and true perfection![59]
Peace, ho! The moon sleeps with Endymion
And would not be awaked.[60]

[*Music ceases.*]

LORENZO

That is the voice,
Or I am much deceived, of Portia.

PORTIA

He knows me as the blind man knows the cuckoo—
By the bad voice.

LORENZO

Dear lady, welcome home.

PORTIA

We have been praying for our husbands' welfare,
Which speed we hope the better for our words.[61]
Are they returned?

LORENZO

Madam, they are not yet,
But there is come a messenger before
To signify[62] their coming.

PORTIA

Go in, Nerissa.
Give order to my servants that they take
No note at all of our being absent hence;
Nor you, Lorenzo; Jessica, nor you.[63]

[*A tucket*[64] *sounds.*]

LORENZO

Your husband is at hand. I hear his trumpet.
We are no tell-tales, madam; fear you not.

59. ***How many ... perfection!:*** So many things are shown to their best advantage when they are seen at the right time.

60. ***The moon ... awaked:*** *In Greek mythology the moon loved Endymion (a shepherd) so much that she put him to sleep forever.*

61. ***Which speed ... words:*** whom we hope are benefitting from our prayers

62. ***signify:*** announce

63. ***Give order ... you:*** Tell my servants not to mention that we were away. You must not tell either, Lorenzo – or you, Jessica.

64. ***tucket:*** a flourish of trumpets

PORTIA

This night methinks is but the daylight sick.
It looks a little paler. 'Tis a day,
Such as the day is when the sun is hid.[65]

Enter BASSANIO, ANTONIO, GRATIANO and their followers.

BASSANIO

We should hold day with the Antipodes,
If you would walk in absence of the sun.[66]

PORTIA

Let me give light, but let me not be light;[67]
For a light wife doth make a heavy[68] husband,
And never be Bassanio so for me.
But God sort[69] all! You are welcome home, my lord.

BASSANIO

I thank you, madam. Give welcome to my friend.
This is the man, this is Antonio,
To whom I am so infinitely bound.[70]

PORTIA

You should in all sense be much bound to him,[71]
For, as I hear, he was much bound[72] for you.

ANTONIO

No more than I am well acquitted[73] of.

PORTIA

Sir, you are very welcome to our house.
It must appear in other ways than words,
Therefore I scant this breathing courtesy.[74]

GRATIANO

[*to NERISSA*] By yonder moon I swear you do me wrong;
In faith, I gave it to the judge's clerk.
Would he were gelt[75] that had it for my part,
Since you do take it, love, so much at heart.

65. *Such as ... hid:* It is like a day when the sun is hidden.
66. *We should ... sun:* We should share daylight with the other side of the world *(Antipodes)* as your radiant presence makes it seem like daylight here in Belmont.
67. *light:* unfaithful
68. *heavy:* sad
69. *sort:* decide
70. *To whom ... bound:* To whom I am so indebted/obliged.
71. *bound to him:* tied/connected to him as a friend
72. *he was much bound:* he was imprisoned
73. *acquitted:* freed
74. *Sir, you ... courtesy:* I had better welcome you to my house with less talk and more action.
75. *Would he were gelt:* I wish he were castrated

PORTIA

A quarrel, ho, already! What's the matter?

GRATIANO

About a hoop of gold, a paltry[76] ring
That she did give me, whose posy[77] was
For all the world like cutlers' poetry
Upon a knife[78]—'Love me and leave me not.'

NERISSA

What talk you of the posy or the value?
You swore to me when I did give it you
That you would wear it till your hour of death,
And that it should lie with you in your grave.
Though not for me, yet for your vehement oaths[79]
You should have been respective[80] and have kept it.
Gave it a judge's clerk!—no, God's my judge,
The clerk will ne'er wear hair on's face that had it.[81]

76. ***paltry:*** *a silly/insignificant thing*

77. ***posy:*** motto/inscription

78. ***like cutlers' ... knife:*** like knife-makers might write on their knives

PLOT POINT

We are now seeing the consequences of Gratiano and Bassanio giving away their rings! This is the denouement (final outcome) of the ring plot. Gratiano is trying to justify giving his ring away. Notice the dramatic irony in Nerissa's words in line 158.

79. ***vehement oaths:*** passionate promises

80. ***respective:*** careful

81. ***The clerk ... it:*** The so-called clerk you gave it to will never grow a beard (because you gave it to a woman).

GRATIANO

He will, an[82] if he live to be a man.

NERISSA

Ay, if a woman live to be a man.

GRATIANO

Now by this hand, I gave it to a youth,
A kind of boy, a little scrubbèd[83] boy
No higher than thyself, the judge's clerk,
A prating[84] boy that begged it as a fee.
I could not for my heart deny it him.

PORTIA

You were to blame, I must be plain[85] with you,
To part so slightly[86] with your wife's first gift,
A thing stuck on with oaths upon your finger
And so riveted[87] with faith unto your flesh.
I gave my love a ring, and made him swear
Never to part with it; and here he stands.
I dare be sworn for him he would not leave it[88]
Nor pluck it from his finger, for the wealth
That the world masters.[89] Now, in faith, Gratiano,
You give your wife too unkind a cause of grief.
An 'twere to me,[90] I should be mad at it.

BASSANIO

[*aside*] Why, I were best to cut my left hand off
And swear I lost the ring defending it.

GRATIANO

My lord Bassanio gave his ring away
Unto the judge that begged it, and indeed
Deserved it, too, and then the boy his clerk,
That took some pains in writing, he begged mine,
And neither man nor master would take aught[91]
But the two rings.

PORTIA

What ring gave you my lord?
Not that, I hope, which you received of me.

82. *an:* if
83. *scrubbèd:* short
84. *prating:* chattering/talkative
85. *plain:* honest/straight
86. *slightly:* carelessly
87. *riveted:* fastened/secured
88. *leave it:* part with it
89. *for the ... masters:* for all the wealth/money in the world
90. *An 'twere to me:* If it were me
91. *aught:* anything

BASSANIO

If I could add a lie unto a fault,
I would deny it; but you see my finger
Hath not the ring upon it. It is gone.

PORTIA

Even so void[92] is your false heart of truth.
By heaven, I will ne'er come in your bed
Until I see the ring.

NERISSA

Nor I in yours
Till I again see mine.

BASSANIO

Sweet Portia,
If you did know to whom I gave the ring,
If you did know for whom I gave the ring,
And would conceive for what I gave the ring,
And how unwillingly I left the ring,
When naught[93] would be accepted but the ring,
You would abate the strength of your displeasure.[94]

PORTIA

If you had known the virtue[95] of the ring,
Or half her worthiness that gave the ring,
Or your own honour to contain[96] the ring,
You would not then have parted with the ring.
What man is there so much unreasonable,
If you had pleased to have defended it
With any terms of zeal,[97] wanted the modesty
To urge the thing held as a ceremony?[98]
Nerissa teaches me what to believe:
I'll die for't but some woman had the ring.[99]

BASSANIO

No, by my honour, madam, by my soul,
No woman had it, but a civil doctor[100]
Which did refuse three thousand ducats of me,
And begged the ring, the which I did deny him,
And suffered him to go displeased away,[101]

92. ***void:*** empty

93. ***naught:*** nothing

94. ***You would ... displeasure:*** You wouldn't be as angry.

95. ***virtue:*** power

96. ***contain:*** retain/keep

97. ***zeal:*** passion/enthusiasm

98. ***What man ... ceremony?:*** What person would insist on taking a ring if it was explained with passion how sacred/precious it was?

99. ***I'll die ... ring:*** I'd swear that you gave the ring away to a woman.

LOOKING AT LANGUAGE

Repetition: Notice that both Bassanio and Portia use repetition here. They mention the ring ten times between them! What is the effect of this, in your opinion?

100. ***civil doctor:*** a doctor of law (lawyer)

101. ***suffered him ... away:*** allowed him to go away unsatisfied

Even he that had held up the very life
Of my dear friend. What should I say, sweet lady?
I was enforced to send it after him.
I was beset with shame and courtesy.
My honour would not let ingratitude
So much besmear it.[102] Pardon me, good lady,
For by these blessèd candles of the night,
Had you been there, I think you would have begged
The ring of me to give the worthy doctor.

PORTIA

Let not that doctor e'er come near my house.
Since he hath got the jewel that I loved,
And that which you did swear to keep for me,
I will become as liberal[103] as you.
I'll not deny him any thing I have,
No, not my body nor my husband's bed.
Know him[104] I shall, I am well sure of it.
Lie not a night from home. Watch me like Argus.[105]
If you do not, if I be left alone,
Now by mine honour, which is yet mine[106] own,
I'll have that doctor for my bedfellow.[107]

NERISSA

And I his clerk, therefore be well advised
How you do leave me to mine own protection.

GRATIANO

Well, do you so. Let not me take him then,[108]
For if I do, I'll mar the young clerk's pen.[109]

ANTONIO

I am th'unhappy subject of these quarrels.

PORTIA

Sir, grieve not you. You are welcome notwithstanding.

BASSANIO

Portia, forgive me this enforcèd wrong,
And in the hearing of these many friends
I swear to thee, even by thine own fair eyes,
Wherein I see myself—

102. ***My honour ... it:*** I couldn't allow him to think I was so ungrateful for his help; it would have ruined my honour.

CHARACTER NOTE

Portia could at this point reveal that she was the doctor of law to whom Bassanio gave the ring. Instead, she goes further with her 'punishment' of Bassanio, even suggesting that, following his example, she would not deny the doctor anything – she would even sleep with him! Why do you think that she prolongs this teasing of him? What is your opinion of Portia here? Do you think she is funny? Cruel? Manipulative? Justified in her behaviour?

103. ***liberal:*** generous/giving

104. ***Know him:*** *'Know him' can mean 'recognise him' or 'sleep with him'.*

105. ***Argus:*** *Argus was a giant from mythology who had 100 eyes.*

106. ***mine:*** my

107. ***bedfellow:*** person who shares a bed

108. ***take him then:*** catch him with you

109. ***I'll mar ... pen:*** I will destroy the young man's pen

PORTIA

Mark you but that!
In both my eyes he doubly sees himself,
In each eye one. Swear by your double[110] self,
And there's an oath of credit.[111]

BASSANIO

Nay, but hear me.
Pardon this fault, and by my soul I swear
I never more will break an oath with thee.[112]

ANTONIO

I once did lend my body for his wealth
Which, but[113] for him that had your husband's ring,
Had quite miscarried.[114] I dare be bound again,
My soul upon the forfeit,[115] that your lord
Will never more break faith advisedly.[116]

PORTIA

Then you shall be his surety.[117] Give him this,
And bid him keep it better than the other.

ANTONIO

Here, lord Bassanio, swear to keep this ring.

BASSANIO

By heaven, it is the same I gave the doctor!

110. ***double:*** two-faced/deceitful
111. ***And there's ... credit:*** Now there's an oath to be believed! *(Portia is being sarcastic.)*
112. ***Pardon this ... thee:*** Forgive this one thing and I swear that I will never again break a promise to you.
113. ***but:*** only
114. ***Had quite miscarried:*** Would have been destroyed
115. ***My soul ... forfeit:*** I would pledge my soul
116. ***advisedly:*** knowingly/deliberately
117. ***surety:*** guarantor

PORTIA

I had it of him. Pardon me, Bassanio,
For by this ring, the doctor lay with me.[118]

NERISSA

And pardon me, my gentle Gratiano,
For that same scrubbèd boy, the doctor's clerk,
In lieu of this[119] last night did lie with me.

GRATIANO

Why, this is like the mending of highways
In summer where the ways are fair enough![120]
What, are we cuckolds[121] ere we have deserved it?

PORTIA

Speak not so grossly.[122] You are all amazed.[123]
Here is a letter. Read it at your leisure.
It comes from Padua, from Bellario.
There you shall find that Portia was the doctor,
Nerissa there her clerk. Lorenzo here
Shall witness I set forth as soon as you,
And even but now[124] returned. I have not yet
Entered my house. Antonio, you are welcome,
And I have better news in store for you
Than you expect. Unseal this letter soon.
There you shall find three of your argosies[125]
Are richly come to harbour suddenly.
You shall not know by what strange accident
I chancèd on this letter.

ANTONIO

I am dumb.[126]

BASSANIO

Were you the doctor and I knew you not?

GRATIANO

Were you the clerk that is to make me cuckold?

NERISSA

Ay, but the clerk that never means to do it,
Unless he live until he be a man.

118. *lay with me:* slept with me

119. *In lieu of this:* In exchange for this

120. *Why, this ... enough!:* There was no need to do that – just like there is no need to mend the roads when the weather is fine!

121. *cuckolds: men whose wives have been unfaithful*

122. *grossly:* rudely

123. *amazed:* confused

124. *even but now:* only just now

125. *argosies:* large merchant ships

PLOT POINT

At last the denouement arrives: Portia reveals the truth – that she was the doctor and Nerissa the doctor's clerk at the court in Venice. She produces a letter from her cousin, Doctor Bellario, to prove this. Not only that, but Portia is now the bearer of great news: three of Antonio's ships are safe.

126. *dumb:* dumbstruck/shocked

SHAKESPEARE'S WORLD

A cuckold was a man whose wife was unfaithful to him. Understandably, there was a real fear of being cuckolded and publicly shamed. Cuckolds were depicted with horns growing out of their heads.

BASSANIO

Sweet doctor, you shall be my bedfellow.
When I am absent, then lie with my wife.

ANTONIO

Sweet lady, you have given me life and living;[127]
For here I read for certain that my ships
Are safely come to road.[128]

PORTIA

How now, Lorenzo?
My clerk hath some good comforts, too, for you.

NERISSA

Ay, and I'll give them him without a fee.
There do I give to you and Jessica
From the rich Jew a special deed of gift,
After his death, of all he dies possessed of.

LORENZO

Fair ladies, you drop manna[129] in the way
Of starvèd people.

PORTIA

It is almost morning,
And yet I am sure you are not satisfied
Of these events at full.[130] Let us go in,
And charge us there upon inter'gatories,[131]
And we will answer all things faithfully.

GRATIANO

Let it be so. The first inter'gatory[132]
That my Nerissa shall be sworn on is
Whether till the next night she had rather stay,
Or go to bed now, being two hours to day.
But were the day come, I should wish it dark,
That I were couching[133] with the doctor's clerk.
Well, while I live I'll fear no other thing
So sore[134] as keeping safe Nerissa's ring.[135]

Exeunt.

PLOT POINT
Antonio acknowledges all that Portia has done for him, saving his life and giving him the news that his ships are safe.

127. ***you have ... living:*** you have saved my life and have given me back my means of living *(i.e. his wealth)*

128. ***road:*** harbour

PLOT POINT
Nerissa also announces to Lorenzo and Jessica that they are to receive a 'special deed of gift', which indicates that they will inherit Shylock's possessions after his death.

129. ***manna:*** food from heaven

130. ***And yet ... full:*** I am sure you still want to know more about all these things that have happened.
131. ***And charge ... inter'gatories:*** you can ask us questions under oath like in a court of law

132. ***inter'gatory:*** question

133. ***couching:*** lying/sleeping

134. ***sore:*** much
135. ***Well, while ... ring:*** *Gratiano is saying that, for as long as he lives, he will respect and value love tokens.*

OVERVIEW OF ACT 5, SCENE 1

- This is a scene of calm at the end of a **turbulent** (unsettled/chaotic) play. The setting, the **idyllic** (perfect) garden paradise of Belmont under the starry night sky, establishes a tranquil, romantic tone at the start of the scene. The music also contributes to the **serene** (calm) atmosphere.
- Lorenzo refers to lovers from mythology such as Troilus and Cressid and Dido and Aeneas. It is interesting that all the lovers he mentions experience great misfortune. He includes Jessica in his list of unfortunate lovers:

  In such a night
  Did Jessica steal from the wealthy Jew,
  And with an unthrift love did run from Venice
  As far as Belmont. (lines 14–17)

- Soon Stephano, a servant, comes to inform Lorenzo of Portia's **imminent** (about to happen) return. Launcelot also has news that Bassanio will be back in Belmont before morning.
- Lorenzo, at first, decides to go in to prepare for Bassanio and Portia's return, but changes his mind, preferring to listen to the musicians in the open air. Lorenzo's language is quite poetic as he gazes at the night sky and **meditates on** (thinks about) the harmonious music:

  How sweet the moonlight sleeps upon this bank!
  Here will we sit, and let the sounds of music
  Creep in our ears. (lines 54–56)

- He also paints very clear visual imagery of the night sky:

  Look how the floor of heaven
  Is thick inlaid with patens of bright gold. (lines 58–59)

- Lorenzo praises music and its power to tame wild animals. He argues that wild herds or horses that hear music become gentle and docile because of the healing power of music:

  Their [the animals'] savage eyes turned to a modest gaze
  By the sweet power of music. (lines 78–79)

- Lorenzo is suspicious of anyone who does not like music, claiming that such a person is capable of **treason** (betrayal), plotting and destruction:

  The man that hath no music in himself,
  Nor is not moved with concord of sweet sounds,
  Is fit for treasons, stratagems, and spoils. (lines 83–85)

- As Portia and Nerissa arrive back in Belmont, Portia notices a candle burning in her house. This causes Nerissa to remark that they didn't even notice the candle when the moon was shining brightly. Portia responds by saying:

  So doth the greater glory dim the less. (line 93)

  This means that something brighter, or more powerful can outshine or eclipse something 'less' than it.
- Next, Portia and Nerissa hear music **emanating** (coming) from Portia's garden. Nerissa observes how the silence of the night enhances the music. Portia agrees, commenting that the nightingale would not sound as nice by day when other more **raucous** (harsh/loud) sounds are competing with it, such as 'When every goose is cackling' (line 105). It is at this point that Lorenzo becomes aware of Portia's voice and welcomes her home.
- Portia tells Nerissa to instruct the servants to say nothing of their absence when Bassanio returns home. Lorenzo and Jessica also vow to keep their absence a secret:

  We are no tell-tales, madam; Fear you not. (line 123)

- Next, Bassanio returns to Belmont, accompanied by Gratiano and Antonio. Bassanio is quick to flatter Portia, claiming that she is so radiant that it would appear like the daytime if Portia 'would walk in absence of the sun' (line 128). Portia **quips** (jokes):

  Let me give light, but let me not be light;
  For a light wife doth make a heavy husband (lines 129–130)

  Portia is suggesting that a 'light' or unfaithful wife causes a 'heavy' or sad husband.

- Bassanio introduces Antonio to Portia, while Nerissa and Gratiano argue about Nerissa's missing ring. Gratiano considers the ring nothing more than 'a hoop of gold, a paltry ring' (line 147), but Nerissa argues that he had sworn that he would keep it until he died. Portia agrees that it was very **remiss** (careless/negligent) of him to give the ring away:

  You were to blame, I must be plain with you,
  To part so slightly with your wife's first gift (lines 166–167)

- Unsurprisingly, Portia now brings up the topic of her own ring that she gave to Bassanio. A **shamefaced** Bassanio is forced to reveal the truth: that he gave the ring away as payment to a civil doctor (lawyer). When Portia accuses him of giving the ring to another woman, he pleads with her to believe him. Bassanio says Portia would have begged him to give the ring away if she had been there:

  Pardon me, good lady,
  For by these blessèd candles of the night,
  Had you been there, I think you would have begged
  The ring of me to give the worthy doctor. (lines 219–222)

- Bassanio asks Portia to forgive him this one 'fault', saying that he will never again break a promise to her. Antonio is quick to vouch for his friend Bassanio once more, saying that he will bet his soul that Bassanio will never deliberately break his word to Portia:

  I dare be bound again,
  My soul upon the forfeit, that your lord
  Will never more break faith advisedly. (lines 251–253)

- Portia then gives Antonio a ring to give Bassanio – the same ring that he gave to the doctor. Portia and Nerissa now engage in teasing their husbands, claiming that they slept with the doctor and his clerk in exchange for the rings. This absurd, outrageous claim shocks their husbands. Gratiano wonders:

  What, are we cuckolds ere we have deserved it? (line 265)

- Portia doesn't keep up the **charade** (pretence) long, however, and soon reveals her part in the court case. She produces a letter from her cousin, the lawyer Bellario, which **corroborates** (supports/backs up) both her own and Nerissa's involvement in the trial. This unravelling of the plot is known as the **denouement**.

- However, the surprises don't stop there. Portia produces yet another letter, this one for Antonio, which reveals that three of his **merchant ships** (argosies) have safely landed in the harbour. Antonio is overjoyed, thanking Portia for her assistance:

  Sweet lady, you have given me life and living (line 286)

- Portia's generosity continues when Nerissa announces that she has a 'special deed of gift' (line 292) from Shylock for Lorenzo and Jessica, which entitles them to all his possessions after his death. Considering Portia's **benevolence** (goodness/generosity) in this scene in bringing news of good fortune to all, it is fitting when Lorenzo remarks:

  Fair ladies, you drop manna in the way
  Of starvèd people. (lines 294–295)

  This conveys the amount of good deeds Portia has done for all, especially Lorenzo, Jessica and Antonio.

- As the scene draws to a close, Portia promises to elaborate on her story. Gratiano appears to have learnt his lesson about the importance of keeping love tokens safe.
- The scene ends with the three couples and Antonio going into Portia's house. There is a sense of harmony and calm being **restored** and the promise of new beginnings for the couples with the new day about to dawn.

REVIEWING

1. What news does Stephano bring Lorenzo?
2. What news does Launcelot bring Lorenzo?
3. What does Lorenzo decide to do instead of going inside?
4. According to Lorenzo, what effect can music have on wild animals? What point is he making about music in general?
5. How does Lorenzo feel about people who do not like music?
6. Why does music sound better at night, according to Nerissa?
7. What does Portia instruct Nerissa to say to her servants?
8. How does Nerissa react to the news that Gratiano gave away her ring?
9. How does Portia respond to Gratiano having given the ring away?
10. Who does Portia think that Bassanio gave his ring to?
11. How does Bassanio try to convince Portia that this is not the case?
12. What does Portia claim she would do if she met the 'doctor'?
13. How does Antonio respond to the conflict between Portia and Bassanio about the ring?
14. How do Gratiano, Antonio and Bassanio react to the revelation that Portia and Nerissa were disguised as the doctor of law and his clerk?

ORAL LANGUAGE

Portia and Bassanio's Conversation about the Rings

Pair Activity

Read aloud Bassanio and Portia's conversation (lines 192–208) in which they discuss the ring.

One person should read Bassanio's lines (shaded in green). The other person should read Portia's lines (shaded in blue).

1. Read the lines, focusing on the appropriate **tone of voice** for your character.
2. Swap roles and read the lines again. Pay particular attention to how the characters deliver the word '**ring**'.
3. Finally, discuss the different **tones of voice** used. Discuss what the tone of voice reveals about **how the character is feeling** at that particular time.

EXPLORING

1. Research: Classical Lovers P

Research the fate of the classical lovers mentioned at the start of Act 5, Scene 1 by Jessica and Lorenzo. Use the internet or your library to help you. Turn to **page 86** of your portfolio to complete the tasks.

2. Visual Images P

This scene contains many clear visual images, especially when Lorenzo is discussing music and the night sky. Choose any **one image** that stood out to you from this scene and illustrate it. Turn to **page 88** of your portfolio to draw your image.

3. Director's Notebook – Music P

If you were directing this scene, what kind of music would you choose to have playing when Portia arrives home? Turn to **page 88** of your portfolio to write down your ideas and explain your choices.

CREATING

Doctor Bellario's Letter P

Imagine that you are **Doctor Bellario**, Portia's cousin. Write the **letter** mentioned in **lines 267–270** in which Portia and Nerissa's part in the court scene is revealed. Turn to **page 89** of your portfolio to write the letter. Feel free to add in your own creative ideas too!

REFLECTING

1. My Reflection on Act 5, Scene 1 P

Complete the scene reflection on **page 90** of your portfolio.

2. A Good Ending? P

Do you think this is a **good ending** for this play? If you were to change it, what would you change? Turn to **page 91** of your portfolio to give reasons for your answer.

3. Character File P

Update the Character File section of your portfolio for **(a) Portia** (**page 130**), **(b) Bassanio** (**page 122**) and **(c) Antonio** (**page 116**) based on what you have learned in this scene.

LOOKING BACK AT ACT 5

1. Overview P

Pair Activity

With your partner, turn to **page 4** of your portfolio to write **one sentence or phrase** in the box for Act 5, Scene 1. This sentence or phrase should **sum up the main action** in the scene.

2. Quotes Quiz P

Turn to **page 92** of your portfolio to review the **important quotes** for Act 5.

3. Individual Assignment – Choose one of the following activities:

(a) **Themes**: Discuss what we have read about the theme of **love and marriage** or the theme of **false appearances** in this scene.

(b) **Setting**: Discuss the importance of **the setting** in this last scene of the play.

(c) **What If…?**: What if the play did not end here in Act 5, Scene 1? Imagine that there is an extra scene – **Act 5**, **Scene 2** – which features **Shylock** alone on stage. Write the **speech** (or **soliloquy**) Shylock would make at the end of the play.

The speech can recap on events, look forward to Shylock's future life, discuss his reaction to the trial or his daughter's elopement with Lorenzo, etc. Write Shylock's speech in **modern English**. The speech should be about **150–200 words**.

DELVING DEEPER

1. Comparing the Original Play with a Film or Theatre Production

After viewing any production (film or theatre) of the play, compare it to the original play you have read in class.

What were the main differences? Which one did you prefer and why?

Here are some things to think about:

- How the **characters** were portrayed.
- How the **settings** were used/shown.
- The **plot/action**. Were events in the production you saw presented in the same order as in the original play? Were there parts left out?
- Your **overall response**. Which production did you prefer?

2. *The Merchant of Venice* Film Poster P

There have been many film adaptations of *The Merchant of Venice*. Turn to **pages 94–96** of your portfolio to learn more about the **key features** and **layout** of film posters, how to **analyse** them and to **design** your own film poster. There is also an examination question on film posters on **page 102** of your portfolio that you might wish to complete.

LINKING TO THE EXAM

1. Writing About Characters' Essential Qualities P

It is important to reflect on the qualities and traits of the main characters in a play and to be able to discuss where we see evidence of those qualities in the important scenes. Use the responses you have written in your **character file** to help you answer questions on the characters' qualities. Turn to **pages 97–101** of your portfolio to complete a question on characters' essential qualities.

2. Conflict Is at the Centre of All Drama P

Conflict is central to drama. It develops the plot, creates crucial tension and provides information about characters' motivations, values and weaknesses. Turn to **page 104** of your portfolio for tips on how to answer a question based on the theme of conflict in a play.

Examining the Play

• Plot Structure • Characters • Themes •
• Approaching Exam Questions •

Important Vocabulary

Plot: The sequence of events in a story.

Protagonist: The main character or one of the main characters in a literary work.

Theme: A recurring topic, message or idea in a literary work. Examples from *The Merchant of Venice* include: Love and Marriage, False Appearances, Money and Conflict.

Looking at the Plot Structure

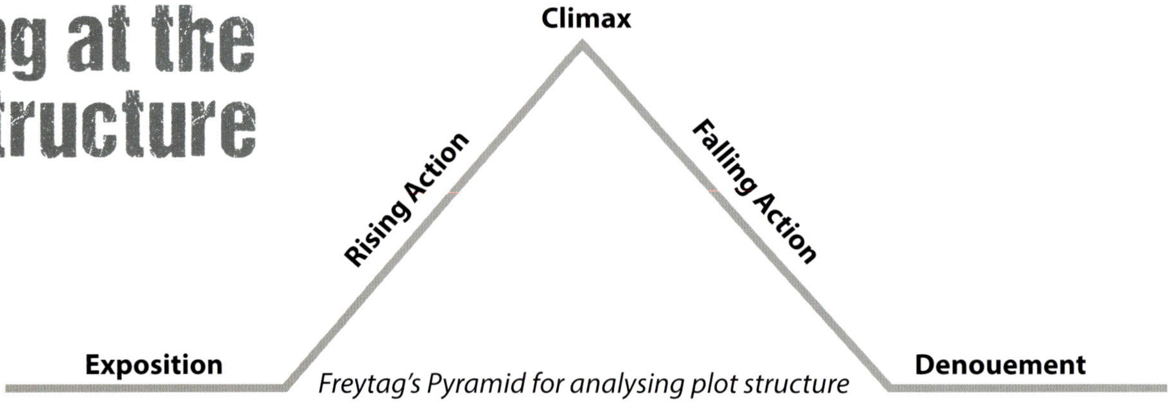

Freytag's Pyramid for analysing plot structure

The plot is the sequence of events in a story. The German writer **Gustav Freytag** (1816–1895) devised the diagram above to examine the plot structure in Shakespearean plays. He identified the following five elements:

1. **Exposition** refers to the audience's introduction to the characters, main setting and events. The main themes may also be introduced.
2. **Rising action** refers to important events (or inciting actions) that cause the story to develop. Rising action leads to the play's climax.
3. The **climax** is the high point of the play. It is also known as the crisis. It may include a dramatic turning point. The climax scene often occurs in the third act of a play.
4. **Falling action** includes the events that occur after the climax. These lead to the play's ending. In scenes of falling action, the main protagonist (character) suffers a period of bad luck or misfortune.
5. **Resolution** (or **denouement**) is the ending of the story, during which the plot details are tied up. Themes and conflicts are resolved and explained.

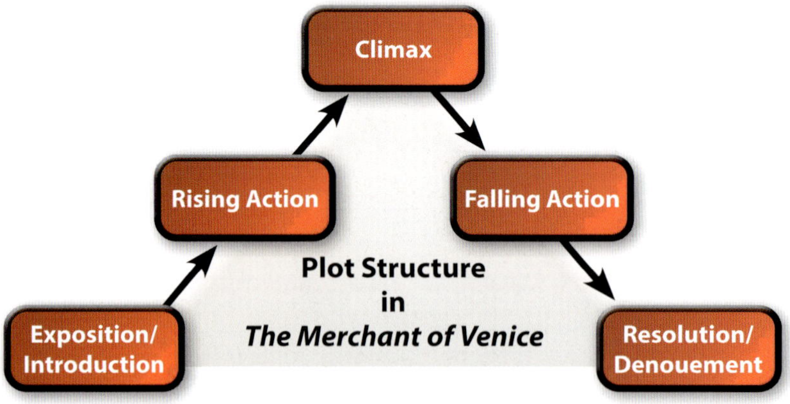

EXPLORING

Plot Structure P

Pair Activity

Turn to **page 142** of your portfolio to complete the activity on plot structure.

Looking at Character Development

Think about **how and why the characters develop** as they do in the play. Use the Character File in your portfolio to reflect on the characters and to form a response to them.

Character Checklist P

Think about:

- What the **character does** or how he/she **behaves** in each key scene.
- The **adjectives** that you would use to describe the character.
- Something that **stands out** to you in a key scene.
- How the character **reacts to situations**.
- A significant **change** in the character.
- Your personal response to the character – reflecting on something that **confuses or surprises you** about the character.
- How the character interacts with other characters – his/her **relationships, both positive and negative**.

CHARACTER TRACKER

Turn to **page 143** of your portfolio to fill in the diagram based on your **favourite character** from the play. (Use the grids showing characters and their scenes on **page 146** of your portfolio as well as the Character File section to help you.)

Bassanio

materialistic
sociable
prodigal
devoted
sincere
honest
affable

When we first meet Bassanio in **Act 1**, **Scene 1**, we get the impression that he is quite **extravagant**, **wasteful** and **superficial**. We learn very quickly that he is a **spendthrift** who has wasted his money on his lavish lifestyle. As he says to Antonio:

> *'Tis not unknown to you, Antonio,*
> *How much I have disabled mine estate,*
> *By something showing a more swelling port*
> *Than my faint means would grant continuance* (Act 1, Scene 1, lines 122–125)

Bassanio has already borrowed money from Antonio to whom he 'owe[s] the most in money and in love' (Act 1, Scene 1, line 131) and cannot pay him back. He asks Antonio for yet another loan which will help him as he prepares to set off to Belmont to woo a rich heiress called Portia.

> *In Belmont is a lady richly left,*
> *And she is fair, and, fairer than that word,*
> *Of wondrous virtues.* (Act 1, Scene 1, lines 161–163)

Bassanio is convinced that he has a very good chance of winning her hand in marriage, but he needs financial assistance in order to woo her:

> *O my Antonio, had I but the means*
> *To hold a rival place with one of them,*
> *I have a mind presages me such thrift*
> *That I should questionless be fortunate.* (Act 1, Scene 1, lines 173–176)

It is interesting that Bassanio identifies with the mythological figure of Jason who went in search of the golden fleece. Bassanio sees Portia's golden locks as resembling the golden fleece and compares her home in Belmont to Colchos, the place where Jason went to steal the fleece. This creates an image of Bassanio as an **opportunist**, who seems more interested in marrying Portia for her wealth than for love.

When we next meet Bassanio, in **Act 1**, **Scene 3**, he is negotiating a loan of 3,000 ducats from Shylock, a Jewish moneylender. As Antonio has agreed to act as guarantor for the loan, Shylock agrees to lend the money to Bassanio. However, Bassanio is **apprehensive** (uneasy) about agreeing to the conditions of the bond and asks Antonio not to accept Shylock's terms:

> *You shall not seal to such a bond for me.*
> *I'll rather dwell in necessity.* (Act 1, Scene 3, lines 150–151)

Bassanio suspects that Shylock's motivations are sinister:

> *I like not fair terms and a villain's mind.* (Act 1, Scene 3, line 175)

Despite his materialistic tendencies, Bassanio seems to be an **affable**, **agreeable** (friendly) character. In **Act 2**, **Scene 2**, he agrees to hire Launcelot as his servant, even offering him a better uniform than Bassanio's existing servants:

> *Give him a livery*
> *More guarded than his fellows* (Act 2, Scene 2, lines 147–148)

In the same scene, he agrees to take Gratiano with him to Belmont, even though Gratiano, with his reputation for being boisterous, could potentially ruin Bassanio's chances of wooing Portia.

It is in **Act 3**, **Scene 2**, as Bassanio prepares to choose his casket that we see greater depth to his character. He reveals himself as **insecure** and **sensitive** as he meditates on the caskets. His reasoning behind his choice of caskets reveals his **thoughtful**, **insightful** nature. He rejects the 'gaudy gold' (line 101) casket because he is not to be fooled by false appearances: 'So may the outward shows be least themselves' (line 73).

Even when Bassanio is successful in choosing the correct casket, he is **deferential** (respectful) and somewhat unsure of himself as he approaches Portia.

> *So, thrice-fair lady, stand I even so,*
> *As doubtful whether what I see be true,*
> *Until confirmed, signed, ratified by you* (Act 3, Scene 2, lines 146–148)

Bassanio's joy is short-lived, however, as he finds out the news of Antonio's bad luck. Bassanio shows real concern and distress for his friend when he realises the extent of Antonio's troubles. He tells Portia that he has misrepresented himself to her when he told her that his 'state was nothing' (line 258). He reveals:

> *I should then have told you*
> *That I was worse than nothing, for indeed*
> *I have engaged myself to a dear friend,*
> *Engaged my friend to his mere enemy,*
> *To feed my means.* (Act 3, Scene 2, lines 258–262)

Bassanio's desire to return to Venice immediately to try to help Antonio is **admirable**. Before he leaves, he tells Portia just how anxious he is to return to her:

> *but till I come again,*
> *No bed shall e'er be guilty of my stay,*
> *Nor rest be interposer 'twixt us twain.* (Act 3, Scene 2, line 324–326)

Bassanio shows tremendous **loyalty** and **devotion** to Antonio during the Trial Scene (Act 4, Scene 1). He offers encouragement to Antonio when Antonio has lost all hope:

> *Good cheer, Antonio. What, man, courage yet!*
> *The Jew shall have my flesh, blood, bones and all*
> *Ere thou shalt lose for me one drop of blood.* (Act 4, Scene 1, lines 110–112)

He pleads with 'Balthasar' to bend the rules in this case and spare Antonio's life:

> *And I beseech you,*
> *Wrest once the law to your authority.*
> *To do a great right, do a little wrong,*
> *And curb this cruel devil of his will.* (Act 4, Scene 1, lines 212–215)

Bassanio shows his true **devotion** to Antonio when tells him how dear he is to him. He says that nothing in the world is more important to him than their friendship:

> *But life itself, my wife, and all the world*
> *Are not with me esteemed above thy life.* (Act 4, Scene 1, lines 282–283)

When Antonio's life is spared, Bassanio insists that 'Balthasar', the lawyer, takes some form of payment. When 'Balthasar' asks for the ring that Portia gave him, he tries to avoid giving it. It is only when Antonio persuades Bassanio that he eventually parts with it:

> *Let his deservings and my love withal*
> *Be valued 'gainst your wife's commandement.* (Antonio, Act 4, Scene 1, lines 450–451)

Finally, in **Act 5**, **Scene 1**, Bassanio returns to Belmont with Antonio to be reunited with Portia. He openly admits to Portia that he gave the ring away and begs her to forgive him:

> *Pardon this fault, and by my soul I swear*
> *I never more will break an oath with thee.* (Act 5, Scene 1, lines 247–248)

Portia

intelligent
resourceful
loyal
compassionate
merciful
mischievous
just

Portia is an **intelligent**, **resourceful**, **three-dimensional** character who develops over the course of the play.

When we first meet Portia in **Act 1**, **Scene 2**, it is clear that she is **discontented** and slightly **depressed**. She tells Nerissa, her waiting-woman and confidante, 'my little body is aweary of this great world' (lines 1–2). We learn the fact that her father has restricted her choice of potential husband has contributed to her **malaise** (unease):

> *I may neither choose who I would nor refuse who I dislike; so is the will of a living daughter curbed by the will of a dead father.* (Act 1, Scene 2, lines 23–25)

However, Portia proves herself **light-hearted** and **good-humoured** in this scene as she playfully mocks the many suitors that have come to woo her.

Even though Portia is restricted by her father's will, she is extremely **dutiful** because she will obey her father's wishes no matter what. This is in contrast to Jessica who rebels against her father, Shylock.

> *If I live to be as old as Sibylla, I will die as chaste*
> *as Diana, unless I be obtained by the manner of*
> *my father's will.* (Act 1, Scene 2, lines 102–104)

The audience may be surprised by Portia's **racism** which is evident in **Act 1**, **Scene 2**. When the Prince of Morocco's messenger arrives announcing his **imminent** (expected) arrival, Portia comments:

> *If he have the*
> *condition of a saint and the complexion of a devil,*
> *I had rather he should shrive me than wive me.* (Act 1, Scene 2, lines 123–125)

Portia's racist response to the colour of the Prince of Morocco's complexion negatively affects our opinion of her. Perhaps Portia – like many others in the play – finds it difficult to identify with people who may be culturally or socially different to her. When she meets the Prince of Morocco in **Act 2**, **Scene 1**, she assures him that were it not for the 'lottery of [her] destiny' (line 15) that her dead father has imposed, he would stand as good a chance as any other suitor of winning her love:

> *Yourself, renownèd prince, then stood as fair*
> *As any comer I have looked on yet*
> *For my affection.* (Act 2, Scene 1, lines 20–22)

However, we know that she does not really mean this as Portia is greatly relieved when the Prince of Morocco chooses incorrectly and leaves:

> *A gentle riddance. Draw the curtains, go.*
> *Let all of his complexion choose me so.* (Act 2, Scene 7, lines 78–79)

Again, in **Act 2**, **Scene 9**, Portia is pleased when the Prince of Arragon fails to choose the correct casket and must leave. She calls these suitors 'deliberate fools' (line 79). This is quite **insensitive** considering that the oath these suitors had to swear before they could participate in the lottery was to leave immediately and never marry anyone else. Portia is **indifferent** to the suitors and becomes excited only when she hears news that a Venetian lord has come to chance his luck. Nerissa rightly suspects that this is Bassanio.

Portia's character undergoes an interesting **transformation** (change) in **Act 3**, **Scene 2** when Bassanio comes to try his luck with the caskets. Up until this point, Portia has proven herself a **confident**, **assertive** young lady, yet in this scene she appears more **vulnerable**, **nervous** and **insecure**. The difference here is that Portia actually likes Bassanio and wants him to be successful. Her desire to ensure that Bassanio chooses the correct casket and her wish to stay loyal to her father's wishes cause Portia to experience **inner conflict**. When Bassanio is choosing the casket, she is overwhelmed with feelings of love that she struggles to control:

> *O love, be moderate! Allay thy ecstasy* (Act 3, Scene 2, line 111)

When Bassanio approaches Portia after choosing the lead casket, Portia seems **modest**, almost insecure.

> *You see me, lord Bassanio, where I stand,*
> *Such as I am. Though for myself alone*
> *I would not be ambitious in my wish*
> *To wish myself much better, yet for you*
> *I would be trebled twenty times myself* (Act 3, Scene 2, lines 149–153)

She wishes to be better than she is to please Bassanio. As she is, she claims that she is 'an unlessoned girl, unschooled, unpractisèd' (line 159), but is willing to learn from Bassanio. She shows her generosity by quickly informing Bassanio that everything she has is his:

> *This house, these servants, and this same myself*
> *Are yours, my lord's.* (Act 3, Scene 2, lines 170–171)

Portia shows great **solicitude** (concern) and **worry** when she learns about the extent of Antonio's bad luck. She wastes no time in offering all the financial assistance she can to help him:

> *You shall have gold*
> *To pay the debt twenty times over.* (Act 3, Scene 2, lines 305–306)

She does not wish Bassanio to have 'an unquiet soul' (line 305) with her in Belmont and urges him to go at once to help Antonio:

> *O love! Dispatch all business, and be gone.* (Act 3, Scene 2, line 322)

One of Portia's best qualities is her **inherent** (fundamental) **sense of justice**. Not content to wait in Belmont, Portia takes an active role in helping Antonio. Portia devises a plan to go to Venice, disguising herself as a young male lawyer and presiding over the trial. Portia is responsible for saving Antonio's life. She displays remarkable **ingenuity** (cleverness) in the Trial Scene (Act 4, Scene 1), calmly appealing to Shylock to show mercy. In her famous, 'The quality of mercy' speech, Portia argues that mercy benefits those who show it as well as those who receive it. When her words have no effect on Shylock, Portia cleverly identifies a legal loophole – or flaw. She allows Shylock his 'pound of flesh', but he must not spill a drop of Antonio's blood. Portia's tactic is successful, but she is not finished with Shylock yet.

We could criticise Portia for being overly harsh on Shylock in this scene. Before Shylock leaves, Portia informs him that the 'law hath yet another hold on' (line 345) him. Apparently, by seeking his forfeit, Shylock is guilty of conspiring to kill a Venetian citizen (Antonio). This has severe consequences.

Portia shows her **devious**, **deceitful** nature at the end of this scene when she insists on Bassanio's ring as payment for her services, knowing that this would be a very difficult moral decision for him to face.

Finally, in **Act 5**, **Scene 1**, Portia shows her playful, mischievous side again by mocking Bassanio about the ring before revealing the extent of her involvement in the trial. Portia's **benevolence** (goodness/kindness) is most evident at the end of the play when she is the bearer of great news for everybody. She relays good news to Antonio about his ships:

> *Sweet lady, you have given me life and living* (Act 5, Scene 1, line 286)

Portia also informs Jessica and Lorenzo about the deed of gift, which means that they will inherit Shylock's goods after he dies.

Overall, Portia has a major role in the play, linking the themes of love and marriage and the bond (money) theme. Portia is a **three-dimensional**, **realistic** character whose actions make her believable to the audience.

Shylock

isolated
vindictive
merciless
callous
vengeful
shrewd
scheming

Shakespeare's **depiction** (presentation) of Shylock in this play is highly **ambiguous** (open to debate). On the one hand, Shylock is treated as the **villain** of the play, especially at the end, but on the other hand, Shakespeare also encourages our **sympathy** for Shylock, especially in his famous 'To bait fish withal' speech in Act 3, Scene 1.

Shylock is a Jewish moneylender who lends Bassanio the money he needs to go to Belmont to woo Portia. We are first introduced to Shylock in **Act 1**, **Scene 3** when Bassanio is negotiating the terms of a loan from him.

In an **aside**, Shylock openly admits that he hates Antonio:

> *I hate him for he is a Christian;*
> *But more, for that in low simplicity*
> *He lends out money gratis, and brings down*
> *The rate of usance here with us in Venice.* (Act 1, Scene 3, lines 37–40)

Shylock hates Antonio because he is a Christian, but mainly because he does not charge interest when he lends money, which has a negative effect on Shylock's business. Shylock is clearly a **vindictive** (nasty) character. His intention to deliberately get revenge on Antonio is made clear in the following lines:

> *If I can catch him once upon the hip,*
> *I will feed fat the ancient grudge I bear him.* (Act 1, Scene 3, lines 41–42)

If only Shylock could catch Antonio at a disadvantage, it would help to 'feed fat' the bitter resentment Shylock feels towards him. While we may be surprised initially by Shylock's strong language, we later learn why his **antipathy** (hatred) for Antonio runs so deep.

Shylock launches a **vicious verbal attack** on Antonio, confronting him about his abusive treatment towards him in the past. Antonio, it emerges, has publicly abused and humiliated Shylock 'many a time and oft in the Rialto' (Act 1, Scene 3, lines 101–102). He accuses Antonio of calling him a 'misbeliever, cut-throat dog' (line 106) and of spitting on him and kicking him. Shylock is **incredulous** (in disbelief) that this same person is now coming to him looking for help:

> *you come to me, and you say*
> *'Shylock, we would have moneys'—you say so,*
> *You, that did void your rheum upon my beard,*
> *And foot me as you spurn a stranger cur* (Act 1, Scene 3, lines 110–113)

Antonio asks him to lend the money, not as a friend, but as an enemy as he thinks it would be easier for Shylock to demand the penalty from someone he dislikes:

> *But lend it rather to thine enemy,*
> *Who if he break, thou mayst with better face*
> *Exact the penalty.* (Act 1, Scene 3, lines 130–132)

In response to this, Shylock claims that he wishes to be friends with Antonio and forgive him for all past **grievances** (wrongs/insults): 'I would be friends with you, and have your love' (Act 1, Scene 3, line 134). To prove it, he says that he will lend the money interest-free and 'take no doit of usance for my moneys' (lines 136–137). Shylock then suggests that just for fun, what he calls a 'merry sport' (line 141), there should be a penalty for not repaying the loan:

> *let the forfeit*
> *Be nominated for an equal pound*
> *Of your fair flesh to be cut off and taken*
> *In what part of your body pleaseth me.* (Act 1, Scene 3, lines 144–147)

Antonio agrees and seems to be taken in by Shylock's **apparent kindness**:

> *I'll seal to such a bond,*
> *And say there is much kindness in the Jew.* (Act 1, Scene 3, lines 148–149)

Shylock is further **isolated** when his only daughter, Jessica, and his servant, Launcelot, abandon him. He is **outraged** when he learns that his daughter has **eloped** with a Christian. Jessica describes her house as 'hell' and is ashamed of her father:

> *But though I am a daughter to his blood,*
> *I am not to his manners.* (Act 2, Scene 3, lines 18–19)

In **Act 2, Scene 5**, we witness Shylock's interaction with his daughter. He appears quite **controlling** and **overprotective** of her. He tells her to lock up all the doors and windows and not to look out into the street:

> *Do as I bid you. Shut doors after you.* (Act 2, Scene 5, line 52)

We next hear about Shylock from Salerio and Solanio in **Act 2**, **Scene 8**. They describe Shylock's reaction to his daughter's escape and theft of his money. Solanio reports how he:

> *never heard a passion so confused,*
> *So strange, outrageous, and so variable*
> *As the dog Jew did utter in the streets.* (Act 2, Scene 8, lines 12–14)

In **Act 3**, **Scene 1**, Solanio and Salerio taunt and tease Shylock when they meet him on the street. Salerio mocks Shylock by saying that 'There is more difference between thy flesh and [Jessica's] than between jet and ivory' (Act 3, Scene 1, lines 34–35).

Salerio asks Shylock what good Antonio's flesh would be if Antonio were unable to keep the terms of the bond. In response, Shylock makes a powerful speech **asserting** (declaring/

stating) his dignity as a Jew and as a human being. Through Shylock's powerful speech Shakespeare is presenting a more **vulnerable** and **human side** to Shylock's character:

> *If you prick us, do we not bleed?*
> *If you tickle us, do we not laugh? If you poison*
> *us, do we not die?* (Act 3, Scene 1, lines 59–61)

Shylock feels that, as a Jew, he has been treated with **contempt** (hatred) and **disrespect**. In his speech he calls on Christians to see Jews as equal. At the end of his speech, Shylock becomes increasingly **bitter** towards Christians whom he accuses of having double standards. He vows that he will practise the lessons in revenge that he has learnt from Christians:

> *The villainy you*
> *teach me I will execute, and it shall go hard but I*
> *will better the instruction.* (Act 3, Scene 1, lines 66–68)

Shylock also finds out from Tubal in this same scene that Jessica has been squandering his money. He is so **incensed** (angry) that he says he wishes that his daughter were dead and he had his jewels back:

> *I would my*
> *daughter were dead at my foot and the jewels in her ear!*
> *Would she were hearsed at my foot, and the ducats in*
> *her coffin!* (Act 3, Scene 1, lines 80–83)

When Tubal informs Shylock that Jessica has exchanged a precious ring for a monkey, he is very upset as he believes this ring to be his 'turquoise' (line 108), a precious ring he associates with Leah, his late wife.

When Tubal tells Shylock that another of Antonio's ships has been wrecked coming from Tripolis, Shylock is **elated** (overjoyed) as, if he eliminates Antonio, he can make up for his (Shylock's) losses by charging more interest:

> *I will have the heart of him, if he forfeit, for were*
> *he out of Venice I can make what merchandise I*
> *will.* (Act 3, Scene 1, lines 113–115)

It seems that, by the end of the scene, any sympathy we may have felt for Shylock rapidly disappears as he appears **callous** (cruel) and **vindictive** (nasty) in planning the death of Antonio.

In **Act 3**, **Scene 3**, Shylock displays great **malice** and **malevolence** (spite/hatred) as he seeks out Antonio. He appears particularly vicious as he says to Antonio:

> *Thou called'st me a dog before thou hadst a cause,*
> *But since I am a dog, beware my fangs.* (Act 3, Scene 3, lines 6–7)

Shylock stubbornly insists on his bond and nothing can change his mind. Solanio sums up Shylock's **stubborn** character very well at this point when he says:

> *It is the most impenetrable cur*
> *That ever kept with men.* (Act 3, Scene 3, lines 18–19)

In the Trial Scene (Act 4, Scene 1), Shylock's good fortune is reversed. Unwilling to back down and take any money as compensation, Shylock is punished and leaves the stage a broken man.

Shylock's unwillingness to get a doctor – as it is not explicitly stated in the agreement – confirms our suspicion that Shylock doesn't just want his 'pound of flesh'; he wants Antonio dead. If Shylock were simply interested in his 'pound of flesh', he should have no problem extracting it and then seeing to it that Antonio has a doctor nearby so that he does not bleed to death. There is no doubt here that Shylock is a **cruel**, **heartless** character who has **no sympathy** for Antonio's plight.

Portia argues that, legally, Shylock is allowed to have the pound of flesh only and no blood must be spilt in the operation of taking the flesh. As it is impossible for Shylock to proceed, he begins to back down. However, Portia does not show him mercy, warning him that he 'shalt have justice more than [he] desir'st' (line 315).

Very **shrewdly** (cleverly), Shylock is now willing to take his money, but Portia refuses to give it as Shylock publicly 'refused it in the open court' (line 336):

> *He shall have merely justice and his bond.* (Act 4, Scene 1, line 337)

Just as Shylock is about to leave, Portia reveals that the law still has a 'hold' on Shylock. It now emerges that by demanding his penalty Shylock was planning to kill a Venetian citizen and must therefore be punished.

The Duke displays 'the difference of our spirit' (line 366) (his Christian spirit) by showing mercy to Shylock. He pardons his life and orders one half of Shylock's wealth to be given to Antonio and the other half to the state of Venice. He reduces the portion due to the state of Venice to a fine. However, instead of seeing this as an act of mercy, Shylock sees this as the worst form of punishment:

> *you take my life*
> *When you do take the means whereby I live.* (Act 4, Scene 1, lines 374–375)

It is now Antonio's turn to display mercy. He asks the Duke to cancel Shylock's fine and says that he will invest his half of Shylock's wealth on behalf of Jessica and Lorenzo. Antonio outlines two more conditions: that Shylock convert to Christianity and that he leave all his possessions to his daughter Jessica and son-in-law Lorenzo when he dies.

Shylock has no choice but to agree to the terms, uttering a feeble 'I am content' (line 392). This image of the **defeated**, **broken** man forms a dramatic contrast to the **powerful**, **vindictive** character we witnessed at the start of this scene. Antonio's generosity of spirit forms a dramatic contrast with Shylock's **lack of compassion** in this scene.

Shylock, as an **outsider** in Venice, is **sceptical** and **suspicious** of others. Perhaps his resentment and stubbornness can be interpreted as **self-preservation**. Shylock may be trying to protect himself against those who mistreat and abuse him. However, this does not excuse his obvious **malice** and **vindictiveness** in the play.

Antonio

entrepreneurial
stoical
generous
resigned
melancholy
self-sacrificing

Despite the fact that Antonio is 'the merchant of Venice' from the title of the play, he plays a relatively minor role and is not a very well-developed character. Antonio is an **entrepreneur** and a **risk-taker**. He is universally liked and displays remarkable **generosity** to his friends, especially Bassanio.

At the start of the play, Antonio is **melancholy** (depressed) but he doesn't know why. His **malaise** (unhappiness) perhaps springs from the fact that he knows his best friend Bassanio is soon to marry:

> *In sooth, I know not why I am so sad.* (Act 1, Scene 1, line 1)

When he encounters Gratiano, he tells him that he thinks being sad is his destiny:

> *I hold the world but as the world, Gratiano—*
> *A stage where every man must play a part,*
> *And mine a sad one.* (Act 1, Scene 1, lines 77–79)

Despite his sadness, he is very **jovial** (cheerful) when he speaks to Bassanio. He is more than willing to help him acquire the money to go to Belmont despite the fact that Antonio has no money available to him at present as it has been invested in his ships. However, he urges Bassanio to 'try what [his] credit can in Venice do' to get him 'to Belmont, to fair Portia' (Act 1, Scene 2, lines 180 and 182).

Antonio is quite **dismissive** of Shylock in **Act 1**, **Scene 3**. He persuades Shylock to lend the money as if 'to thine enemy' (line 130):

> *I'll seal to such a bond,*
> *And say there is much kindness in the Jew.* (Act 1, Scene 3, lines 148–149)

Antonio is confident that he can repay the loan in time, so he doesn't forsee any danger with the bond:

> *Come on. In this there can be no dismay.*
> *My ships come home a month before the day.* (Act 1, Scene 3, lines 176–177)

Unfortunately, Antonio experiences bad luck. All his ships are wrecked which means he cannot repay the loan to Shylock and must pay the forfeit. Antonio tries to plead with Shylock in **Act 3**, **Scene 3**, but realises that Shylock cannot be persuaded:

> *Let him alone.*
> *I'll follow him no more with bootless prayers.* (Act 3, Scene 3, lines 19–20)

At this stage, Antonio is **resigned** to his fate and is unwilling to plead with Shylock any further.

Antonio is very **stoical** (uncomplaining/patient) in his suffering. He takes full responsibility for the bond and is prepared to face the consequences. He asks Bassanio to plead no further with Shylock and to give him his 'will'.

Antonio's **loyalty** and **devotion** are evident in **Act 4**, **Scene 1** when he is preparing to die. He tells Bassanio not to blame himself for what has happened, showing great **selflessness**:

> *Repent but you that you shall lose your friend,*
> *And he repents not that he pays your debt;*
> *For if the Jew do cut but deep enough,*
> *I'll pay it instantly with all my heart.* (Act 4, Scene 1, lines 276–279)

When Antonio's fortune is reversed, he shows mercy to Shylock. He asks the Duke to waive the fine for one half of Shylock's goods and wishes to invest the other half for Lorenzo and Jessica following Shylock's death. However, controversially, he demands that Shylock convert to Christianity, which is possibly the worst punishment he could inflict on him.

Antonio accompanies Bassanio and Gratiano to Belmont and he is **conspicuous** (stands out) as the only single person on stage at the end of the play. Perhaps this suggests that Antonio is destined to be alone. Antonio does experience good fortune in **Act 5**, **Scene 1** when Portia informs him that three of his ships 'Are richly come to harbour suddenly' (line 277). This news causes Antonio to reflect on the positive impact Portia has had on his life:

> *Sweet lady, you have given me life and living* (Act 5, Scene 1, line 286)

Overall, Antonio is a **magnanimous** (generous), **selfless** character in the play. Bassanio sums up Antonio's character perfectly in the following quote:

> *The dearest friend to me, the kindest man,*
> *The best-conditioned and unwearied spirit*
> *In doing courtesies* (Bassanio, Act 3, Scene 2, lines 291–293)

Looking at Themes

False Appearances

The theme of **false appearances** is central to *The Merchant of Venice*. In the play, things are often not what they appear to be:

- The **casket test** reminds us that appearances can be deceptive.
- Shylock **pretends that the 'pound of flesh' is simply a 'merry sport'**, when we know in reality he wishes to have revenge on Antonio and would like to see him dead.
- Jessica, Portia and Nerissa **disguise themselves as men** to deceive others.

False Appearances and the Casket Test

The casket test is basically a test to see which suitor does not judge on appearances. Appearances can be deceptive. The Prince of Morocco is first to find this out when he tries his luck at the caskets in **Act 2**, **Scene 7**. The Prince of Morocco rejects the lead casket, saying that ''Twere damnation to think so base a thought' (Act 2, Scene 7, lines 49–50).
He also dismisses the silver casket as 'Being ten times undervalued to tried gold' (line 53). When he chooses the gold casket, he finds a skull and a scroll inside which warns: 'All that glisters is not gold' (line 65). The Prince of Morocco, having chosen the most obvious casket, leaves disappointed.

The next suitor, the Prince of Arragon also bases his judgements on appearances and is unsuccessful. He interprets the inscription 'Who chooseth me shall have as much as he deserves' (Act 2, Scene 9, line 35) to mean that he deserves Portia, when in fact this is false. Again, he is punished for judging by appearances.

Bassanio doesn't judge by appearances and he is therefore rewarded with Portia's hand in marriage in **Act 3**, **Scene 2**. Before choosing he contemplates the idea of false appearances:

> *So may the outward show be least themselves:*
> *The world is still deceived by ornament.* (Act 3, Scene 2, lines 73–74)

Bassanio comments that women adopt false appearances by wearing fake hair and make-up 'purchased by the weight' (line 89). He claims that even though this may work 'a miracle in nature' (line 90), it makes those who wear it seem shallow. With this logic, he rejects the 'gaudy gold' (line 101) casket in favour of the 'meagre lead' (line 104) one. He is rewarded for his reluctance to be drawn in by outward displays or false appearances.

However, it could be argued that Bassanio himself is guilty of projecting a false appearance. When he arrives to woo Portia, he appears to be a wealthy suitor, but in reality he has had to borrow money to put on this elaborate show. When he lands at Belmont bringing 'Gifts of rich value' (Act 2, Scene 9, line 90) Bassanio is misrepresenting himself.

False Appearances and Shylock

Another character who **assumes** (puts on) a false appearance is Shylock. On the surface, Shylock appears to be friends with Antonio:

I would be friends with you, and have your love (Act 1, Scene 3, line 134)

The audience knows, however, from his earlier **aside** that in reality he hates Antonio and wants to take revenge on him. When Antonio agrees to the terms of the bond and the forfeit of the pound of flesh, Shylock suggests that it is all just a 'merry sport' (Act 1, Scene 3, line 141). Antonio seems to be taken in by Shylock's false appearance, but Bassanio is suspicious of him and tries to **dissuade** (stop/prevent) Antonio from agreeing to the bond on his behalf:

I like not fair terms and a villain's mind. (Act 1, Scene 3, line 175)

False Appearances and Disguises

In the play, we also witness female characters adopting false identities by disguising themselves as men. Jessica, Shylock's daughter, dresses as a page boy to make her escape easier, Portia disguises herself as a male lawyer and Nerissa assumes the identity of his clerk. Portia uses her false appearance for good in the play. By presenting herself as the young doctor of law, Portia deceives everybody but succeeds in saving Antonio's life.

Portia and Nerissa take advantage of their disguises to trick their husbands. They request the rings they have given their husbands as payment. When the couples are reunited in Belmont, it appears that their husbands have been unfaithful as they are without the rings, when in reality they were **compelled** (forced) to give them up. When Portia and Nerissa's involvement in the Trial Scene is revealed, their husbands are **incredulous** (in disbelief):

Were you the doctor and I knew you not? (Bassanio, Act 5, Scene 1, line 280)

The play teaches us not to judge on appearances; appearances can be deceptive. However, not all false appearances are bad, as is proven in the case of Portia and Nerissa whose new identities helped to save Antonio from certain death. In order to do a 'great right' they did 'a little wrong' (Act 4, Scene 1, line 214).

Love and Marriage

Love and marriage is one of the main themes in the play. The main plot revolves around Portia, a wealthy heiress in Belmont, whose father has devised an unusual way for his daughter to acquire a husband. Before he died, he created a lottery of three caskets: gold, silver and lead. The suitor who chooses the correct casket (the one which contains Portia's portrait) wins her hand in marriage. In **Act 1**, **Scene 1**, we learn about Portia from Bassanio:

> *In Belmont is a lady richly left*
> *And she is fair* (Act 1, Scene 1, lines 161–162)

Bassanio also informs us that many suitors come from all over the world. Bassanio asks Antonio for a loan so he too can have a chance to journey to Belmont to woo Portia: 'To hold a rival place with one of them' (line 174). Bassanio is confident that he will be successful.

At this stage, it is clear that Portia, being very rich and beautiful, would be a desirable match for any man. However, Bassanio is also motivated by his desire for money to clear his debts. It is evident that love is not Bassanio's only motivation in his **pursuit** (quest) of Portia.

In **Act 1**, **Scene 2**, Portia confides in Nerissa about her opinion of the lottery. She tells her that she is 'aweary of this great world' (lines 1–2) and that:

> *I may neither choose who I would nor refuse who*
> *I dislike; so is the will of a living daughter curbed*
> *by the will of a dead father.* (Act 1, Scene 2, lines 23–25)

Portia enjoys mocking the suitors who have arrived, stereotyping them according to the countries they come from. At the end of **Act 1**, **Scene 2**, when Nerissa reminds Portia of Bassanio, a Venetian 'scholar and a soldier' (line 109) whom she once met at Belmont, it is clear that Portia is attracted to him. She tells Nerissa that she remembers that he was worthy of her praise. When the Prince of Morocco and the Prince of Arragon fail to choose the correct casket, the audience is now hoping that Bassanio will choose the lead casket.

A **key scene of love is Act 3**, **Scene 2** when Bassanio chooses the correct casket. Even though the desire for money and wealth was a big factor in Bassanio's pursuit of Portia, it is clear in this scene that he has genuine feelings for her. When Portia asks Bassanio to delay his choice because she doesn't want to lose him, he replies that he is in torture. He says he needs to choose immediately 'For as I am, I live upon the rack' (line 25).

It is abundantly clear that Portia favours Bassanio. Portia even plays music while he chooses which offers a slight hint at the correct casket. Portia is overjoyed when Bassanio chooses the lead casket and expresses her love to him very openly. In fact, Portia appears very vulnerable and insecure as she states:

> *You see me, lord Bassanio, where I stand,*
> *Such as I am. Though for myself alone*
> *I would not be ambitious in my wish*
> *To wish myself much better, yet for you*
> *I would be trebled twenty times myself,*
> *At thousand times more fair* (Act 3, Scene 2, lines 149–154)

Portia's love appears honest and genuine, but she somehow feels unworthy.

Also in this scene, Nerissa and Gratiano announce that they are to wed which comes as a lighthearted, almost comical, surprise. Gratiano **jests** (jokes) to Bassanio: 'You saw the mistress, I beheld the maid' (Act 3, Scene 2, line 198). It reminds us that the play is meant to be a comedy and that love is universal. The world of Belmont seems to be a world where romance flourishes. Even Jessica and Lorenzo end up in Belmont in this scene, having fled from Venice.

However, just as Portia and Bassanio are preparing to get married, a **major obstacle** threatens their love. News of Antonio's bad luck arrives and Bassanio is filled with grief. Bassanio displays true regard for Portia when he openly admits that he misrepresented himself to her:

> *I have engaged myself to a dear friend,*
> *Engaged my friend to his mere enemy,*
> *To feed my means.* (Act 3, Scene 2, lines 260–262)

Portia's reaction shows her love for Bassanio. She tells him that he can pay whatever it takes to 'deface the bond' (line 298) and tells him to leave to help Antonio:

> *For never shall you lie by Portia's side*
> *With an unquiet soul. You shall have gold*
> *To pay the debt twenty times over.* (Act 3, Scene 2, lines 304–306)

Portia also displays her love for Bassanio when she is not content to simply stay in Belmont and do nothing. Instead, she plays an active part in saving Antonio's life. All of this is motivated by her love for Bassanio as she knows that Bassanio feels responsible for Antonio's predicament.

The rings test that both Nerissa and Portia participate in is designed to test the loyalty of their husbands. When Portia and Nerissa both insist on having the rings from their husbands as payment for their legal services, a note of comedy is sounded as we await the consequences in the final scene.

The final scene of the play, **Act 5**, **Scene 1** is a celebration of romantic love. In fact, the setting with the moon and the sounds of music creates a suitably romantic atmosphere. The play that contained so much strife and conflict ends with love with the three new couples on stage. There is a sense of harmony and new beginnings as the scene ends and the couples and Antonio enter Portia's house. Ultimately, love triumphs over hatred in the play.

Money

Money is a very important theme in the play and is linked to other themes such as love, conflict and false appearances.

Bassanio's lack of money at the start of the play is what sets the plot in motion. Bassanio requires 3,000 ducats to 'furnish [him] to Belmont, to fair Portia' (Act 1, Scene 1, line 182). We know that Bassanio is an extravagant spendthrift who is already deeply indebted to his friend Antonio when he seeks the loan he needs to go to Belmont in Act 1, Scene 1:

'Tis not unknown to you, Antonio,
How much I have disabled mine estate,
By something showing a more swelling port
Than my faint means would grant continuance (Act 1, Scene 1, lines 122–125)

Bassanio believes that by acquiring a loan of 3,000 to go to Belmont, he will solve all his financial problems. In this way the theme of money is connected to the theme of love.

Jessica, Shylock's daughter, steals her father's money and jewels when she escapes. As the daughter of a rich Jewish person, it could be argued that Jessica, like Portia, is a very attractive potential wife for anyone. Lorenzo sets his sights on Jessica and they plan to elope together. When Jessica is escaping from her father's house she steals money and jewels. After she has already thrown down a casket filled with riches, she says:

I will make fast the doors, and gild myself
With some more ducats, and be with you straight. (Act 2, Scene 6, lines 49–50)

This means that she will cover herself with more gold coins before descending to Lorenzo.

As Antonio's money is tied up in his ships, Bassanio's only option is to borrow the money from someone else. Antonio will be Bassanio's guarantor, or security for the loan. They approach Shylock, a Jewish moneylender, to secure the funds they need.

The conflict between Shylock and Antonio stems from their different attitudes to lending money. Antonio, as a Christian, does not charge interest on loans, whereas Shylock charges interest, a practice known as **usury**.

> *He lends out money gratis, and brings down*
> *The rate of usance here with us in Venice.* (Act 1, Scene 3, lines 39–40)

Shylock believes that Antonio undermines his business as he believes it is right to charge interest on loans:

> *And thrift is blessing, if men steal it not.* (Act 1, Scene 3, line 85)

However, it is clear that Shylock is not motivated by money or interest when lending Bassanio the sum he needs. He lends the money interest-free and, as a 'merry sport' (line 141), sets the penalty for not repaying the loan as a pound of Antonio's flesh:

> *If you repay me not on such a day,*
> *… let the forfeit*
> *Be nominated for an equal pound*
> *Of your fair flesh to be cut off and taken*
> *In what part of your body pleaseth me.* (Act 1, Scene 3, lines 142–147)

It appears that Shylock has been waiting for such an opportunity to get revenge on Antonio for his over-generous lending practices.

It is clear that Shylock wants only revenge. This is obvious since Shylock, someone who is so interested in money, does not seem to care that his money has not been repaid. Shylock is overjoyed when he finds out that Antonio's ships have been destroyed, indicating that the loan cannot be repaid.

Shylock is even more intent on seeking revenge on the Christian, Antonio, when he learns that his daughter has fled with a Christian, Lorenzo, and has stolen gold and valuable jewellery. Shylock tells Tubal in **Act 3**, **Scene 1**:

> *I would my*
> *daughter were dead at my foot and the jewels in her ear!* (Act 3, Scene 1, lines 80–81)

It would appear that Shylock values money above all else, including family, but later in the scene when he learns that his daughter exchanged a 'turquoise' ring for a monkey, he is devastated. This is not because of the value of the ring, but because of its association with his late wife, Leah:

> *Thou torturest me, Tubal…*
> *I would not have given it for a wilderness of monkeys.* (Act 3, Scene 1, lines 107–109)

In the Trial Scene, Shylock flatly refuses to take any money, insisting on the terms of the bond. Bassanio offers to repay the full amount and later Shylock is offered three times the original sum of money Bassanio borrowed:

> *Shylock, there's thrice thy money offered thee.* (Act 4, Scene 1, line 225)

However, Shylock claims that he has sworn an oath and cannot commit **perjury** (break an oath).

When Portia finds the legal loophole (that Shylock may take his pound of flesh, but not a drop of blood) Shylock experiences a reversal of fortune. Realising that he has been defeated, Shylock backs down and is now prepared to take three times the money. As Bassanio is about to give the money to Shylock, Portia intervenes saying that 'He shall have nothing but the penalty' (Act 4, Scene 1, line 320). Shylock asks if he can have the original sum, his 'principal', but is denied it.

Next, Portia claims that Shylock conspired against the life of a Venetian and therefore must pay a penalty. The usual punishment is that half of the perpetrator's goods goes to the Duke of Venice and the other half goes to the person against whom he conspired, Antonio. The Duke **waives** (gives up) his right to half of Shylock's fortune, reducing it to a fine, while Antonio decides to invest the other half to be inherited by Lorenzo and Jessica after Shylock's death. Portia (as Balthasar, the lawyer) demands that 'a deed of gift' (line 392) be drawn up and signed by Shylock to secure the agreement.

Shylock is outraged at his **sudden loss of wealth**:

you take my life
When you do take the means whereby I live. (Act 4, Scene 1, lines 374–375)

Bassanio offers to pay Portia the 3,000 ducats that were meant for Shylock as a reward for saving Antonio's life. However, she refuses the money, saying that 'He is well paid that is well satisfied' (Act 4, Scene 1, line 413), emphasising that not every good deed needs a financial reward. Bassanio, who is very insistent that she takes some payment or 'remembrance', is eventually **coerced** (forced) into parting with the ring his wife gave him.

At the end of the play, Portia brings news of good fortune for Lorenzo, Jessica and Antonio. Three of Antonio's ships have safely arrived in the harbour meaning his wealth has now been restored. He says to Portia:

Sweet lady, you have given me life and living (Act 5, Scene 1, line 286)

Lorenzo echoes this **sentiment** (opinion) when Portia informs him of the deed of gift from Shylock which entitles Lorenzo and Jessica to inherit Shylock's wealth after he dies:

Fair ladies, you drop manna in the way
Of starvèd people. (Act 5, Scene 1, line 294–295)

Money is responsible for almost all of the action in the play:

- Bassanio needs money to go to Belmont.
- Shylock goes after Antonio because Antonio cannot repay the money.
- Shylock is humbled and humiliated when half his money is taken from him in the Trial Scene.

Conflict

The main conflict in the play occurs between Shylock and Antonio.

The conflict between Shylock and Antonio stems from their different attitudes to lending money as mentioned previously in the **theme of money**. Antonio, as a Christian, does not charge interest on loans, whereas Shylock, a Jew, charges interest, a practice known as **usury**.

In his **aside** in **Act 1**, **Scene 3**, Shylock reveals his hatred towards Antonio:

> *I hate him for he is a Christian;*
> *But more, for that in low simplicity*
> *He lends out money gratis* (Act 1, Scene 3, lines 37–39)

So the two reasons he outlines for hating Antonio are because he is a Christian and because he does not charge interest which undermines Shylock's business. Shylock also makes it clear that he is looking for an opportunity to get revenge on Antonio for this and 'feed fat the ancient grudge I bear him' (Act 1, Scene 3, line 42).

When Antonio approaches Shylock for the loan of 3,000 ducats, Shylock is surprised as the two are **adversaries** (enemies) and Antonio has abused him publicly in the past by calling him names and spitting on him:

> *You call me misbeliever, cut-throat dog,*
> *And spit upon my Jewish gaberdine* (Act 1, Scene 3, lines 106–107)

Despite this, Shylock agrees to lend the money, **stipulating** (demanding) the forfeit as a pound of Antonio's flesh if he fails to repay the money within three months. Antonio does not see the agreement as a threat as he is confident that his ships will 'come home a month before the day' (line 177) the money needs to be repaid. Bassanio, however, is suspicious of Shylock's motivations: 'I like not fair terms and a villain's mind' (Act 1, Scene 3, line 175).

In **Act 3**, **Scene 3**, Shylock calls a jailer to arrest Antonio:

> *Jailer, look to him. Tell me not of mercy.*
>
> *This is the fool that lent out money gratis.* (Act 3, Scene 3, lines 1–2)

Antonio begs Shylock to listen to him, 'Hear me yet, good Shylock' (Act 3, Scene 3, line 3) but he refuses:

> *Thou called'st me a dog before thou hadst a cause,*
>
> *But since I am a dog, beware my fangs.* (Act 3, Scene 3, lines 6–7)

Antonio realises that it is **futile** (useless) trying to reason with Shylock; he wants him dead:

> *I'll follow him no more with bootless prayers.*
>
> *He seeks my life.* (Act 3, Scene 3, lines 20–21)

Antonio realises that the reason that Shylock hates him so much is that Antonio often helped people who owed Shylock money. Antonio is resigned to his fate – certain death – as he knows there is very little the Duke can do for him:

> *The Duke cannot deny the course of law* (Act 3, Scene 3, line 26)

Antonio faces his 'bloody creditor' (line 34) Shylock in court the next day. Again, Shylock is extremely stubborn in this scene, wanting nothing but his 'pound of flesh' from Antonio. Only a miracle can save Antonio against such a vindictive, vengeful enemy – 'A stony adversary' (Act 4, Scene 1, line 3) – and this miracle arrives in the form of Portia, disguised as 'Balthasar', a young lawyer and his clerk (Nerissa).

Portia's arrival on the scene signals a change in fortunes for Shylock. Again, like the Duke before her, Portia begs Shylock to show mercy. Her words go unheeded as Shylock replies:

> *There is no power in the tongue of man*
>
> *To alter me. I stay here on my bond.* (Act 4, Scene 1, lines 239–240)

Portia informs Antonio that he must 'prepare [his] bosom for [Shylock's] knife' (Act 4, Scene 1, line 243). Shylock is ready to cut Antonio's flesh, which will mean certain death.

Portia asks Shylock to have a doctor available to 'stop [Antonio's] wounds lest he bleed to death' (line 256). Shylock's reluctance to do so makes it abundantly clear that he wishes to take Antonio's life. He wants him to bleed to death without the aid of a doctor. Shylock's callousness is apparent here.

Portia then informs Shylock that he must take the pound of flesh **at his peril** (at his own risk). Shylock is entitled to the pound of flesh only, so if he spills one drop of Antonio's blood, his lands will be **confiscated** (taken away).

Shylock has no choice but to back down. He is denied any money and shown little mercy by Portia. It now appears that Antonio has beaten his rival, Shylock. Portia finds another law that Shylock has broken. By trying to get his pound of flesh from Antonio, he has conspired against the life of a Venetian and so must be punished.

Antonio emerges **triumphant** from the Trial Scene, while Shylock is a broken man. Antonio **stipulates** (demands) that half of Shylock's wealth be given to Lorenzo, a Christian, and his daughter Jessica after Shylock's death and, worst of all, Shylock must now convert to Christianity. All Shylock can now do is utter a feeble 'I am content' (Act 4, Scene 1, line 392) when Portia asks him what he has to say. Antonio's powerful, vindictive enemy now leaves abruptly saying he is not well. Thus, the conflict comes to an end between Shylock and Antonio.

Approaching Examination Questions

KEY AREAS FOR STUDY

- **Characters**
- **Key scenes**
- **Themes**
- **Relationships – positive or negative**
- **Your evaluation of the play**

The TED Approach to Answering Examination Questions

For each main point:

include a **Topic sentence**
give **Examples/evidence**
and then **Discuss**

A **topic sentence** expresses the main **idea/point** of the paragraph in which it occurs. It usually comes at the **start** of the paragraph, but can also be found at the end of the paragraph. For example, if you wish to write about the **challenges** that Portia faces as a character, you might write a topic sentence such as: **The fact that Portia's dead father has created a lottery/test to choose her potential husband causes Portia to feel frustrated and disillusioned.**

Next, try to include **examples** to support your point. These could be quotes or references to the play.

Finally, discuss how your examples help to expand on your topic sentence.

Approaching a Merchant of Venice Character Question

EXPLORING AN IMPORTANT CHARACTER

Sample Question

Identify a **hero**, **heroine** or **villain** from a play you have studied. Explain why, in your opinion, this character deserves the title of **hero**, **heroine** or **villain**. Support your answer with reference to the play.

For this answer, you could choose Portia as the heroine of the play, or Shylock as the villain. We will take Portia as an example of a heroine from a play we have studied.

1. Planning Your Answer

Brainstorm your points. Make brief notes for yourself about Portia's heroic or good qualities:

- Her loyalty to her father's wishes, despite her frustration and weariness.
- Her compassion, intelligence and ingenuity – she is selfless in allowing Bassanio to leave immediately to return to Venice when his friend's life is in danger and shows great ingenuity in devising the plan to help Antonio.
- She saves the life of Antonio in the Trial Scene.
- She brings good news to Lorenzo, Jessica and Antonio at the end of the play.

2. Structuring Your Answer

Now that you have **brainstormed** your points, decide which ones you will discuss in detail. Your answer needs:

- An **introduction**.
- Three or four **developed points** (one point per paragraph).
- A brief **conclusion**.

3. Writing Your Answer

Write your introduction, develop three or four points, including plenty of **quotes** or **references** to expand on each point, and then write a brief conclusion summing up your answer.

Writing About an Important Scene in the Play

When writing about an important scene, consider the following:

Characters

Who are the main characters in this scene? What do they say and do? How do the characters interact with each other in this scene? For example, a scene might show how a character has changed or developed. Where do we see this in the scene?

Action

What happens in this scene to further the plot? Is this a climax scene? Is this a key scene for a major theme in the play such as love or conflict?

Does anything **surprising/shocking/memorable/unexpected** take place in this scene?

Atmosphere

How is the atmosphere created? Is the mood tense or calm, romantic or sorrowful? How is this mood established? What images contribute to this mood?

Audience's Response

How did you respond to this scene? How do you feel about the events that take place in the scene and the characters?

Staging the Scene

Imagine that you will be staging/directing this scene. How would you stage it to maximise its impact? Consider the type of stage, advice to actors, visual and sound effects, the positioning of the characters on the stage, etc.